Photoshop® CS2
QuickSteps

CAROLE MATTHEWS

DOUG SAHLIN

McGraw-Hill/Osborne

New York Chicago San Francisco
Lisbon London Madrid Mexico City
Milan New Delhi San Juan
Seoul Singapore Sydney Toronto

McGraw-Hill/Osborne

2100 Powell Street, 10th Floor
Emeryville, California 94608
U.S.A.

To arrange bulk purchase discounts for sales promotions, premiums, or fund-raisers, please contact McGraw-Hill/Osborne at the above address. For information on translations or book distributors outside the U.S.A., please see the International Contact Information page immediately following the index of this book.

PHOTOSHOP® CS2 QUICKSTEPS

1234567890 WCK WCK 0198765

ISBN 0-07-226159-5

VICE PRESIDENT, GROUP PUBLISHER / Phillip Ruppel

VICE PRESIDENT, PUBLISHER / Jeffrey Krames

ACQUISITIONS EDITOR / Roger Stewart

ACQUISITIONS COORDINATOR / Agatha Kim

SERIES CREATORS & EDITORS / Martin and Carole Matthews

TECHNICAL EDITORS / Carole Matthews and Doug Sahlin

COPY EDITOR / Lisa McCoy

PROOFREADER / Harriet O'Neal and Kellen Diamanti

INDEXER / Valerie Perry

LAYOUT ARTIST / Laura Canby

ILLUSTRATORS / Kathleen Edwards, Pattie Lee, Bruce Hopkins

SERIES DESIGN / Bailey Cunningham

COVER DESIGN / Pattie Lee

Contents at a Glance

Chapter 1 **Stepping into Photoshop CS2** 1
Get acquainted with Photoshop CS2, use its tools and palettes, assign keyboard shortcuts, work with colors, and calibrate your monitor.

Chapter 2 **Creating, Importing, and Saving Images** 25
Learn about working with image types and use the Bridge to search and work with files, user scanners, and digital cameras.

Chapter 3 **Making Selections** 51
Use Photoshop's selection tools; modify, crop, and manipulate selections; extract images from backgrounds; and use Quick Masks.

Chapter 4 **Using Layers** 75
Create layers, and then rearrange, copy, merge, and group layers. Work with layer masks and layer effects, and use blending modes.

Chapter 5 **Using Paths, Shapes, and Painting Tools** 103
Use the Pen and Shape tools to create shapes and paths. Paint with the Brush tool. Personalize artwork with patterns and tools.

Chapter 6 **Color Correcting, Retouching, and Repairing** 129
Rotate, flip, straighten, crop, resize, and trim images. Color-correct with curves and levels. Sharpen, blur, and retouch images.

Chapter 7 **Using Type and Type Effects** 159
Create and edit text and use text tasks, such as the spelling checker. Warp text; transform text and use paths, layer styles, and text masks.

Chapter 8 **Printing and Exporting Images** 175
Print all or part of an image. Create a contact sheet or a picture package, and save images. Add a digital copyright or metadata.

Chapter 9 **Preparing Your Images for the Web** 195
Optimize images for web site viewing. Learn how to use the Folder Browser and how to automate image-processing tasks.

Chapter 10 **Saving Time with Actions and Automation** 219
Automate images, work with the Actions palette to record actions, and use the Automate menu and the Web Photo Gallery.

Index 241

1
2
3
4
5
6
7
8
9
10

About the Authors

For Lorian, bright stars all — **Carole Matthews**
For Emily, Wherever I May Find Her — **Doug Sahlin**

Carole Matthews:

Carole Boggs Matthews has been around computers as a programmer, systems analyst, technical consultant, and founder, co-owner, and vice president of a software company. She has been on all sides of computer software products, from designer and builder, to an accomplished user of software in her business. Together with Marty Matthews, her husband, she has authored or co-authored over 50 books, including *Adobe Photoshop CS QuickSteps*, *Adobe Photoshop Elements 3 QuickSteps*, *Microsoft Office PowerPoint 2003 QuickSteps*, *Microsoft Office FrontPage 2003*, *The Complete Reference*, and *The Official Guide to CorelDraw! 6*.

Doug Sahlin:

Doug Sahlin is an author, photographer, videographer, and web site designer living in Central Florida. He uses Photoshop CS2 as his digital darkroom to edit and create images for client multimedia presentations and web sites. He is the author or co-author of 14 books on computer graphics and web animation, including *Digital Photography QuickSteps*, *Adobe Photoshop Elements 3 QuickSteps*, *Adobe Photoshop CS QuickSteps*, *How To Do Everything with Macromedia Contribute*, and *How To Do Everything with Adobe Acrobat 7.0*. He has authored online Flash courses, presented on-location seminars, and co-authored a book on digital video.

Acknowledgments

A wonderful part of working with this QuickSteps series is the people who have worked on it. This book, as the others in the series, has been blessed with an exceptionally talented and hard-working team. Each person has been dedicated to making this book one to match their capabilities, which are substantial. One by-product of the book has been the supportive and cohesive team that has been developed. Although many members of the team may never personally meet, they have interacted in a professional and caring way.

Lisa McCoy, copy editor extraordinaire, has made our two distinctive authoring voices readable and consistent. She gave us that secure feeling that comes from knowing that our mistakes and awkward wording would be discovered and corrected. Thank you, Lisa, for your dedication and professionalism.

Laura Canby, layout artist, worked precisely and with artistic flair to lay out the book chapters with creative skill. The "look" of the pages belongs largely to her, who took our writings and made them beautiful—sometimes with amazing intuition. Thanks, Laura, for your attention to detail and perfection.

Harriet O'Neal, proofreader, always so sharp-eyed and professional, found those hidden and elusive errors that escaped all the other pairs of bleary eyes, and made the book so much better. Thanks, Harriet, for being responsive and thorough, even when you were so busy with other activities.

Kellen Diamante, proofreader, again stepped in to help out when the schedule was particularly demanding. Thanks, Kellen, for your supportiveness and willingness to step in at the last minute.

Valerie Perry, indexer, found the important words and ideas and placed them into a comprehensive and highly usable index. Always at the last minute. Thanks, Valerie, for your planning and preparation to pull it all together at the end of the cycle.

Mark Clarkson, an author on the first edition of this book, kindly gave us permission to use some of his photos. We greatly appreciate his generosity.

Contents

Acknowledgments...iv

Introduction..x

Conventions Used in this Book x

Chapter 1 **Stepping into Photoshop CS2** 1

Get Acquainted with Photoshop **1**
   Start and Close Photoshop...2
   Use the Photoshop Workspace...3
   Creating Shortcuts...5
   Open and Create Images...6
   Work with Photoshop's Interface...8
   Creating a Preset..9
   Navigating within a Document..10
   Using Photoshop's Online Help...11
   Work with Photoshop Controls..11
   Sliding a Numeric List...12
   Using the Palette Well..13
   Work with Palettes...13
   Prepare and Save the Workspace...14
   Assign Keyboard Shortcuts 15
   Selecting Screen Modes...16
Introducing Photoshop's Tools..**17**
   Work with Tool Options...19
   Set Foreground and Background Colors 20
   Use the History Palette..21
   Undoing Actions..22
   Work with the History Brush 23
Work with Color..**24**
   Working with Hue, Saturation and Luminance..............................24

Chapter 2 **Creating, Importing, and Saving Images** 25

Work with Image Types..**25**
   Understand Bitmaps..25
   Understand Vector Shapes...26
   Understanding Compression..27
   Changing Image Size and Resolution 28
   Understand Dimension vs. Resolution 28
   Choose a Color Mode 28
   Convert a Color Mode 30
Use the Bridge **31**
   View, Select, and Open files...31
   Sort and Rearrange Files 33
   Renaming Labels..34
   Select Files 34
   Label Your Files 34
   Rename Images in a Folder..36

1

2

Customize the Bridge 37
Saving and Loading a Bridge Workspace 37
Renaming, Moving, Copying, and Deleting Files 40
Search for Files...40
Use Scanners and Digital Cameras **41**
Scan an Image in Photoshop..41
Import Digital Photos 43
Find Adobe Stock Photos 44
Save Your Files..46
Work with Camera RAW Images...47

Chapter 3 **Making Selections** 51

Create New Selections **51**
Use the Marquee Tool 52
Constraining Your Selections..53
Use the Magic Wand Tool 53
Use the Lasso Tools 54
Select a Range of Colors 57
Feathering and Anti-Aliasing..59
Exclude Areas Using Selections 59
Change, Save, and Load Selections **59**
Modify a Selection...59
Crop to Fit a Selection 62
Delete Using Selections 62
Remove Fringe Pixels 63
Save and Load Selections 63
Extract Images from Backgrounds **64**
Copying Layer Styles...65
Copy to a New Layer 65
Copy to a New Document 66
Extract Background Elements...**66**
Moving and Duplicating 67
Expanding Selections 70
Use the Magic Eraser Tool 70
Use the Background Eraser Tool 70
Paint Selections with Quick Masks **72**
Work with Quick Masks..72
Use the Pen Tool 74

Chapter 4 **Using Layers**...75

Work with Layers...**75**
Hiding and Revealing Layers...76
Create New Layers...77
Linking and Unlinking Layers 78
Edit with Layers 78

Manipulating Layer Groups 82
Consolidate Layers into Layer Groups **82**
   Create a Layer Group 82
Flattening an Image 83
Merge Layers **83**
   Merge a Layer with the Layer Beneath It 83
   Merge Linked Layers 84
   Merge Visible Layers 84
Work with Layer Masks **84**
   Create Layer Masks 85
Editing a Mask 86
Work with Layer Effects **87**
Masking a Layer Group 88
   Add Layer Drop Shadows 89
   Create a Frame with Layer Effects 90
   Save and Load Layer Styles 94
Use Blending Modes and Transparency **95**
   Work with Opacity and Fill 95
   Use Blend Modes 97
   Create a CD Label 99

Chapter 5   **Using Paths, Shapes, and Painting Tools** 103

Use the Pen Tool as a Drawing Tool **103**
   Use the Pen Tool 104
   Use the Magnetic Pen Tool 106
Using the Freeform Pen Tool 107
Understanding Paths 108
   Use Paths to Create Artwork 108
   Stroke and Fill Paths 109
Converting Selections 110
   Use the Shape Tools 110
Converting Paths 111
Work with Paint **112**
   Use the Brush Tool 112
Editing Shapes 112
   Manage Brush Presets 115
Using the Eraser Tool 116
   Erase Pixels..116
   Use the Gradient Tool 118
   Use the Paint Bucket Tool 121
   Create and Manage Patterns...122
Using the Preset Manager 124
   Use the Art History Brush..124
Work with Filters **125**
   Use the Filter Gallery 125
   Use the Liquify Filter 127

6   Chapter 6   **Color Correcting, Retouching, and Repairing Images**
....129

     Perform Simple Image Corrections **129**
         Rotate and Flip Images 130
         Straighten a Photo with Free Transform 130
     Straightening a Photo 131
         Resize and Trim Images 132
     Color-Correct with Curves and Levels **135**
         Use a Histogram to View the Tonal Range 135
         Manually Adjust Levels 138
         Use the Curves Command 139
         Color-Correct Images 144
     Using Color Balance 145
         Change Hue and Saturation 147
     Working with Adjustment Layers 150
         Sharpen and Blur Images 151
     Editing in 32-Bit Mode 152
     Fine-Tuning with the Sharpen, Blur, and Smudge Tools 153
         Retouch and Repair Images 153
     Changing Image Colors 154
         Use the Dust & Scratches Filter 157
     Creating a Sepia-Tone Photo 158

7   Chapter 7   **Using Type and Type Effects** 159

     Create and Edit Text **160**
     Committing Type 161
     Hyphenating and Justifying Type 164
         Use the Spelling Checker 166
         Find and Replace Text 166
     Transforming Type 167
         Warp Text 167
         Create Text on a Path 168
         Add Special Type Effects with Layer Styles 170
     Finding and Using Layer Styles 171
         Create Text Masks 174

8   Chapter 8   **Printing and Exporting Images** 179

     Print Your Work **175**
     Resizing an Image for Printing 176
         Print Images with a Desktop Printer 176
     Printing a Single Copy of a Page 180
         Use Color Management When Printing 180
     Printing Part of an Image 181
     Using a Proof Setup 182
         Create a Contact Sheet 182
         Create a Picture Package 185
     Creating a Digital Quickmat 187

Save Images..**187**
🎨Saving a Document...188
   Add File Information and Metadata 190
   Create a Digital Copyright..191
   Import Document Metadata...193
   Create a PDF Presentation 193

Chapter 9 **Preparing Your Images for the Web**........................191   9

Optimize Images for the Web..**195**
🎨Making Part of an Image Transparent...198
   Work with Image Maps..202
🎨Using Layers to Create Image Maps...204
   Set Output Options 204
✒️ Working with Rollovers and States 206
Animate Your Images..**207**
🎨Optimizing Animations...210
🎨Importing Files and Folders as Animations 212
Work with ImageReady **215**
   Slice an Image 215
🎨Saving Sliced Images..217

Chapter 10 **Saving Time with Actions and Automation** 219   10

Automate Sequences of Frequently Used Commands **219**
   Work with the Actions Palette..220
   Record an Action to Automate a Multistep Task..221
✒️ Using Modal Controls and Tools 222
   Play and Undo Actions..222
   Edit Actions..223
🎨Setting Playback Options...223
🎨Rerecording and Duplicating Actions and Commands...............................224
Work with the Automate Menu **224**
   Use the Batch Command..224
🎨Changing Action Options 226
   Create a Droplet from an Action 227
   Crop and Straighten Photos..228
🎨Fitting an Image...229
   Create a Picture Package 229
🎨Adding Copyright Information to an Image...233
   Create a Web Photo Gallery..235
   Create a Panorama with Photomerge 238

Index...241

Introduction

QuickSteps books are recipe books for computer users. They answer the question "How do I...?" by providing a quick set of steps to accomplish the most common tasks with a particular program. The sets of steps are the central focus of the book. QuickSteps sidebars show you how to quickly do many small functions or tasks that support the primary functions. Notes, Tips, and Cautions augment the steps, yet they are presented in a such a manner as to not interrupt the flow of the steps. The brief introductions are minimal rather than narrative, and numerous illustrations and figures, many with callouts, support the steps.

QuickSteps books are organized by function and the tasks needed to perform those functions. Each function is a chapter. Each task, or "How To," contains the steps needed for its accomplishment along with the relevant Notes, Tips, Cautions, and screenshots. Tasks are easy to find through:

- The Table of Contents, which lists the functional areas (chapters) and tasks in the order they are presented

- A How To list of tasks on the opening page of each chapter

- The index with its alphabetical list of the terms used in describing the functions and tasks

- Color-coded tabs for each chapter or functional area with an index to the tabs just before Table of Contents

Conventions Used in this Book

Photoshop CS2 QuickSteps uses several conventions designed to make the book easier for you to follow. Among these are:

- A insert clock icon ⊕ or an insert check mark icon ⊘ in the Table of Contents or the How To list in each chapter references a QuickSteps or a QuickFacts sidebar in a chapter.

- **Bold type** is used for words on the screen that you are to do something with, such as click **Save As** or click the **File** menu.

- *Italic type* is used for a word or phrase that is being defined or otherwise deserves special emphasis.

- <u>Underlined type</u> is used for text that you are to type from the keyboard.

- SMALL CAPITAL LETTERS are used for keys on the keyboard, such as ENTER and SHIFT.

- When you are expected to enter a command, you are told to press the key(s). If you are to enter text or numbers, you are told to type them. Specific letters or numbers to be entered will be underlined.

- When you are to click the mouse button on a screen command or menu, you will be told to "Click File, click Open.", or sometimes, "Click File and select Save For Web."

How to...

- Start and Close Photoshop
- Use the Photoshop Workspace
- Creating Shortcuts
- Open and Create Images
- Work with Photoshop's Interface
- Creating a Preset
- Navigating within a Document
- Using Photoshop's Online Help
- Work with Photoshop Controls
- Sliding a Numeric List
- Using the Palette Well
- Work with Palettes
- Prepare and Save the Workspace
- Assign Keyboard Shortcuts
- Selecting Screen Modes
- Work with Tool Options
- Set Foreground and Background Colors
- Use the History Palette
- Undoing Actions
- Work with the History Brush
- Working with Hue, Saturation, and Luminance

Chapter 1
Stepping into Photoshop

This chapter will introduce you to some of Photoshop's basic capabilities and its user interface. You will learn how to open and close Photoshop, how to understand its screens and toolbars, and how to set up the program according to your personal needs. You will learn how to use Photoshop's Help and how to find additional help and tutorials online. You will also get a glimpse into the tools that Photoshop offers and an introduction to working with color and calibration.

Get Acquainted with Photoshop

Getting acquainted with Photoshop involves starting and closing it; setting preferences, such as how to display the mouse pointer; working with the Photoshop workspace and its menus, palettes, and other components; opening and creating images; and using Photoshop's interface, including navigating, zooming, and working with palettes.

This chapter assumes that you already know how to turn on the computer and load Windows and that Photoshop has been installed on your computer. Once Photoshop is installed, you start it as you would any other program. A quick and common way is to double-click the Photoshop icon on your desktop. Another common way is to use the Start menu.

Start and Close Photoshop

You can start Photoshop with a menu, shortcut, or keyboard combination.

USE THE START MENU TO START PHOTOSHOP

To start Photoshop using the Start menu on the Windows task pane:

1. Start your computer and log on to Windows, if necessary.

2. Click **Start**. The Start menu opens.

3. Click **All Programs** and click **Adobe Photoshop CS2**. The Photoshop application opens, as shown in Figure 1-1.

4. After using the Welcome screen to become acquainted with Photoshop CS2, click **Close** on the dialog box so you can begin working with images in Photoshop CS2.

When Photoshop first starts, the Welcome screen is displayed, which provides you with quick access to what's new in Photoshop and tutorials of Photoshop features. If you don't want to see this screen every time Photoshop starts, deselect the **Show This Dialog At Startup** check box.

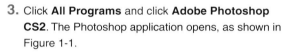

Click **Help** to find many great tutorials, such as "How to Create Web Images" or "How to Customize and Automate" (a task, palettes, or tool presets, for instance).

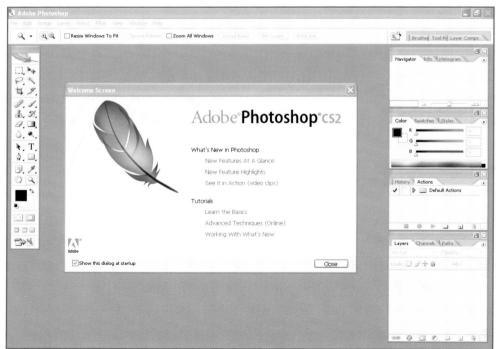

Figure 1-1: By default, the Welcome screen appears every time you start Photoshop unless you deselect this option.

START PHOTOSHOP FROM THE KEYBOARD

1. Press **CTRL+ESC** or press the **Windows** icon key (⊞) on your keyboard to open the Start menu.

2. Press **P** to select the All Programs menu (you may have to press it more than once if other program names also begin with P and are selected before All Programs), and press the **RIGHT ARROW** key to open it.

3. Press the **DOWN ARROW** key until Adobe Photoshop CS2 is selected. Then press **ENTER** to start it.

CLOSE PHOTOSHOP

1. Click **File** on the Menu bar.

2. Click **Exit**. You will be prompted to save any unsaved work.

–Or–

Click the **Close** icon in the upper-right corner of the Photoshop CS2 window.

Figure 1-2: The Photoshop workspace looks something like this.

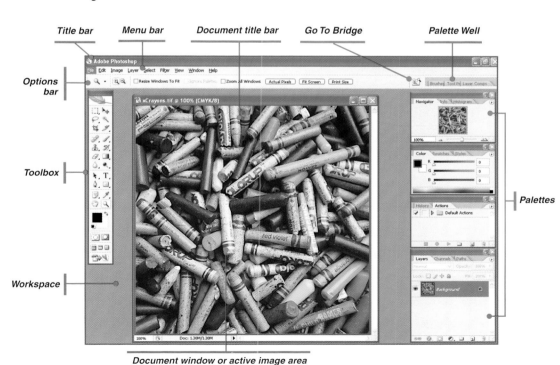

Title bar   Menu bar   Document title bar   Go To Bridge   Palette Well

Options bar

Toolbox

Palettes

Workspace

Document window or active image area

Use the Photoshop Workspace

Figure 1-2 shows an example of the Photoshop workspace. Yours may look slightly different, depending on what tools, documents, and windows you have open. Any of the items can be closed or moved about on the screen. In Windows, the empty workspace is gray.

SET PHOTOSHOP PREFERENCES

You can change the way Photoshop works by setting its *preferences*. You can change the look of the tool pointers, the color of guidelines, which units of measurement you prefer to work in (for example, inches, centimeters, or pixels), and more.

NOTE

Photoshop CS2 comes with several filters and software programs that work in conjunction with it to add features to Photoshop. When you install Photoshop CS2, these filters and programs are automatically installed in special subfolders of Photoshop's Plug-In folder. You may own other Photoshop-compatible filters or programs that are stored in different directories or that were installed prior to installing Photoshop CS2. To let Photoshop CS2 know where they are located so that you can still use them, click the **Edit** menu, click **Preferences**, and click **Plug-Ins & Scratch Disks**. In the Plug-Ins Preferences dialog box, click **Additional Plug-Ins Folder** and then browse for the folder where the plug-ins are stored. Once Photoshop knows where the plug-ins can be found, they will be included as options in various menus, depending on what the plug-in does. For instance, they will be added to the list of filters in the Filter menu or to the list of file types in the Open, Save As, and Export dialog boxes. If there are too many plug-ins, the overflow options will be listed in the Other submenu (accessed by clicking the Filter menu).

When you are first learning Photoshop, it is best to leave the default preferences intact. When you understand the implications, however, you can make changes.

1. On the Menu bar, click **Edit**, click **Preferences**, and then click **General Preferences**. The Photoshop Preferences dialog box appears, as shown in Figure 1-3.

2. Click **Next** and then click **Previous** to cycle through Photoshop's nine pages of preferences. You will see these choices:

- **General** provides general-purpose options, such as those pertaining to the Color Picker, the number of history states, whether to show Tool Tips, whether to automatically launch the Bridge, or whether to zoom with the scroll wheel.

- **File Handling** provides options for saving files, determining file compatibility, and whether to use Version Cue workgroup file management, and the number of files retained for the list. Version Cue is used to track and manage projects where multiple people are working on versions of data.

Figure 1-3: Photoshop CS2 has many preferences you can change, beginning with the General preferences.

- **Display And Cursors** provides options regarding whether to display color channels in color or to use pixel doubling—a technique for doubling the size of pixels with half the resolution for quicker previewing, or how to display the painting cursors. (See "Change Cursor Preferences" next for specific recommendations.)

- **Transparency And Gamut** provides default settings for transparency, such as grid size and grid colors, and gamut warning color and opacity.

QUICKSTEPS

CREATING SHORTCUTS

CREATE A DESKTOP SHORTCUT

Another way to start Photoshop is to create and use a shortcut icon on your desktop.

1. Click **Start**, click **All Programs**, and move your pointer to **Adobe Photoshop CS2**.

2. Right-click **Adobe Photoshop CS2**, click **Send To**, and click **Desktop (Create Shortcut)**.

3. Double-click the shortcut icon on your desktop to start Photoshop.

CREATE A KEYBOARD SHORTCUT

You can also start Photoshop using a keyboard shortcut.

1. Click **Start**, click **All Programs**, and move your pointer to **Adobe Photoshop CS2**.

2. Right-click **Adobe Photoshop CS2** and then click **Properties**.

3. Click in the **Shortcut Key** box (next to None), and type or press any letter, number, or function key. If you select a number or letter, Windows will add "**CTRL+ALT**" to the shortcut command. If you change your mind, press **ESC** to reset the shortcut to "None."

4. Click **Apply**. Click **OK**. Photoshop creates the keyboard shortcut.

5. From anywhere within Windows, press the key combination you defined (for example, **CTRL+ALT+P** or **F9**) to start Photoshop.

- **Units And Rulers** provides default units for ruler measurements and type and for column width and gutter size, new document default print and screen resolutions, and whether the point/pica size default is in PostScript or traditional typefaces.

- **Guides, Grid And Slices** provides color and style defaults for guides; color defaults for Smart Guides; color, style, and grid structure defaults for grids; color defaults for slices; and whether to show slice numbers.

- **Plug-Ins And Scratch Disks** provides an additional Plug-Ins folder, records the legacy Photoshop serial number to validate the use of some plug-ins, and determines where scratch disks are located and how many you will have.

- **Memory And Image Cache** determines how many cache levels you will have and how much of the available RAM will be used by Photoshop.

- **Type** determines whether to use smart quotes and whether to show Asian text options or English font names. You can set the size for previewing fonts.

3. All of the preferences can be left at their default settings for now. Click **Cancel** to close the dialog box.

CHANGE CURSOR PREFERENCES

One preference that you might want to change is how tool cursors are displayed. By default, Photoshop shows each tool cursor as an icon, indicating which tool is active. Instead, you might want to use a cursor that shows the size and shape of the active tool.

1. From the Menu bar, click **Edit**, click **Preferences**, and click **Display And Cursors**.

2. Click **Next** until the Display And Cursors page appears.

3. Under Painting Cursors, click the **Full Size Brush Tip** button. This shows an outline of the full size and shape of the current brush.

4. Under Other Cursors, click the **Precise** button.

5. Click **OK** to close the dialog box.

Open and Create Images

You open a file in Photoshop in much the same way you open a file in almost any Windows program.

OPEN AN IMAGE FROM THE MENU BAR

To open a file in Photoshop from the Menu bar:

1. With Photoshop open, click **File** and then click **Open**. The Open dialog box appears, as shown in Figure 1-4.

2. Use standard Windows navigation techniques to find the folder containing your image.

3. Select the file name. A thumbnail of the image appears at the bottom of the dialog box.

4. Click **Open** or double-click the file's name to open the file in Photoshop.

Figure 1-4: The Open dialog box shows a thumbnail of the selected file.

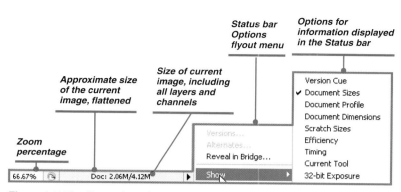

Status bar
Options
flyout menu

Options for
information displayed
in the Status bar

Size of current
image, including
all layers and
channels

Approximate size
of the current
image, flattened

Zoom
percentage

Figure 1-5: The Status bar gives useful information about the current document and tool.

OPEN AN IMAGE WITH THE BRIDGE

Photoshop's Bridge is a powerful way to browse, manage, and open your files. See Chapter 2 for in-depth information on how to use the Bridge. To open a file with the Bridge:

1. With Photoshop open, click the **Go To Bridge** button at the right of the Options bar next to the Palette Well. The Bridge window opens, as shown in Figure 1-6.

2. Use the Folders pane of the window to navigate to a folder containing images. Thumbnails of all images in the folder will appear in the Thumbnails pane.

3. Click any thumbnail to select that file. A preview appears in the preview pane.

4. Double-click a thumbnail to open the file in Photoshop.

TIP

The Status bar, shown in Figure 1-5, gives useful information about your currently selected document and tool. You can change the information displayed by opening the Options flyout menu on the Status bar and choosing the information to be displayed.

NOTE

Press **CTRL** while you click to select multiple files; or press **SHIFT** while you click to select a range of files; then click **Open** to open multiple files in Photoshop.

Double-click a thumbnail of the
image to open it in Photoshop

Sources
of images:
Favorites or
Folders

Preview of
selected image
thumbnail

Information
that may be
available on
each photo

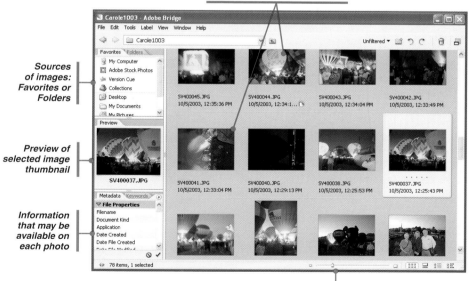

Slide to increase or decrease the size of thumbnails

Figure 1-6: The Photoshop Bridge is a powerful tool for finding, managing, and opening files.

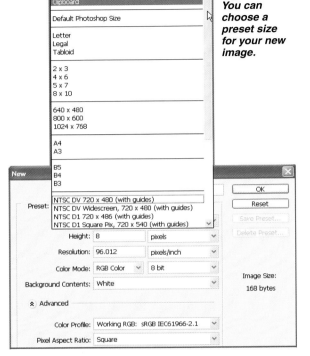

Figure 1-7: You can choose a preset size for your new image.

CREATE A NEW IMAGE CANVAS FROM A PRESET

Photoshop allows you to easily create an image canvas from a list of preset sizes and resolutions. To create a new, blank canvas for your image:

1. From the Menu bar, click **File** and then click **New**. The New dialog box appears.
2. Type a name for the new image.
3. Click the **Preset** drop-down list box, and choose a preset image size, such as **640 x 480**, as shown in Figure 1-7.
4. You then have these options:
   - Specify the **Width** and **Height** by typing the values in pixels, inches, centimeters, millimeters, points, picas, or columns.
   - Type a **Resolution** and choose between pixels per inch or per centimeter.
   - Leave the **Color Mode** in either RGB (for color images) or Grayscale (for black-and-white images). We'll examine the other color modes in later chapters.
   - Choose a white or transparent **Background**, or you can set it to the current background color.
   - Click **Advanced** for advanced options relating to color profiles (a record of the color type of an image so that the image color is as accurate as it can be when read by various devices) and the pixel aspect ratios (this allows for a square pixel image to be displayed on a non-square device).
5. Click **OK** to create a new image canvas.

Work with Photoshop's Interface

For the most part, Photoshop uses standard interface conventions for opening and closing dialog boxes and windows, entering and changing values, and so forth, but it also offers some unique controls.

ZOOM IN AND OUT

Being able to work as close up or as far away in your image as you want is a big advantage. When working with images in Photoshop, you can zoom in until the image is displayed at 16 times its actual size (that is, 1600 percent larger). At 1600 percent, each pixel in the image is 16 by 16 pixels on the screen. Similarly, you can zoom out until an entire image is only a few pixels wide.

NOTE

Zooming in and out does not in any way alter the actual image.

QUICKSTEPS

CREATING A PRESET

You can create a new preset image size for a frequently created image, such as a 120-pixel-by-60-pixel banner for a web page.

1. If the New File dialog box is not displayed, click **File** and then click **New**.

2. Set the size, resolution, color mode, and background color; and then click **Save Preset**.

3. Name the preset and click **OK** to create it.

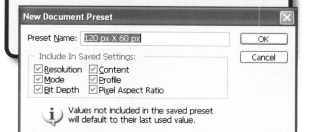

New Document Preset

Preset Name: 120 px X 60 px

OK
Cancel

Include In Saved Settings:
☑ Resolution ☑ Content
☑ Mode ☑ Profile
☑ Bit Depth ☑ Pixel Aspect Ratio

ⓘ Values not included in the saved preset will default to their last used value.

ZOOM WITH THE ZOOM TOOL

1. With an image open and selected in Photoshop, click the **Zoom** tool in the Toolbox, or press **z**, to select the Zoom tool. The Zoom tool, which includes Zoom In and Zoom Out, is displayed in the Options bar:

   • Click repeatedly within the image to zoom in.

   • To zoom out, press and hold the **ALT** key. The Zoom tool changes from a plus sign (+) to a minus sign (–). Press **ALT** and click repeatedly within the image to zoom out. Release the **ALT** key to zoom in again. You can also click the **Zoom Out** tool in the Options bar.

   • Click and drag the part of the image you want to zoom in on. A marquee is created that specifies the area on which to zoom. You will then either zoom in or out, depending on the Zoom tool selected.

ZOOM WITH THE KEYBOARD

1. With an image open and selected in Photoshop, hold down **CTRL** and repeatedly press the plus (**+**) key to zoom in.

2. Hold down **CTRL** – and repeatedly press the minus (**–**) key to zoom out.

3. Press **CTRL+0** to zoom the current image to fit on the screen. Press **ALT+CTRL+0** to zoom the current image to 100 percent.

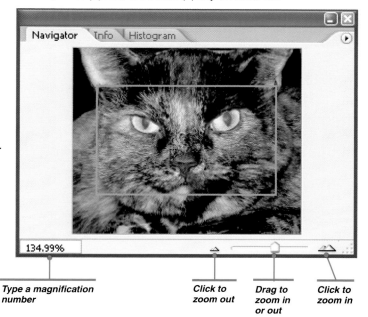

Navigator Info Histogram

134.99%

Type a magnification number

Click to zoom out

Drag to zoom in or out

Click to zoom in

QUICKSTEPS

NAVIGATING WITHIN A DOCUMENT

You need to be able to move around within your image, especially when you are zoomed in for detail work.

MOVE AROUND WITH THE NAVIGATOR PALETTE

1. Open an image. If the Navigator palette is not displayed, click **Window** and then click **Navigator**.

2. Drag the slider to the right until your image is larger than the Navigator window.

3. Locate the red rectangle within the image thumbnail in the Navigator palette. This represents the visible area of your image.

4. Drag the rectangle to move around within your image, as shown in Figure 1-8.

MOVE AROUND WITH THE HAND TOOL

1. Open an image. Hold down **CTRL** and repeatedly press the **plus (+)** key until your image is larger than the Navigator window.

2. Click the **Hand** tool in the Toolbox, or press **H** to select the Hand tool.

3. Drag your image to move it around the window.

TIP

To zoom using other techniques you can:

- **Status bar**: Type a zoom amount in the text box at the far left of the Status bar.

- **Hand tool**: Double-click the **Hand** tool in the Toolbox to zoom the current image to fit on the screen.

Figure 1-8: Drag the red rectangle in the Navigator to move around within your image.

ZOOM WITH THE NAVIGATOR PALETTE

1. Open and select an image in Photoshop. If the Navigator palette is not displayed, click **Window** and then click **Navigator**.

2. Drag the slider to the right to zoom in; drag it to the left to zoom out.

   –Or–

   Click the large mountains at the right of the slider to zoom in, and click the small mountain at the left of the slider to zoom out.

   –Or–

   Type a zoom amount in the Navigator text box, and press **ENTER**. To display your image at twice its actual size, type 200; for half the image's actual size, type 50.

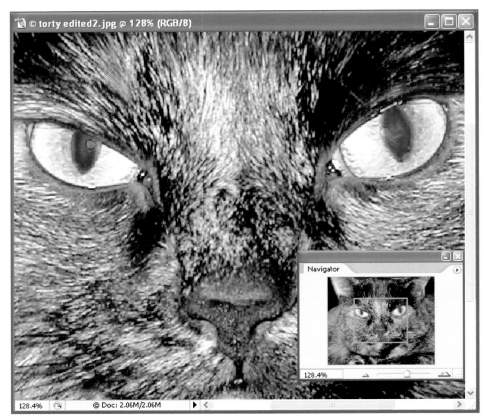

UICKSTEPS

QUICKSTEPS

USING PHOTOSHOP'S ONLINE HELP

Photoshop has a comprehensive online Help system available. To access Help:

- Press **F1**.

  –Or–

- On the Menu bar, click **Help** and then click **Photoshop Help**.

Photoshop's Help opens in your default web browser, as shown in Figure 1-9. Navigate through Help from the left pane by searching for keywords or by browsing the alphabetical index, site map, or table of contents.

Figure 1-9: Photoshop's online Help displays in your default web browser.

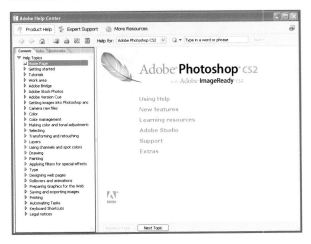

Work with Photoshop Controls

Use sliders, drop-down lists and controls, flyout menus, and swatches when working with Photoshop.

USE SLIDERS

Many Photoshop controls use sliders to change values. To use a slider control in Photoshop, click the down arrow to open the slider, and drag the slider to the left to decrease the value; drag it to the right to increase the value.

USE DROP-DOWN LISTS

Drop-down lists in Photoshop and ImageReady are indicated by a little down arrow.

To access a drop-down list:

1. Click the down arrow.
2. Click your selection in the list.

   –Or–

1. Click within the displayed text of the drop-down list.
2. Use the **UP ARROW** and **DOWN ARROW** keys to scroll through the list.

USE DROP-DOWN CONTROLS

To access a drop-down control:

1. Click and hold the right arrow.
2. Drag the control.

NOTE

In Full Screen mode, you can move your image around the screen by holding down the **SPACEBAR** to temporarily select the Hand tool and then dragging the image.

QUICKSTEPS

SLIDING A NUMERIC LIST

Any list that displays a text box for a numerical value, such as font size, can be operated like a slider.

1. Drag the cursor over the contents of the text box so that it is highlighted.

2. Press and hold the **CTRL** key. The cursor changes to a hand with arrows.

3. Move the cursor to the left to decrease the displayed number; move the cursor to the right to increase it.

USE FLYOUT MENUS

Flyout menus are indicated in Photoshop and ImageReady by a small arrow in a dialog box or by a small arrow at the corner of a tool in the Toolbox.

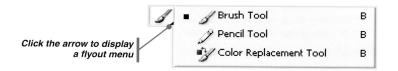

Click the arrow to display a flyout menu

To use a flyout menu:

1. Click the flyout arrow.
2. Click your selection in the menu.

USE SHORTCUT MENUS

You access shortcut menus, also called context menus, which display additional options, by right-clicking within the canvas, that is, right-clicking the image. You can also access shortcut menus for various palettes by right-clicking inside them. To close a shortcut menu, either select an option and begin using the tool, or click anywhere outside of the current canvas or image.

USE SWATCHES

Photoshop has several palettes and dialog boxes for picking colors. These include the Swatches palette and the Color palette, as well as the foreground and background swatches, which, when clicked, open the Color Picker. From a swatch, simply click a color to select it.

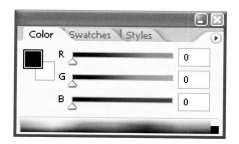
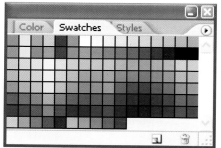

USING THE PALETTE WELL

You can dock palettes using the Palette Well, located to the right of Photoshop's Options bar. By default, you'll find the Brushes, Histogram, Info, and Layer Comp palettes docked in the Palette Well, but you can replace any or all of these with the palettes you use most frequently. The Palette Well gives you access to palettes without cluttering your workspace.

USE A PALETTE IN THE PALETTE WELL

To use a palette in the Palette Well, click the tab and use the palette as you normally would.

CLOSE A PALETTE

To close a palette, click outside the palette area.

REMOVE A PALETTE FROM THE PALETTE WELL

To remove a palette from the Palette Well, click the palette's tab and drag the palette out of the Palette Well and into the workspace.

PLACE A NEW PALETTE IN THE PALETTE WELL

Open the palette you want to place in the Palette Well. Then:

1. Click the **Options** menu button near the top right of the palette.
2. Click **Dock To Palette Well**.

–Or–

Click and drag the palette tab into the Palette Well.

Work with Palettes

Photoshop has a number of small windows, called *palettes*, that you can use to choose colors, set paragraph formatting options, sample the RGB (Red, Green, Blue) values of pixels in an image, manage paths and layers, and so forth.

- To open a palette, click **Window** and click the name of the palette you want to work with, for example, **Layers**.

Palettes are grouped together with other related palettes. Each palette has a tab with its name extending from the top.

- To switch between palettes in a group, click the name tab, as shown here.

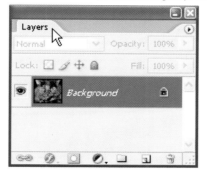 

- To restore the original location and contents of the palettes, click **Window**, click **Workspace**, and then click **Reset Palette Location**.
- To move a palette from a group of palettes, click the tab and drag it to the Palette Well, to another group of palettes, to the bottom of another palette to dock it to that palette, or into the workspace to separate it into its own palette window.
- To move a single palette or a group of palettes docked together, drag the title bar.
- If you delete a palette by clicking its Close icon in the upper-right corner, you can restore it by clicking **Window** and then clicking the name of the palette.
- You can resize a palette in the Palette Well by dragging its lower-right corner. Some palettes cannot be resized.
- Press the **TAB** key to hide all palettes and toolbars and have an uncluttered workspace. Press **TAB** again to restore them to their original positions. While still displaying any toolbars currently open, press **SHIFT+TAB** to hide or show only the palettes.

TIP

To minimize or restore palettes, click **Minimize** or **Maximize** at the top of the palette, or double-click the top of the palette.

Prepare and Save the Workspace

Photoshop allows you to customize your workspace—decide which palettes are open, what their positions are on the screen, and so forth—and then save that workspace. You can create one workspace suitable for browsing through large folders or images and another suitable for retouching scanned photos.

1. Close any palettes you don't want open.

2. Open any additional palettes and windows you require, and position them where you want them.

3. Click **Window**, click **Workspace**, and click **Save Workspace**. The Save Workspace dialog box appears.

4. Type a name for the workspace, such as Retouching.

5. Click **OK**.

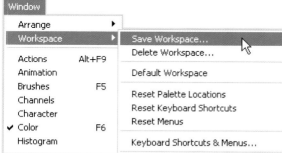

To retrieve a custom workspace, click **Window**, click **Workspace**, and click the name of the workspace from the menu.

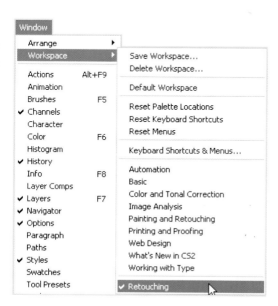

NOTE

If you encounter a problem in the layout of your workspace—for example, a palette gets pushed partially off screen and you can't reach it—click **Window**, click **Workspace**, and click **Reset Palette Locations** to restore the workspace to its original layout.

Assign Keyboard Shortcuts

Photoshop allows you to assign keyboard shortcuts for selecting tools, opening palettes, and selecting menu commands. Some keyboard shortcuts are assigned by default: **B** selects the Brush or Pencil tool, for example; and **F5** opens and closes the Brushes palette. You can change these defaults and create new shortcuts to suit the way you work.

ASSIGN A KEYBOARD SHORTCUT TO A MENU COMMAND

This procedure assigns the keyboard shortcut **ALT+F6** to open and close the Navigator palette. The process is basically the same to create any shortcut.

1. Click **Edit** and click **Keyboard Shortcuts**. The Keyboard Shortcuts And Menus dialog box appears.

2. Click the **Keyboard Shortcuts** tab, click the **Shortcut For** drop-down menu, and click **Application Menus**, as shown in Figure 1-10.

3. Under Application Menu Command, double-click **Window** to expand the list of menu items.

4. Scroll down and click **Navigator**. A text box appears to the right of the command name.

5. Press the key combination you want to assign to the Navigator palette, such as **ALT+F6**. Shortcuts must include the **ALT** or **CTRL** key, a function key, or both. Click **OK** to accept the change.

Pressing this key combination will now open and close the Navigator palette.

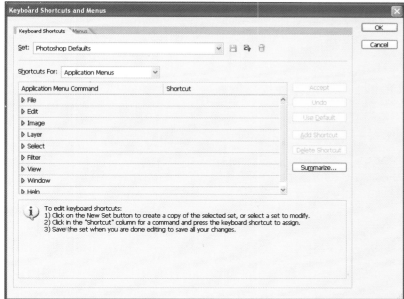

Figure 1-10: Use the Keyboard Shortcuts And Menus dialog box to assign new keyboard shortcuts.

SELECTING SCREEN MODES

Photoshop offers three different screen modes. You can display them one at a time by pressing **F** repeatedly to cycle through the screen modes.

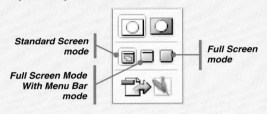

Standard Screen mode

Full Screen mode

Full Screen Mode With Menu Bar mode

USE THE STANDARD SCREEN MODE

In Standard Screen mode, your image is placed within a window. You can view multiple images at once in Standard Screen mode, as shown in Figure 1-11. To select Standard Screen mode, click the **Standard Screen Mode** button in the Toolbox.

SELECT FULL SCREEN MODE

In Full Screen mode, only your currently selected document is visible. All frames, scroll bars, title bars, menus, and so forth are hidden, as shown in Figure 1-12. To select Full Screen mode, click the **Full Screen Mode** button in the Toolbox. In Full Screen mode, the main menu is moved to the top of the Toolbox.

USE FULL SCREEN MODE WITH MENU BAR MODE

Full Screen Mode With Menu Bar mode is the same as Full Screen mode, but the menu remains at the top of the workspace. To select Full Screen Mode With Menu Bar mode, click the **Full Screen Mode With Menu Bar Mode** button in the Toolbox.

Continued...

Figure 1-11: Standard Screen mode shows all open documents.

Figure 1-12: Full Screen Mode hides all documents but the one currently selected.

Introducing Photoshop's Tools

Photoshop's primary tools are kept in a palette called the Toolbox. The Toolbox, shown in Figure 1-13, is open by default. If it is not visible, click **Window** on the Menu bar, and then click **Tools**.

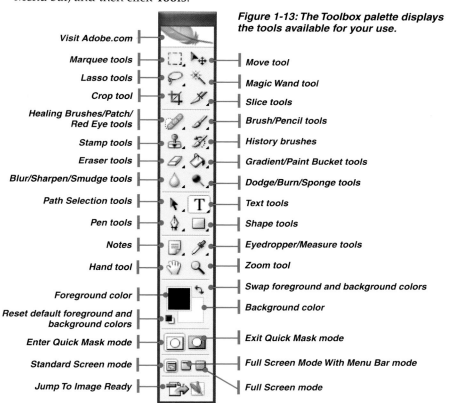

Figure 1-13: The Toolbox palette displays the tools available for your use.

Visit Adobe.com	
Marquee tools	Move tool
Lasso tools	Magic Wand tool
Crop tool	Slice tools
Healing Brushes/Patch/Red Eye tools	Brush/Pencil tools
Stamp tools	History brushes
Eraser tools	Gradient/Paint Bucket tools
Blur/Sharpen/Smudge tools	Dodge/Burn/Sponge tools
Path Selection tools	Text tools
Pen tools	Shape tools
Notes	Eyedropper/Measure tools
Hand tool	Zoom tool
	Swap foreground and background colors
Foreground color	Background color
Reset default foreground and background colors	
Enter Quick Mask mode	Exit Quick Mask mode
Standard Screen mode	Full Screen Mode With Menu Bar mode
Jump To Image Ready	Full Screen mode

While up to 33 buttons and controls are shown in the Toolbox at any given time, more tools are available for you to use. Many of Photoshop's tools are hidden beneath other tools in the Toolbox. Whenever a tool icon has a small black triangle at the bottom, that indicates you can access a flyout menu containing additional tools.

Figure 1-14 provides some examples of the functions of several tools in Photoshop.

Figure 1-14: Photoshop's basic tools offer a wide variety of options.

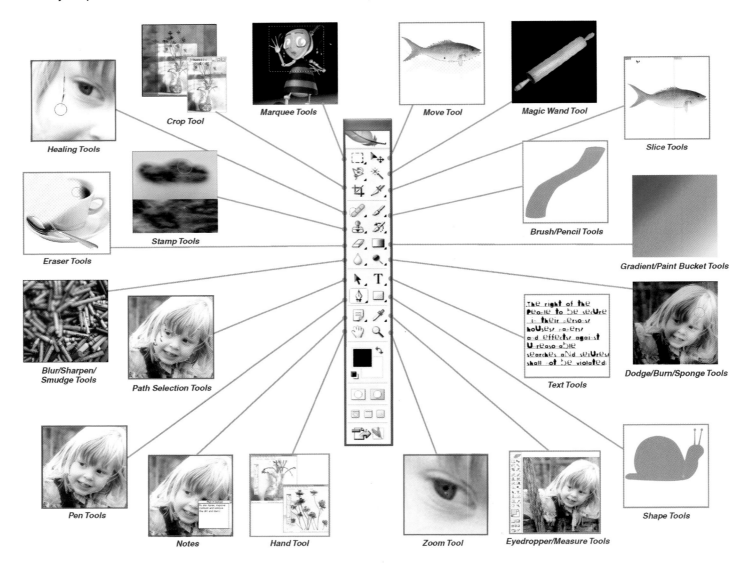

Crop Tool

Marquee Tools

Move Tool

Magic Wand Tool

Slice Tools

Healing Tools

Brush/Pencil Tools

Stamp Tools

Eraser Tools

Gradient/Paint Bucket Tools

Blur/Sharpen/ Smudge Tools

Path Selection Tools

Text Tools

Dodge/Burn/Sponge Tools

Pen Tools

Notes

Hand Tool

Zoom Tool

Eyedropper/Measure Tools

Shape Tools

Work with Tool Options

All tools in Photoshop have options you can control: size, shape, color, and so forth. Let's take a close look at setting the options for a common tool.

CHANGE THE BRUSH TOOL OPTIONS

The Brush tool serves as a good introduction to setting tool options in Photoshop; the same controls are available for many other tools, including the Smudge, Blur, Burn, Dodge, and Eraser tools. Some guidelines to keep in mind are:

- Access basic options for most tools, including the Brush tool, by right-clicking the image and changing settings from the shortcut menu that appears, as shown here for the Brush tool.

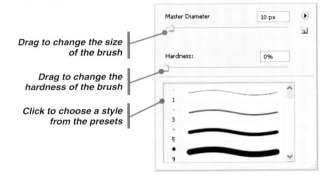

Drag to change the size of the brush

Drag to change the hardness of the brush

Click to choose a style from the presets

- From this menu, you can change the size of the brush, as well as its hardness, by dragging the **Master Diameter** and **Hardness** sliders to the right or left. The harder the brush (drag right), the more distinct the brush strokes created, as shown here, where the top brush stroke is set to 0 percent hardness (soft, almost fuzzy) and the bottom is set to 100 percent (very distinct and abrupt).

- Choose a brush tip from the Presets menu at the bottom of the Brush Options dialog box.

- Close the Options dialog box, either by starting to paint or by clicking somewhere outside the dialog box.

More options are available on the Brush tool Options bar, located beneath the main menu, as shown in Figure 1-15. The one you'll probably use most is Opacity, which controls the maximum paint opacity of the paintbrush.

TIP

Many tool shortcuts actually toggle between multiple tools within the same Toolbox flyout menu. Press **B**, for example, to select the Brush tool. Press **B** again to switch to the Pencil tool. Press **B** once more to switch to the Color Replacement tool, before finally pressing **B** to return to the Brush tool again.

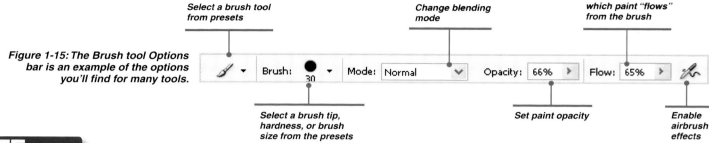

Select a brush tool from presets

Change blending mode

Set the rate at which paint "flows" from the brush

Figure 1-15: The Brush tool Options bar is an example of the options you'll find for many tools.

Select a brush tip, hardness, or brush size from the presets

Set paint opacity

Enable airbrush effects

NOTE

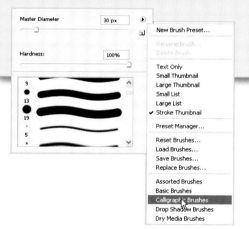

To load new sets of brushes from the context menu, click the **Palette Options** button in the upper-right area, and choose a new set of brushes from the menu.

To really get the most out of the paintbrush, press **F5** or click **Window** and then click **Brushes** to open the Brushes palette. You'll learn more about advanced Brush options in Chapters 5 and 6.

Set Foreground and Background Colors

Painting, drawing, fills, type, and many Photoshop filters depend on the current foreground and background colors. You can set these manually by taking a sample of a color, thereby changing the foreground or background color. Then you can select the paint, drawing, fill, type, or other tool to use with the sampled color.

SAMPLE A FOREGROUND COLOR FROM AN IMAGE

With an image file open in Photoshop:

1. Select the **Eyedropper** tool from the Toolbox.
2. Click a color in the image that you want to use as the foreground color.

SAMPLE A BACKGROUND COLOR FROM AN IMAGE

With an image file open in Photoshop:

1. Select the **Eyedropper** tool from the Toolbox.
2. Press **ALT** and click a color in the image that you want to use as the background color.

TIP

Clicking the **Airbrush** option on the Brush tool Options bar allows you to build up spray-painted effects with the Brush tool.

TIP

Press **X** to swap foreground and background colors.

NOTE

By default, Photoshop allows you to undo the last 20 changes to a document. To increase or decrease this number, press **CTRL+K** to open the General Preferences dialog box, and change the number in the **History States** field.

TIP

If you're not sure if a change is an improvement or not, press **CTRL+Z** repeatedly to switch between the original image and the changed image to compare them.

RESTORE DEFAULT FOREGROUND AND BACKGROUND COLORS (BLACK & WHITE)

To restore Photoshop to its default black and white foreground and background colors, do one of the following:

- Press **D**.

    –Or–

- Click the **Default Foreground And Background Color** button on the Toolbox.

Use the History Palette

The History palette contains a snapshot of the 20 most recent changes in your document. Every time you make a change to the image, Photoshop adds a new image state to the History palette. When the number of changes exceeds 20, the older states are discarded from the History palette. Each state is named for the tool, filter, or other operation that created it—Brush tool, Pencil tool, Invert, and so forth. The Open layer is at the top, unless you have made more than 20 changes and then that initial layer is overlaid with a more recent one. Click the **Open** layer to view the state of the image when it was first opened. Click any of the other layers to view the state of the image created by performing the change named on the layer.

To revert to a previous state, click that layer in the History palette, and save the file or begin working on it again. Any changes that existed in the palette after this state will be discarded from the History palette as soon as you save the work or make new changes.

The following procedure will help you understand how Photoshop's History palette keeps track of recent changes and allows you to easily compare earlier states and to revert to an earlier state.

1. Open an image in Photoshop, and make at least three major changes to it. You might paint a circle with the Brush tool, invert the colors (press **CTRL+I**), or apply a filter.

2. Click **Window** and then click **History** to open the History palette.

 **UICKSTEPS**

UNDOING ACTIONS

USE UNDO

To undo your most recent action:

- Press **CTRL+Z**.

–Or–

- Click **Edit** and then click **Undo**.

REDO A CHANGE

To redo the most recent change:

- Press **CTRL+Z**.

–Or–

- Click **Edit** and then click **Redo [operation]**.

USE STEP BACKWARD

The Undo command only undoes the most recent operation. If you want to undo more than one operation, use the Step Backward command. To move backward through recent changes:

- Press **ALT+CTRL+Z**.

–Or–

- Click **Edit** and click **Step Backward**.

USE STEP FORWARD

To move forward again through recent changes:

- Press **SHIFT+CTRL+Z**.

–Or–

- Click **Edit** and click **Step Forward**.

 TIP

You can double-click a default snapshot name to rename it with a more meaningful name.

---

3. Click a layer to select it. The image will revert to that state. All states after the selected state will be dimmed, but they are still available if you click them. If you begin to work with the image at this point, all succeeding states are deleted.

MAKE A HISTORY PALETTE SNAPSHOT

Twenty undo actions may seem like a lot, but you can use them up before you know it. Twenty quick strokes with the Brush tool, for example, will do it. The History palette can take a snapshot of an image at a particular point in time. This snapshot will remain available until you delete it or close the document.

To take a snapshot of an image:

1. If the History palette is not open, click **Window** and click **History**.
2. If you want to take a snapshot of an earlier state, click that layer in the History palette. The image reverts to that state.
3. Click the **Create New Snapshot** button at the bottom of the palette.

REVERT TO A SNAPSHOT

1. If the History palette is not open, open it by clicking **Window** and then clicking **History**.
2. In the History palette, click the snapshot. The image reverts to that state.

Work with the History Brush

The History Brush allows you to revert *parts* of your image to an earlier state while leaving changes intact across the rest of the image. You are essentially painting over the current image with the older image. You might, for example, open a photo of a person, remove the color from it, and then paint the color back in with the History Brush tool.

1. Open a color photograph in Photoshop.

2. Press **CTRL+SHIFT+U** (Desaturate), or click **Image**, click **Adjustments**, and click **Desaturate** to remove the color from the image.

3. If the History palette is not open, open it by clicking **Window** and then clicking **History**.

4. Find the layer just above the Desaturate state, but do *not* click it. In your photo, this would be the state you want to restore.

5. Click the blank square to the left of the layer just above the Desaturate layer. The History Brush icon appears, as shown in Figure 1-16.

6. Click the **History Brush** tool from the Toolbox, and then paint on the image. Where you paint with the History Brush, the older, colored version of the photo replaces the newer black-and-white version.

Figure 1-16: Click above the Desaturate state to activate the History Brush tool in order to revert to an earlier color.

NOTE

History information is not preserved when you save your files.

See Chapter 5 for more information on using the History Brush to create special effects in your images.

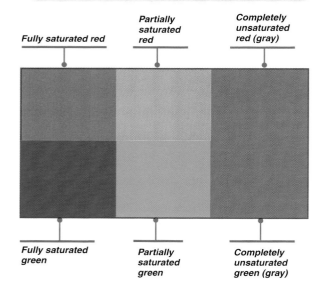

Fully saturated red · Partially saturated red · Completely unsaturated red (gray)

Fully saturated green · Partially saturated green · Completely unsaturated green (gray)

Work with Color

Certain colors in Photoshop are described using specific terms, known as color modes, color models, or color spaces. Your computer monitor primarily uses the RGB (Red, Green, Blue) color space. The colors on your computer monitor are created by mixing together different amounts of red, green, and blue light. Printers and photographs can exist in either the RGB or the CMYK (Cyan, Magenta, Yellow, Black) color space. Most color printing done by a large commercial press or expensive computer printers is done with CMYK. Inexpensive computer printers, such as inkjet printers, use RGB.

RGB and CMYK color spaces differ quite fundamentally. RGB is *additive*. As mentioned, it creates colors by mixing red, green, and blue light. The amount of each color can range from 0 to 255. If you use R 255, G 255, and B 255, you get white light. Keeping the numbers constant between the three colors, any value less than 255 will give you a shade of gray; values of 0 for the three colors give you black. Varying the numbers among the colors, of course, gives you varying colors.

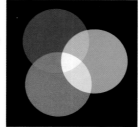

CMYK, on the other hand, is *subtractive*. It creates colors by subtracting colors from white by percentages. A 100 percentage of cyan ink, magenta ink, and yellow ink equals black. In printing, white is (usually) the complete absence of ink on the paper (0 percent). The more ink you add, the darker the color gets.

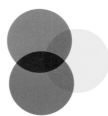

On your computer monitor, a photo of a red ball is red because your monitor is actually emitting red light. However, a red ball sitting in your driveway is red because the ball absorbs every color of sunlight *except* red, which it reflects.

The problem of getting RGB images created on the computer to look the same when printed out in CMYK ink is a difficult one. We'll look at it in more detail in Chapter 8.

How to...

- *Understand Bitmaps*
- *Understand Vector Shapes*
- *Understanding Compression*
- *Changing Image Size and Resolution*
- *Understand Dimension vs. Resolution*
- *Choose a Color Mode*
- *Convert a Color Mode*
- *View, Select, and Open Files*
- *Sort and Rearrange Files*
- *Renaming Labels*
- *Select Files*
- *Label Your Files*
- *Rename Images in a Folder*
- *Customize the Bridge*
- *Saving and Loading a Bridge Workspace*
- *Renaming, Moving, Copying, and Deleting Files*
- *Search for Files*
- *Scan an Image in Photoshop*
- *Import Digital Photos*
- *Find Adobe Stock Photos*
- *Save Your Files*
- *Work with Camera RAW Images*

Chapter 2
Creating, Importing, and Saving Images

With Photoshop, you can organize, sort, search for, preview, and open files on your hard drive or network, as well as import images from digital scanners and cameras. First you will learn about the differences between vector-based and bitmap-based images.

Work with Image Types

Dozens of different types of computer-image files are in existence, each employing different file formats, color models, and compression schemes. Fortunately, Photoshop allows you to work with almost any image file in use today.

Understand Bitmaps

Bitmap images (sometimes called *raster images*) are composed of lots and lots of tiny square dots called *pixels*. The larger the image, the more tiny dots it has. A typical piece of desktop wallpaper has a half-million to three-quarters of a million pixels. If you open a color photograph in Photoshop and zoom all the way in by holding down the **CTRL** key and pressing the plus (**+**) key ten times, you can clearly see the pixels that make up the photograph. The number of pixels is closely related to resolution: the more pixels per inch, the higher the resolution. Most of the different image-file formats you'll encounter—including BMP, PICT, GIF, JPG, TIF, and PNG—are bitmap formats.

Understand Vector Shapes

While bitmaps are made up of pixels, vector-based images are made up of points, lines, and curves, which combine to form the paths that make up the vector shape. A vector-based image file doesn't record the position and color of every pixel; rather, it records the position and color of every curve. Where a bitmap-based image file is like a drawing or painting, a vector-based image file is like a *description* of that drawing or painting.

Because they are composed of shapes rather than individual pixels, vectors can be scaled up or down as far as you like without losing image quality. When vectors are resized, the positions of the points, lines, curves, and paths are mathematically calculated. For example, these two images look identical:

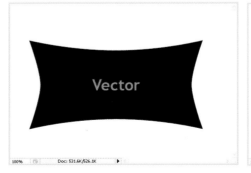

QUICKFACTS

UNDERSTANDING COMPRESSION

To mitigate the size of bitmap images, you can *compress* them. Consider a red circle on a white background.

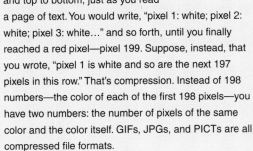

Imagine recording every pixel in that image, starting with the upper-left corner and reading from left to right and top to bottom, just as you read a page of text. You would write, "pixel 1: white; pixel 2: white; pixel 3: white…" and so forth, until you finally reached a red pixel—pixel 199. Suppose, instead, that you wrote, "pixel 1 is white and so are the next 197 pixels in this row." That's compression. Instead of 198 numbers—the color of each of the first 198 pixels—you have two numbers: the number of pixels of the same color and the color itself. GIFs, JPGs, and PICTs are all compressed file formats.

Compression is a good thing, but there's a catch. Compression can cause an image to lose information. Once image information is gone, you cannot get it back. JPG (or JPEG) compression is the worst offender. JPG uses what is called a lossy algorithm. It actually throws away information in order to squeeze the image down to a smaller size, and at higher compression settings, the degradation becomes quite apparent. For instance, JPEG compression discards pixels with similar hues. Keep in mind that a pixel is a mixture of colors. For example, in the RGB (Red, Green, Blue) format, the pixel is a mixture of a shade of red, green, and blue, so some adjacent pixels with similar mixtures of red, green, and blue hues might be lost.

Original image

Image heavily compressed as a JPEG file

But when you scale them up, the differences become apparent:

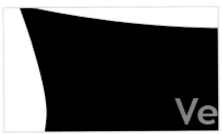

Vector-based image files are generally much smaller than raster image files. If a vector-based image file of a red circle on a white background weighs in at 2000 bytes (2K) in vector format, it will be about the same file size *regardless of the image size*. A ten-inch circle will be the same file size as a one-inch circle. In contrast, a bitmap of the same circle grows larger as you increase the dimensions. Nevertheless, vector-based image files with complex fills and gradients can get quite large.

Vector-based files are best suited to such things as clip art, logos, and bold graphics with relatively large, smooth areas filled with relatively simple colors. Common vector file formats include Adobe Illustrator (AI), Macromedia Flash (SWF), and Encapsulated PostScript (EPS).

Photoshop files can include both vector and raster components. A given Photoshop PSD file can have all vector components, all raster components, or some combination of the two. Photoshop files can include several forms of vector objects: text, shapes, and paths. You will learn more about these in Chapters 5 and 7.

 **UICKSTEPS**

CHANGING IMAGE SIZE AND RESOLUTION

You can change the size of an image and its resolution.

RESIZE AN IMAGE

To change the pixel dimensions of an image:

1. Click **Image** and then click **Image Size**. The Image Size dialog box appears.

2. Under Pixel Dimensions, type a new **Width** or **Height** for the image. The other dimensions automatically update.

   –Or–

   Under Document Size, type a new **Width** or **Height** for the image. Photoshop automatically updates the other dimensions.

CHANGE IMAGE RESOLUTION

To change an image's resolution *without* changing its pixel dimensions at the same time:

1. Click **Image** and click **Image Size**. The Image Size dialog box appears.

2. Deselect **Resample Image**.

3. Type a new **Resolution**, and click **OK**.

To change an image's resolution *and* its pixel dimensions:

1. Click **Image** and click **Image Size**. The Image Size dialog box appears.

2. Click the **Resample Image** check box.

3. Type a new **Resolution**. Under Pixel Dimensions, the Width and Height fields automatically update to reflect the new resolution.

4. Click **OK.**

Understand Dimension vs. Resolution

The difference between an image's *dimensions* and its *resolution* is the source of some confusion. Resolution is generally measured in dots or pixels per inch—*dpi* or *ppi*. An image's resolution determines what document size the image will be when printed. Consider an image of 300 x 300 pixels. At a resolution of 72 dpi, the *document* dimensions will print out a bit larger than four inches square. At a resolution of 150 dpi, it will print out at two inches square. At a resolution of 300 dpi, document dimensions will print out at an inch square. However, the image's *pixel* dimensions remain unchanged at 300 x 300 pixels. You can examine and change an image's dimensions, resolution, and printed size by clicking the **Image** menu and clicking **Image Size**. See Chapter 6 for additional information.

Choose a Color Mode

Taking the time to think about color when you are creating an image can be a wise decision. Four common color modes are grayscale, RGB, CYMK, and indexed color. The one you choose depends on whether you will be printing your images on paper, using a printing press, or using them on the computer, such as in a web page.

CREATE A NEW GRAYSCALE IMAGE

Grayscale images have no color; rather, a grayscale image is 256 shades of gray, from pure black (0) to pure white (255). In photography, grayscale is known as "black and white."

1. Click **File** and click **New**. The New dialog box appears.

2. Select a file size from the Preset drop-down list, or manually enter image dimensions and resolution.

3. Click the **Color Mode** down arrow, and click **Grayscale**.

4. Click **OK** to create the file.

USE RGB

RGB (Red, Green, Blue) is the standard color mode for images displayed on the computer. Images for web pages and other computer applications should almost

CAUTION

You cannot turn a grayscale image into a color image by converting it to RGB.

TIP

When you create a new image for printing in Photoshop, match the resolution of your image with the resolution at which you'll be printing it. Even though some new printers support resolutions of 1200 dpi or more, anything beyond 300-400 dpi is probably overkill.

always be RGB. Common computer printers (less-expensive inkjet printers, for instance) also use RGB color mode.

1. From the Menu bar, click **File** and click **New**. The New dialog box appears.
2. Choose a preset from the Preset drop-down list, or type values in the **Width**, **Height**, and **Resolution** fields.
3. Click the **Color Mode** down arrow, and click **RGB**.
4. Click **OK**.

USE CMYK

CMYK (Cyan, Magenta, Yellow, Black) is the standard color mode for more-expensive computer printers. Images destined to be published on a commercial printer will be more accurately displayed in Photoshop if they are in CMYK color mode.

1. From the Menu bar, click **File** and then click **New**. The New dialog box appears.
2. Choose a preset from the Preset drop-down list, or type values in the **Width**, **Height**, and **Resolution** fields.
3. Click the **Color Mode** down arrow, and click **CMYK**.
4. Click **OK**.

USE INDEXED COLOR MODE

Indexed color mode is a unique animal. Every pixel in the image is in full RGB color, but there can be, at most, only 256 different colors. RGB images, in contrast, can include as many as 16 million colors. The subset of colors used by an indexed color image is called its *palette*. Indexed color images can be much smaller than RGB images unless you start with a photorealistic image. Photoshop *dithers* (mixes color into pixels) the indexed color palette to simulate missing colors, which often makes the file size larger than a full-color JPEG. In most cases, readers should use indexed color mode only for the Web and on images with large areas of solid color, such as logos. GIF is the most common file type that uses indexed color mode.

You cannot create a new indexed-color-mode file in Photoshop or ImageReady, but you can convert an existing RGB image to indexed color mode, or you can save an RGB or CMYK file as an indexed-color-mode GIF file via Photoshop's Save For Web command.

Convert a Color Mode

Even though an image is formatted in a certain color mode, such as RGB or CMYK, you can change it.

CONVERT A COLOR IMAGE TO GRAYSCALE

Click **Image**, click **Adjustments**, and then click **Desaturate**. This removes the color but leaves the image in its color mode. You can, for example, paint on color with the Brush tool.

–Or–

1. Click **Image**, click **Mode**, and then click **Grayscale**. Photoshop prompts you to confirm that you either want to flatten the image or that you want to discard color information.

2. Click **Flatten** to reduce the image to one layer, or click **OK** to discard the color information. You can now only paint on the image in shades of gray.

CONVERT AN IMAGE TO RGB

From the Menu bar, click **Image**, click **Mode**, and click **RGB Color**.

CONVERT AN IMAGE TO CMYK

From the Menu bar, click **Image**, click **Mode**, and then click **CMYK Color**.

CONVERT AN RGB IMAGE TO INDEXED COLOR MODE

1. From the Menu bar, click **Image**, click **Mode**, and click **Indexed Color**. The Indexed Color dialog box appears.

2. In the Colors box, type a number between 2 and 256 to set the number of colors to be used. Photoshop shows you a preview of the image as it is when converted to that number of colors.

3. Click **OK** to accept the conversion.

Chapter 9 explores the other options—Palette, Dither, Transparency, and so forth—in more depth.

TIP

You can use the Channel Mixer feature as an alternate to creating a grayscale image. Click **Image**, click **Adjustments**, and then click **Channel Mixer**. In the Channel Mixer dialog box, click the **Monochrome** check box, and then mix the channels so they add up to 100 percent. You get a much better looking image. A good choice is 40 percent in the Red channel and 60 percent in the Green channel. The added benefit is the image is still in RGB color mode, which means all color heads in your printer will fire to create the image.

Use the Bridge

While you can browse, open, rename, and delete your files using the standard Windows interface, the Photoshop Bridge offers a much more powerful, customizable way to work with your files. It is the primary tool used to find and obtain photos and images for Photoshop. The Bridge is part of the Creative Suite available from Adobe, and it is used with Adobe Illustrator, Adobe InDesign, and Adobe GoLive, as well as with Photoshop CS2.

View, Select, and Open Files

To manipulate files in Photoshop:

1. On the Options bar, click the **Go To Bridge** button to the left of the Palette Well; or click **File** and click **Close And Go To Bridge**. The Bridge appears as shown in Figure 2-1.

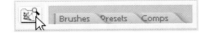

Figure 2-1: The Adobe Bridge provides access to your photos and ways to manage and identify them.

Click Favorites or Folders to find your images

The Preview panel shows the selected image

The Metadata panel contains Information about the selected image

Shortcut buttons provide quick access to file actions

Thumbnails show photos in the selected folder

Drag to change the size of thumbnails (or click the buttons on either side)

Click to change the display of images

NOTE

To return to Photoshop CS2 from the Bridge, click **File** and then click **Return to Adobe Photoshop CS2**. If you have an image you want to work with, double-click it and it will open in Photoshop.

2. Click the **Look In** down arrow to list possible image sources, including Favorites and most recent folders accessed. Click a folder name, **Desktop**, or **My Computer**. The image area will contain icons of the computer disks, networked disks, and files. Double-click the devices or file names to open the folder containing the images you want. You'll see thumbnails of the images.

–Or–

Use the Folders panel as you would Windows Explorer to navigate to a folder containing images. Click the plus sign (+) next to a name to expand it, revealing a layer of folders. When you see the folder containing images you want, double-click it to display thumbnails of the images.

3. Click an image thumbnail to select it (or double-click it to open it immediately).

–Or–

Press and hold **CTRL** while you click two or more noncontiguous images.

–Or–

Press and hold **SHIFT** while you click a second image to select a range of images.

4. Right-click the image and click **Open** from the context menu, as shown in Figure 2-2. The images open in Photoshop CS2.

Figure 2-2: Select multiple images by pressing and holding CTRL while clicking their thumbnails.

TIP

To remove a label, right-click the thumbnail, click **Label**, and click **No Label**.

NOTE

Certain files will not support XMP metadata (a standard format for storing metadata), and label and rating data for these files will be stored only in cache (which can be deleted). These files include BMP, DCS, PICT, PS6, PDF, PSB, locked files, and read-only files. For files that can support XMP metadata, indicate that you want labels and ratings included in the metadata contents by clicking **Edit**, clicking **Preferences**, clicking **Metadata**, and clicking the **Label** and **Ratings** check boxes.

✔ Label
✔ Rating

Sort and Rearrange Files

Within the Bridge, you can arrange your files, making them easier to find and manage.

SORT YOUR FILES

From the Bridge menu, click **View**, click **Sort**, and choose a sort order:

- To sort in descending order (for example, Z to A), deselect **Ascending Order.**
- To view thumbnails with the ratings or colored labels you have assigned to them, click **By Rating** or **By Label**.
- To view thumbnails as manually ordered, click **Manually**.

REARRANGE YOUR IMAGE THUMBNAILS

In addition to sorting your thumbnails in various ways, you can manually rearrange them within the Thumbnails pane.

1. Click an image thumbnail and hold down the mouse button. You'll see a shadow image appear.

2. Drag the shadow thumbnail to a new position, marked by a vertical stripe to indicate where the image will be placed.

3. Release the mouse button.

QUICKSTEPS

RENAMING LABELS

By default, labels are named for five colors: red, blue, green, purple, and yellow. If these labels don't evoke meaning for you, you can rename them to whatever you want. To rename a label from its default color name:

1. Click the **Edit** menu, click **Preferences**, and then click **Labels**.

2. Highlight the name of the color in the text box, and type the new label.

3. Click **OK**.

The typed text will replace the label color in the menu and on the label, as shown in Figure 2-4.

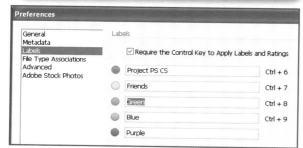

Set the label names in the Preferences dialog box

Figure 2-4: When you change the name of a label, the new name is reflected in the label menus.

The new label names will appear in the label menu

Select Files

You can select files to copy, place in Photoshop, delete, or otherwise work with.

Click **Edit** and choose from the following options:

- **Select All** selects all files currently open on the Bridge.
- **Select Labeled** selects all labeled files.
- **Select Unlabeled** selects only unlabeled files.
- **Invert Selection** selects only the currently unselected files.
- **Deselect All** clears your selections.

Label Your Files

You can label image files in the Bridge. Figure 2-3 shows examples of labels. The labels do not carry preassigned meanings, but will have the particular meanings you assign to them. You can label images with one of five colored labels and add ratings or names to the labels. You can display just the images with a particular label. You can label your family files, files to be deleted, files to be copied, images for a specific project, and so on. To label one or more files:

Figure 2-3: Labels can help you sort and view images for specific purposes.

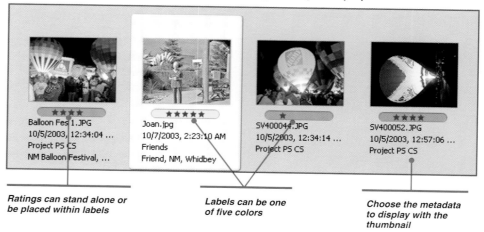

Ratings can stand alone or be placed within labels

Labels can be one of five colors

Choose the metadata to display with the thumbnail

CAUTION

When you change the name of the label in the Preferences dialog box after assigning it to an image, the label will lose its original color and will now be white or gray, indicating that there is a difference between the new and current label names. You can reclaim the original color of the label (red, green, and so on) by reassigning the label to the image.

1. For noncontiguous selections, hold down **CTRL** while you click; for contiguous selections hold down **SHIFT** while you click one or more image thumbnails in the Bridge to select them.

2. Click the **Label** menu and click the label type you want.

   –Or–

   Right-click a selected thumbnail, click **Label**, and then click the label color you want.

3. You will see a warning message that XMP metadata may be stored in cache only. Click **OK**. The labels are applied to the image file.

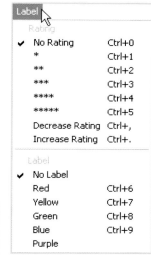

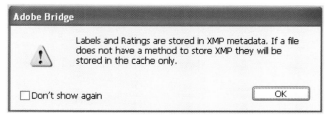

VIEW LABELED OR RATED IMAGES

To view images containing a specific label or rating:

1. Click the **Unfiltered** button.

2. Click the group of rated or labeled items you want to see.

RATE YOUR FILES

You can assign a rating of one to five stars to a file and then sort your files by rating. A rating can represent anything you want it to.

To rate one or more files:

> To rate an image, click the image to select it. A row of dots appears. Click the dot representing the number of stars you want: click the leftmost dot for one star; click the rightmost dot for five stars.
>
> –Or–

1. Hold down CTRL while you click to select noncontiguous files, or hold down SHIFT while you click one or more contiguous image thumbnails in the Bridge to select them.

2. Click the **Label** menu and then click the number of stars you want for the file.

Rename Images in a Folder

To rename all files in a folder:

1. Click **Tools** and then click **Batch Rename**. You can also right-click an image, and click **Batch Rename** from the context menu. The Batch Rename dialog box appears.

2. Under **New Filenames**, open the three drop-down list boxes, and then choose what will change:

   - To change the name of the file, click **Text** and type the new file name. If you don't assign a sequence number for each newly named file, a sequence number will be added in parentheses.

   - To add a sequence number by which files will be numerically sorted, click the plus sign (+). To add a second naming change, click **Sequence Number** from the first drop-down list, type the first number from the second drop-down list, and select the number of digits from the third drop-down list.

3. To preserve the XMP metadata name as it is currently recorded, place a check mark in the **Options** check box.

4. Under Preview, verify that the first name and the replacement name are correct and that the number of files to be renamed is correct.

5. Click **Rename**.

NOTE

You can open several images at once by selecting them, right-clicking, and clicking **Open**.

NOTE

You cannot close the Bridge's Thumbnails pane.

QUICKSTEPS

SAVING AND LOADING A BRIDGE WORKSPACE

You can save your Bridge configuration—thumbnail size, palette size, which palettes are open or closed—as a custom workspace and recall it again at any time.

SAVE YOUR BRIDGE WORKSPACE

1. From the Menu bar, click **Window**, click **Workspace**, and then click **Save Workspace**.
2. Type a name for the workspace, and click **Save**.

LOAD A BRIDGE WORKSPACE

From the Menu bar, click **Window**, click **Workspace**, and select your named workspace from the bottom of the submenu.

Customize the Bridge

You can alter the appearance of the Bridge to better suit your needs.

RESIZE THE PANES

You can change the relative size of the various panes—the Thumbnails, the preview, and so forth. Simply drag the frames between the panels.

Drag any panel divider to resize the palette

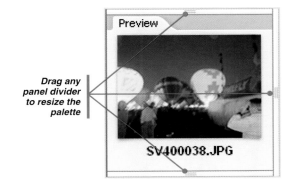

OPEN AND CLOSE THE BRIDGE PALETTES

To open and close palettes in the Bridge:

- Double-click the **Name** tab at the top of a closed palette to open it.
- Double-click the **Name** tab at the top of an open palette to close it.

CHANGE THUMBNAIL SIZE

You can change the size of image thumbnails displayed in the Bridge by dragging the slider or clicking one of the buttons at either end of the slider: left for the smallest size; right for the largest.

CHANGE FILE DISPLAY

By default, image files in the Bridge are displayed as thumbnails. If you want to change this:

Click **View** and choose one of the following:

- **As Thumbnails**—The default, displays a thumbnail of the file image.
- **As Filmstrip**—Displays the images along with the filmstrip of the video. The filmstrip can be vertical or horizontal. When a thumbnail is selected, the filmstrip format displays a large version of the image in the window above (horizontal alignment) or to the left of the filmstrip (vertical alignment).
- **As Details**—Displays the thumbnail along with essential information regarding the file, such as file name, size, date created, date last modified, and so on.
- **As Versions And Alternatives**—Displays the thumbnails of all image versions.

When you have selected the file display, the image area will be refreshed with the new display.

CHANGE DETAIL DISPLAYED WITH THUMBNAILS

To change the information shown on the thumbnail display of the image files:

1. From the Menu bar, click **Edit** and click **Preferences**.

2. Click **General**. Choose from the following options:

   - **Background**—Drag the slider to change the color from black to white.

   - **Show Tooltips**—This is se-
     lected by default. Deselect the
     check box if you don't want to
     show Tool Tips.

   - **Show Date Created**—The first
     of three possibilities for display-
     ing data with the thumbnails.
     Date Created is selected by
     default. Click the down arrow to
     display a menu of what can be
     displayed with the image.

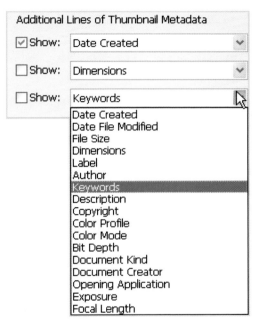

*Thumbnail with
date created,
labels, and file
size metadata
shown*

   - **Show Dimensions**—This is not selected by default. Click the down arrow to display a menu of additional metadata that can be displayed.

   - **Show Keywords**—This is not selected by default. Click the down arrow to display additional metadata items.

3. Click **OK**.

![NOTE]

Find results will be displayed in a separate window by default. You can change this by deselecting the **Show Find Result In A New Browser Window** check box.

QUICKSTEPS

RENAMING, MOVING, COPYING, AND DELETING FILES

You can perform basic file operations—rename, move, copy, delete—from within Adobe Bridge.

RENAME A FILE

1. In the Bridge, double-click the file name located beneath the thumbnail.

2. Type a new name and then press **ENTER**.

MOVE A FILE

1. In the File Browser, click one or more image thumbnails, and then hold down the mouse button.

2. Drag the thumbnail to a new folder in the Folders pane. Release to move the files to that folder.

COPY ONE OR MORE FILES

1. In the Bridge, click one or more image thumbnails, and hold down the mouse button.

2. As you begin dragging the file to the new folder, hold down the **CTRL** key. A plus sign (+) appears next to the cursor, indicating that you are copying the file(s).

3. Press **CTRL** while you drag the thumbnail(s) to a new folder in the Folders pane. Release to copy the file(s) to that folder.

DELETE ONE OR MORE FILES

1. In the Bridge, click one or more image thumbnails.

2. Press **DELETE**. Photoshop asks you to confirm the deletion.

3. Click **OK** to delete the files.

SV400034.JPG
10/5/2003, 12:...

1.82 MB

SV400075.JPG
10/20/2003, 4:...

237 KB

Search for Files

To search your computer or network for image files from within the Bridge:

1. Click **Find** on the Edit menu. An example of using Find is shown in Figure 2-5.

2. In the Look In text box, locate the device or folder you want to search.

3. Choose a criterion to search by, such as **Label**, **File Name**, or **Keyword**.

4. To add another search criterion, click the **plus sign** (+) button to the right of the current criterion. (To delete a criterion, click the **minus sign** (−) button.)

5. Click the **Match** down arrow, and choose how a match is determined.

6. Click **Find** to initiate the search.

Figure 2-5: Search for files with the Find dialog box.

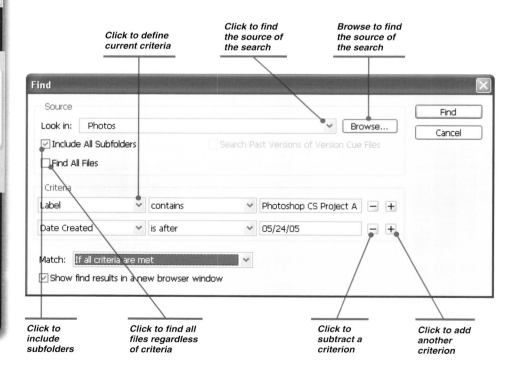

Click to define current criteria

Click to find the source of the search

Browse to find the source of the search

Click to include subfolders

Click to find all files regardless of criteria

Click to subtract a criterion

Click to add another criterion

Use Scanners and Digital Cameras

Photoshop allows you to import images directly from scanners and digital cameras connected to your computer.

Scan an Image in Photoshop

To scan an image from within Photoshop:

1. From the Menu bar, click **File** and click **Import**. A submenu appears, listing the devices from which Photoshop can import.

2. Click to select your scanner from the list. The scanning software starts. The exact appearance and operation will depend on your scanner.

3. Use your scanner software to perform the scan (see Figure 2-6). The scanned image opens in Photoshop.

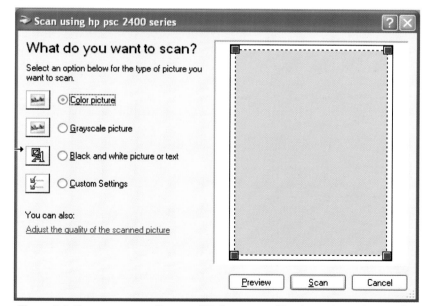

Figure 2-6: Your scanner software will take over and lead you through scanning your images.

SCAN A COLOR PHOTOGRAPH

1. From the Menu bar, click **File** and click **Import**. A submenu appears, listing the devices from which Photoshop can import.

2. Click to select your scanner from the list. The scanning software starts.

3. Choose applicable color photograph settings. The details will depend on your scanner.

4. Perform the scan. The scanned image will open in Photoshop.

SCAN A BLACK-AND-WHITE PHOTOGRAPH

Although most scanning software has a setting for scanning grayscale (black-and-white) photographs, you will often get better results by scanning the photo as a *color photograph* and then converting it within Photoshop. When you convert from color to grayscale, you throw away image data, but if you make the conversion within Photoshop, you can at least control the process.

1. Scan the photo into Photoshop as a color photograph.

2. To convert to grayscale, click **Image**, click **Adjustments**, and click **Desaturate**.

You'll learn about retouching and color-correcting photos in Chapter 6.

SCAN LINE ART

Although most scanning software has a setting for scanning line art, you will get better results by scanning the image as a grayscale photograph.

1. Scan the photo into Photoshop as a grayscale (black-and-white) photograph.

2. Press **ALT+CTRL+0** or double-click the **Zoom** tool to zoom to 100 percent.

3. Click **Image**, click **Adjustments**, and click **Threshold.** The Threshold dialog box appears.

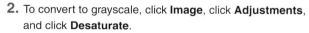

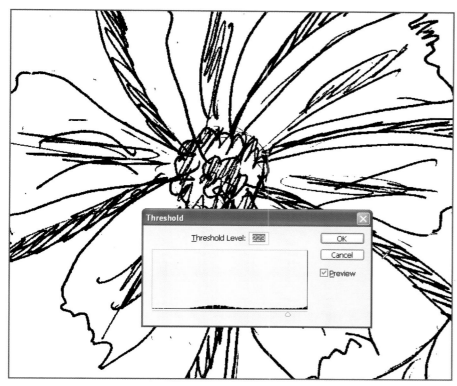

Figure 2-7: You can scan a line drawing and change the line weight with Photoshop CS2.

4. Using the Threshold command will render your image in black and white. Drag the **threshold** slider to the left to make lines lighter; drag it to the right to make lines heavier (see Figure 2-7).

5. Click **OK** to accept the threshold adjustment.

6. Use the **Eraser** and **Brush** tools to clean up any extra spots and specks.

You'll learn more about converting and retouching images in Chapter 6.

Import Digital Photos

To import digital photos into Photoshop:

1. From the Menu bar, click **File** and click **Import**. A submenu appears, listing the devices from which Photoshop can import.

2. Click to select your camera from the list. The camera's software starts.

   –Or–

   The Adobe Photo Downloader will automatically retrieve your photos if the card reader is detected on the computer (see Figure 2-8).

3. Select one or more photos, complete any settings, and click the appropriate button (**OK**, **Get Pictures**, and so on) to import the photos into Photoshop. The exact appearance and operation will depend on your camera.

TIP

If you transfer a photo from the camera to a file on your hard drive or network, you can open the file normally in Photoshop.

Figure 2-8: The Adobe Photo Downloader will automatically retrieve your photos from your digital camera, store them in the folder you want, and number and rename the files.

NOTE

You can vary the size of the thumbnails in the photo area by dragging the slider at the bottom of the window.

Find Adobe Stock Photos

Adobe has joined with other organizations to provide Adobe users with libraries of stock photos that can be used, some for royalty-free fees. For no charge, you can review and download low-resolution comp images to use in trial compositions. Once you determine that you want a high-resolution image (or after a defined length of time), you can decide whether to purchase the photo. You establish an account with Adobe and provide billing information that can be used on an ongoing basis as needed. To find stock photos:

1. Within the Bridge, click the **Favorites** tab in the Favorites panel. Click **Adobe Stock Photos**. The Adobe Stock Photos window opens, as shown in Figure 2-9.

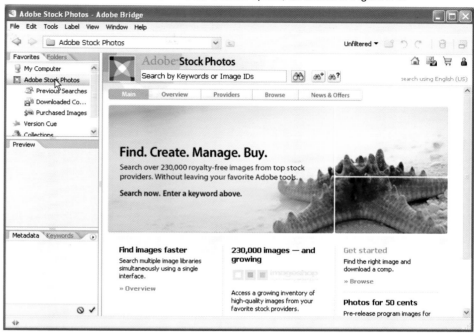

Figure 2-9: Adobe stock photos provide thousands of photos for your use in Adobe products.

Abstract	Children	Lifestyle
Animals	City scenes	Messages and signs
Appearance	Education	Objects
Architecture and structures	Environment	Scenic
Artistic	Ethnicity	Science and technology
Behavior	Family and friends	Shopping
Business and office	Food and dining	Sports
Careers	Industry	Transportation

Abstract
Ambiguous · Angles · Colors · Cosmos · Curves · Circles · Fantasy · Human forms · Icons · Illusions · Matrix · Metallic · Metaphors · Mutations · Neon · Patterns · Psychedelic · Speed · Textures Transformation

Animals
Apes and primates · Amphibians · Animal faces · Animal families · Big cats · Birds · Cats · Dangerous animals · Dogs · Farm animals · Fish · Hunting · Insects · Ocean mammals · Pets · Predators · Reptiles · Safari · Snow wildlife · Wildlife

2. Under Get Started, click **Browse**. You will see a directory of photo types. Click a subject, such as **Animals**, and you will see a thumbnail with the types of animals contained within the selection.

3. If you find a photo that you want to see in more detail, click the thumbnail to see a preview of it.

4. To try the photo out in your trial composition, either double-click the image or click **Download Comp**. The downloaded photo appears in your Photoshop CS2 document area for you to review.

5. Click **Add To Cart** if you want to buy the photo.

6. Click **Get Price & Keywords** to find out how much the photo will cost. You will also be able to perform another search using keywords that apply to the selected photo to find other possibilities.

FIND DOWNLOADED COMPS

To find Adobe stock photos that you have purchased:

1. Click the **Favorites** panel in the Bridge.

2. Click **Adobe Stock Photos** and then click **Downloaded Comps**.

3. To find out about prices, select a downloaded image and then click
Get Prices & Keywords.

4. To purchase the photo, click **Add To Cart**.

Save Your Files

*Figure 2-10: The Save As dialog box presents
alternatives for saving a file, including with another
format or with a new name.*

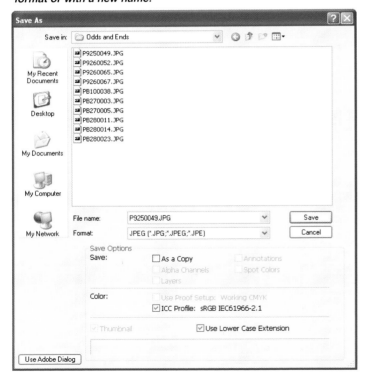

Photoshop allows you to save your work in the original format, as a new file
type, or optimized for the Web.

SAVE AN EXISTING FILE

To save changes to an existing file, click the **File** menu and click **Save**, or
press **CTRL+S**.

SAVE A NEW, RENAMED, OR REFORMATTED FILE

To save a new file or to save a previous file with a new name or file format
(for example, to save a JPG as a BMP):

1. Click **File** and click **Save As**. The Save As dialog box appears, as shown in
Figure 2-10.

2. Type a file name in the File Name field.

3. Choose a file format from the Format drop-down list.

4. Click **Save**.

SAVE A FILE CONTAINING LAYERS AND TRANSPARENCY

To save a file containing multiple layers or varying transparencies, your best option is to save it as a Photoshop file.

1. From the Menu bar, click **File** and click **Save As**. The Save As dialog box appears.
2. Type a new name in the File Name field.
3. Choose a file format from the Format drop-down list. Photoshop will only display those file types capable of storing layers and transparency.
4. Click **Save**.

Work with Camera RAW Images

Some cameras will save photos as camera RAW files. A camera RAW file contains the original, or raw, data captured by the hardware of a digital camera; it hasn't been compressed or modified in any way. Think of a camera RAW file as the digital equivalent of a film negative. By working with camera RAW files, *you* get to decide how deep the shadows are, how much contrast the image has, or how saturated the sky is, rather than leaving it up to your camera's built-in computer.

Not every camera allows you to capture images as RAW files. In some instances, you may not want to bother with camera RAW files, even if the feature is available for your camera. For snapshots and the like, images photographed in the JPEG format are smaller and more convenient if you only need a quick snapshot to share with a friend through e-mail. If your camera can create RAW files, then that means the camera manufacturer supplied an application to decode and process RAW images. However, Photoshop's Camera RAW dialog box offers you more options and flexibility than most applications supplied by camera manufacturers.

The camera RAW file contains more data than a JPG or TIF, making it possible to compensate for a wider range of problems, such as underexposed or overexposed images, bad lighting, incorrect camera settings, and so forth. It also enables you to exercise creative control when processing an image, similar to

NOTE

Unlike JPG or GIF, RAW is not an acronym. Each camera manufacturer has its own proprietary file format and extension for its camera RAW files, including RAW, RAF, CRF, NEF, RAF, ORF, MRW, and THM.

NOTE

Refer to your camera manual for advanced information on your camera's settings.

TIP

Click the **White Balance** tool (it looks like an eyedropper above the image), and click a white area to adjust the white balance of the image.

Press **ALT** while dragging the **Exposure** or **Shadows** slider to reveal any areas of the image that will be clipped to white (Exposure slider) or clipped to black (Shadows slider). (Clipped to black is 0,0,0. If you have a shadow that is 16, 16, 16, that's a shade of gray, albeit a very dark shade, but it is not jet black. If a shadow is clipped to black, the shadow is now 0,0,0.)

the latitude enjoyed by technicians processing film in a darkroom, but without the caustic chemicals.

OPEN AND PROCESS A CAMERA RAW FILE

Open a camera RAW file from the Adobe Bridge; or click **File**, click **Open**, and then select the RAW file you want to process. The Camera RAW dialog box appears, as shown in Figure 2-11. By default, Photoshop analyzes the image and applies suggested settings for exposure, shadows, contrast, and brightness. These settings may be different from what your camera selected when you took the picture. The Photoshop-applied settings may process the image to perfection; however, you can modify the settings by deselecting the **Auto** check box to the right of the Exposure, Shadows, Brightness, and Contrast sliders for a setting and then applying your own settings.

Figure 2-11: You can process RAW files using the Camera RAW dialog box.

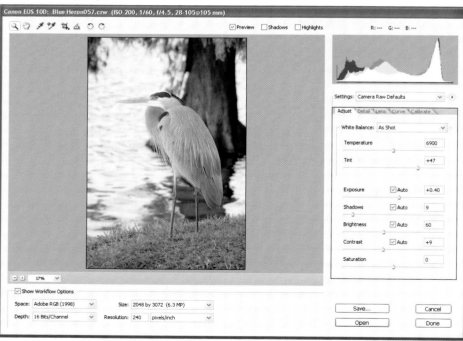

Click the **Adjust** tab (if it isn't already displayed), and make any needed adjustments:

- **White Balance**—Choose a white balance from the White Balance menu to reflect the lighting conditions under which the photo was taken. White balance alters the Temperature and Tint settings.

- **Temperature**—Adjust the color temperature of the photo by dragging the **Temperature** slider to the left for cooler, bluer light or to the right for warmer, more yellow light.

- **Tint**—Adjust the tint by dragging the **Tint** slider to the left to add more green or to the right to add more magenta.

- **Exposure**—Adjust the exposure by dragging the **Exposure** slider to the left to darken or to the right to lighten. A setting of 1.0 is equivalent to setting the camera aperture one F-stop wider. A setting of –1.0 is equivalent to setting the camera aperture one F-stop narrower. If you lighten the image too much, you'll clip highlights to white.

TIP

If you're editing the RAW file for a specific destination, click the down arrow in the lower-right corner of the Crop tool, and click one of the options (which are actually image-aspect ratios) from the drop-down list. For example, if the image is destined to be printed as an 8 x 10-inch image, click 4 x 5. When you drag the Crop tool around the image, the tool will crop to a 4 to 5 aspect ratio, the same aspect ratio as an 8 x 10-inch image.

NOTE

The Crop tool in the Camera RAW dialog box does not enable you to crop the image to a specific size. If you need to do this, process the RAW image without cropping it in the RAW dialog box, and then use the Crop tool in Photoshop. If you do not need to crop the image, use the Size menu on the Camera RAW dialog box.

CAUTION

When you click outside the image, your crop and straighten changes will be lost.

TIP

Press **ALT**, and the Cancel button becomes the Reset button. Click the **Reset** button to undo all changes and have the file revert to the default settings.

- **Shadows**—Drag the **Shadows** slider to the right to darken the shadows in the photo or to the left to lighten them. The Shadows slider will clip off dark areas, forcing them to black.

- **Brightness**—Adjust the overall brightness of the photo by dragging the **Brightness** slider to the left to darken it or to the right to lighten it. Unlike the Exposure and Shadows sliders, the Brightness slider will not clip off dark and light areas.

- **Contrast**—Adjust the overall contrast of the photo by dragging the **Contrast** slider to the left to decrease contrast or to the right to increase contrast.

- **Saturation**—Adjust the overall saturation (color brightness) of the photo by dragging the **Saturation** slider to the left to decrease saturation or to the right to increase saturation.

You can also make these changes to your photo:

- **Image Rotation**—Rotate the image clockwise or counterclockwise by clicking the rotate image buttons above the image.

- **Crop**—Drag to select the part of the image you want to crop. After you release the mouse button, a marquee appears, designating the area to which the image will be cropped. Resizing handles appear at the perimeter of the crop box, which enable you to resize it. You can also click inside the crop box and drag it to a different location. The file will be cropped when you click **Open** to exit the Camera RAW dialog box. To clear a crop, press **CTRL+Z** or click the **Down Arrow** in the lower-right corner of the Crop tool icon, and click **Clear Crop**.

- **Straighten**—Click the **Straighten** tool and drag in the image. When you release the mouse button, a transform box will be applied to the image. Move your pointer away from the box, and rotate it as needed to straighten it. The file will be straightened when you click **Open** to exit the Camera RAW dialog box.

- **Space**—Change the photo's color space by selecting an option from the Space drop-down menu. A *color space* is a scheme or way of defining how color is represented in a computer, camera, scanner, or printer. Each can have its own unique color space. The default color space is the one your camera assigned to the image. Many cameras have menu commands that enable you to change the color space. In most instances, Adobe RGB 1998 is a good choice, as it offers the most latitude in colors.

- **Depth**—Change the photo's depth (bits/channel) by choosing an option of **8** or **16** bits/channel from the Depth drop-down menu.

- **Resolution**—Change the photo's resolution by typing a new value in the Resolution field at the bottom of the Camera RAW window.

TIP

You also have other options in the Camera RAW dialog box. Click the **Details** tab to adjust sharpness, luminance smoothing, and color noise reduction; click the **Lens** tab to adjust chromatic aberration and vignetting (a circular halo from the center to the perimeter of the image); click the **Curve** tab to adjust the tonal contrast of the image; or click the **Calibrate** tab to adjust the automatic settings for hue, tint, and saturation to adjust for the qualities in your camera.

TIP

If you've taken several RAW images with similar camera settings at the same location and the same lighting conditions, you can process all of these files at once. Select the files you want to process in the Adobe Bridge, right-click, and then click **Open** In Camera RAW to open the Camera RAW dialog box. A thumbnail for each image is displayed, which you can click and process separately; or you can click **Select All** or press **CTRL** and press the **plus (+)** key to select all images. If you click **Synchronize**, you can select the settings to apply to all images, and then click the desired button to apply the changes, cancel the changes, or open the images in Photoshop.

NOTE

To find the latest information on which cameras are supported by Photoshop CS2 for RAW images, click **Help** and click **Photoshop Online**. From the Adobe Photoshop CS2 Web site, click **Camera RAW Support**.

● **Size**—Change the photo's dimensions by choosing a new size from the Size drop-down list at the bottom of the Camera RAW window.

When you are done:

● Click **Open** to accept your adjustments and open the photo in Photoshop.

–Or–

● Click **Cancel** to abandon your adjustments. The photo will not open in Photoshop.

–Or–

● Click **Done** to apply your settings to the file but not open the file in Photoshop.

–Or–

● Click **Save** to open the Save dialog box shown in Figure 2-12. From within this dialog box, you can specify destination options, file naming options, and which format the processed RAW file is saved in. You can save the file as a digital negative, JPEG, TIFF, or Photoshop PSD file.

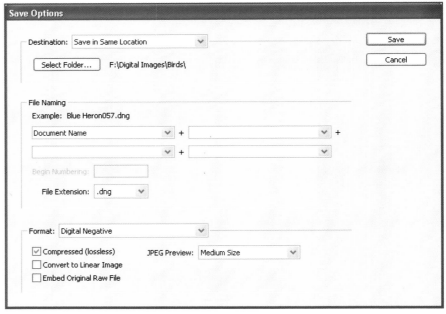

Figure 2-12: You can save a processed file directly from the Camera RAW dialog box.

How to...

- *Use the Marquee Tool*
- *Constraining Your Selections*
- *Use the Magic Wand Tool*
- *Use the Lasso Tools*
- *Select a Range of Colors*
- *Feathering and Anti-Aliasing*
- *Exclude Areas Using Selections*
- *Modify a Selection*
- *Crop to Fit a Selection*
- *Delete Using Selections*
- *Remove Fringe Pixels*
- *Save and Load Selections*
- *Copying Layer Styles*
- *Copy to a New Layer*
- *Copy to a New Document*
- *Extract Background Elements*
- *Moving and Duplicating*
- *Expanding Selections*
- *Use the Magic Eraser Tool*
- *Use the Background Eraser Tool*
- *Work with Quick Masks*
- *Use the Pen Tool*

Chapter 3
Making Selections

Selections are the key to using Photoshop to its fullest. Selections allow you to confine your edits to a limited area of an image. Any operations you perform on the image will affect only these pixels, as shown in Figure 3-1. You can perform almost any Photoshop operation—applying filters, adjusting colors, painting, erasing, and so forth—on the pixels within a selection; any unselected pixels are unaffected. You can also copy the selected pixels to a layer within your document or to a new document.

Create New Selections

Photoshop provides a number of ways to create new selections. You can make selections manually or let Photoshop take the reins, as with the Magic Wand tool. You can also modify selections once they are created. Photoshop has your normal selecting tools, such as the Marquee and Lasso tools or the Magic Wand tool; however, some selections can be made using techniques rather than using formal selection tools, such as using the Crop feature.

Figure 3-1: Filters and adjustments are only applied to the active selection.

Use the Marquee Tool

You can use the Marquee tool to select a rectangular or elliptically shaped area. You also have options for a single-pixel-wide row or column tool.

MAKE A RECTANGULAR SELECTION

You can make a rectangular selection with the Rectangular Marquee tool.

1. If the Rectangular Marquee tool isn't selected, click the current **Marquee** tool icon in the Toolbox palette, and hold down the mouse button. The Marquee tool pop-up menu appears.

2. Click the **Rectangular Marquee** tool.

3. Drag within the image to create the marquee selection.

   –Or–

   Hold down **SHIFT** while dragging to constrain the selection to a square.

MAKE AN ELLIPTICAL SELECTION

To make a circular or elliptical selection with the Elliptical Marquee tool:

1. If the Elliptical Marquee tool isn't selected, click the current **Marquee** tool icon in the Toolbox palette, and hold down the mouse button. The Marquee tool pop-up menu is displayed.

2. Click the **Elliptical Marquee** tool.

3. Click within the image and then drag to create the selection.

   –Or–

   Hold down **SHIFT** while dragging to constrain the selection to a circle.

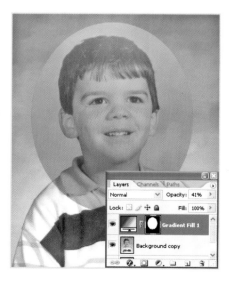

NOTE

Only the pixels *inside* of the marquee are selected.

NOTE

To place a marquee selection around the entire image, press **CTRL+A** (Select All).

NOTE

You can select the Marquee tool and switch between the Rectangular and Elliptical Marquee tools by pressing **SHIFT+M**.

CONSTRAINING YOUR SELECTIONS

MAKE A SELECTION OF A FIXED SIZE

You can tell Photoshop exactly what size you want future rectangular or elliptical selections to be. With the Rectangular Marquee or Elliptical Marquee tool selected:

Style: Fixed Size
- Normal
- Fixed Aspect Ratio
- Fixed Size

1. From the Options bar, click the **Style** drop-down list, and click **Fixed Size**.
2. Type the **Width** and **Height** in pixels (px), inches (in), centimeters (cm), or millimeters (mm).
3. Click to establish the upper-left corner of the selection, and drag to position it.

MAKE A SELECTION OF A FIXED-ASPECT RATIO

You can constrain the aspect ratio of a selection so that, for example, it is twice as tall as it is wide, regardless of the actual size of the area selected. With the Rectangular Marquee or Elliptical Marquee tool selected:

1. From the Options bar, click the **Style** down arrow, and click **Fixed Aspect Ratio**.
2. Type the **Width** and **Height**.
3. Click the image and drag to create the selection.

TIP

If you need to move the selection while creating it, press the **SPACEBAR** while dragging to move the selection without sizing it.

Use the Magic Wand Tool

Marquee selections are great for selecting circular and rectangular areas of an image, but sometimes you need to select all the pixels of the same *color*, regardless of the shape. Then it's time for the Magic Wand tool.

SELECT AN AREA WITH THE MAGIC WAND TOOL

1. Select the **Magic Wand** tool from the Toolbox.
2. Set the **Tolerance** level on the Magic Wand Options bar. This tells Photoshop how similar in color pixels must be to be included in the selection. The larger the tolerance, the more colors will be selected. A tolerance level of 32 (the default) is a good place to start.
3. Click the **Anti-Alias** check box to soften the edges of the selection.
4. From the Options bar, click **Contiguous**.
5. Click within the area you want to select.
6. If too many pixels are selected, reduce the tolerance. If too few pixels are selected, increase the tolerance. Click twice within the selection to reselect the area using the new tolerance level.

The Magic Wand tool's Options bar, shown in Figure 3-2, gives you more control over the tool's selections.

Figure 3-2: For more control, use the Magic Wand Options bar.

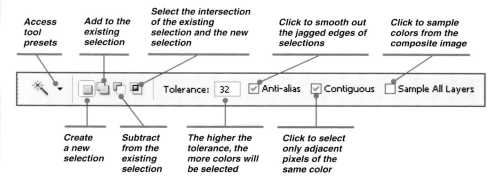

Access tool presets

Add to the existing selection

Select the intersection of the existing selection and the new selection

Click to smooth out the jagged edges of selections

Click to sample colors from the composite image

Create a new selection

Subtract from the existing selection

The higher the tolerance, the more colors will be selected

Click to select only adjacent pixels of the same color

MAKE CONTIGUOUS AND NONCONTIGUOUS SELECTIONS WITH THE MAGIC WAND TOOL

- If you click **Contiguous** on the Magic Wand Options bar, the tool will select only a single contiguous area. Pixels of the same color elsewhere in the image will not be selected.

- If you deselect **Contiguous** on the Magic Wand Options bar, the tool will select all pixels of the same color, regardless of their location within the image.

TIP

When you have a complicated selection to make, you can sometimes use the Magic Wand tool to select the background based on color, and then use the Inverse feature to select what you really want. This only works if the background is of a similar color—it won't work on a scenic background when you're trying to select a person, for instance.

Use the Lasso Tools

Photoshop has three different Lasso tools: the Lasso tool, the Polygonal Lasso tool, and the Magnetic Lasso tool.

SKETCH A FREEHAND SELECTION

You can make a freehand sketch of the outline of your selection.

1. If the Lasso tool is not selected, click the current **Lasso** tool icon in the Toolbox palette, and hold down the mouse button. The Lasso Tool pop-up menu appears.

2. Click the **Lasso** tool.

3. Click within the image and drag to sketch a selection.

4. Release the mouse button to close the selection.

You can fine-tune the way the Lasso tool works by changing its options, shown in Figure 3-3.

Access tool presets

Add to the existing selection

Select the intersection of the existing selection and the new selection

Click to smooth out the jagged edges of selections

Figure 3-3: Change the Lasso tool and Polygonal Lasso tool options.

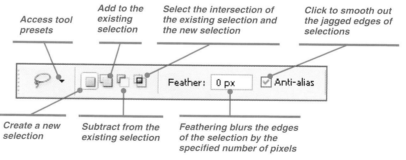

Feather: 0 px ☑ Anti-alias

Create a new selection

Subtract from the existing selection

Feathering blurs the edges of the selection by the specified number of pixels

SELECT AN AREA WITH THE POLYGONAL LASSO TOOL

You can create a selection made up of a number of straight segments, although what you're really doing is creating points that define the area of the selection.

1. If the Polygonal Lasso tool is not selected, click the current **Lasso** tool icon in the Toolbox palette, and hold down the mouse button. The Lasso tool pop-up menu is displayed.

TIP

You can add to a selection by pressing **SHIFT** and then using a tool, or you can subtract from a selection by pressing **ALT** and using a tool.

2. Click the **Polygonal Lasso** tool.

3. Click inside the image to define the starting point of your selection.

4. Move the mouse to a new position. A line segment follows the cursor.

5. Click the image repeatedly to create your selection.

6. Double-click to finish the selection.

You can fine-tune the way the Polygonal Lasso tool works by changing its options, shown in Figure 3-3.

SELECT AN AREA WITH THE MAGNETIC LASSO TOOL

Use the Magnetic Lasso tool to select an image with sharp contrast in its edges. The Magnetic Lasso tool will attempt to automatically follow and "snap to" edges. You can fine-tune the way the Magnetic Lasso tool works by changing its options, shown in Figure 3-4.

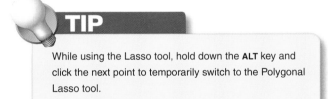

TIP

While using the Lasso tool, hold down the **ALT** key and click the next point to temporarily switch to the Polygonal Lasso tool.

Figure 3-4: Change the Magnetic Lasso tool options to gain greater control.

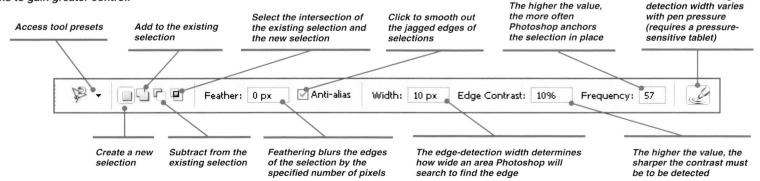

Access tool presets

Add to the existing selection

Select the intersection of the existing selection and the new selection

Click to smooth out the jagged edges of selections

The higher the value, the more often Photoshop anchors the selection in place

When selected, edge-detection width varies with pen pressure (requires a pressure-sensitive tablet)

Create a new selection

Subtract from the existing selection

Feathering blurs the edges of the selection by the specified number of pixels

The edge-detection width determines how wide an area Photoshop will search to find the edge

The higher the value, the sharper the contrast must be to be detected

1. If the Magnetic Lasso tool is not selected, click the current **Lasso** tool icon in the Toolbox palette, and hold down the mouse button. The Lasso tool pop-up menu is displayed.

2. Click the **Magnetic Lasso** tool.

3. Click your image once to begin creating a selection.

4. Move the mouse to a new position. A line segment follows the cursor. Photoshop places small, square "anchors" as it goes.

5. Press **BACKSPACE** at any time to delete the last anchor.

6. Click the image at any time to force the Magnetic Lasso tool to place an anchor at the cursor location.

7. Double-click to finish the selection. The selection end will "snap to" the beginning of the selection.

Select a Range of Colors

The Color Range command can be used to select a color or a range of colors within a selection or in the image itself. You can change an existing selection or replace it. The selections can be cumulative: make one selection, click **OK**, open the Color Range dialog box again to make another selection, and so on. To replace a selection, the previous selection must be deselected. To select all pixels within a range of colors:

1. From the Menu bar, click **Select** and then click **Color Range**. The Color Range dialog box appears.

2. Click the **Select** down arrow to select the color type that will be tested and selected.

3. Click the **Selection Preview** down arrow to select how the image selection will be displayed.

4. Click the **Selection** preview button to see the selection as it is being built, or click the **Image** preview button to preview the whole image. You can switch back and forth between them, sampling and previewing as you work.

5. Click within the image to sample the color you want to select. The Color Range dialog box displays a thumbnail of the selection: white areas in the preview will be selected; black areas will not; gray areas will be partially selected. An example is shown in Figure 3-5.

Figure 3-5: Selecting colors using the Color Range command allows you to select more precisely and to use a masking tool to perfect the selection.

Click to select the type
of color to be selected

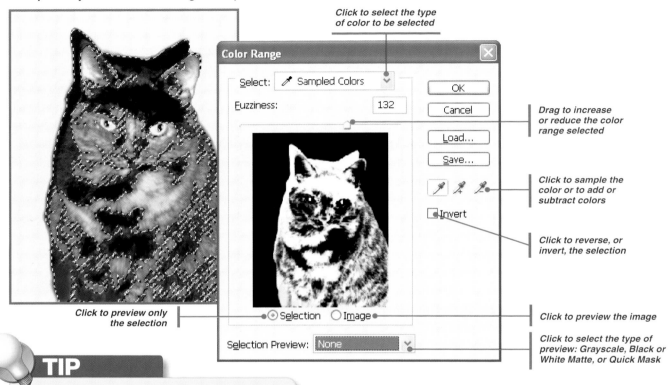

Drag to increase
or reduce the color
range selected

Click to sample the
color or to add or
subtract colors

Click to reverse, or
invert, the selection

Click to preview only
the selection

Click to preview the image

Click to select the type of
preview: Grayscale, Black or
White Matte, or Quick Mask

TIP

When using the Color Range command, press **ALT**, and the Cancel button changes to a Reset button. Click **Reset** to restore the original selection.

NOTE

To deselect a selection, click **Select** and then click **Deselect**.

6. Use the **Fuzziness** slider to adjust the range of colors selected. The greater the fuzziness, the more colors will be selected.

7. To select additional colors, hold down the **SHIFT** key while clicking the image. This activates the plus (+) eyedropper.

8. To subtract colors from the selection, hold down the **ALT** key while clicking the image. This activates the minus (−) eyedropper.

9. To make subtle refinements, click **Select** and click **Sampled Colors**, **RGB**, **CMYK**, **Highlights**, **Midtones**, **Shadows**, or **Out Of Gamut** colors.

10. When finished, click **OK**.

FEATHERING AND ANTI-ALIASING

Feathering and anti-aliasing smooth the edges of your selections. *Feathering* softens a selection by blurring the selection's edges. The pixels at the edge of the selection are only *partially* selected. When they are copied, they will be partially transparent. If an effect or filter is applied to them, that filter or effect is rendered partially transparent.

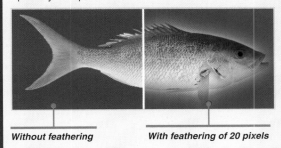

Without feathering   *With feathering of 20 pixels*

Continued...

NOTE

You cannot apply anti-aliasing to an existing selection.

Exclude Areas Using Selections

Sometimes, the elements you *don't* want to work with are easier to select than the elements you *do* want, as in the case of a complicated object on a simple background. In that case, select the background elements first, and then invert the selection.

1. Use any combination of selection tools to select the background elements you do not ultimately want selected.

2. Click **Select** and then click **Inverse**, or press **SHIFT+CTRL+I**, to invert the selection. Everything that was selected is deselected, and everything that was deselected is now selected.

Change, Save, and Load Selections

Once you have created a selection, you can change it.

Modify a Selection

You can modify a selection in a number of ways: repositioning, resizing, expanding or contracting, adding to it, or subtracting from it.

MOVE A SELECTION BORDER

To move a selection border:

1. Using any selection tool, click inside the active selection border.

2. Hold down the mouse button, and drag the border to a new position.

FEATHERING *(Continued)*

FEATHER AN EXISTING SELECTION

1. From the Menu bar, click **Select** and click **Feather**.

2. Type a **Feather Radius** value between 0.2 and 250 pixels. The larger the number, the more the edges of the selection will be blurred.

You can also press **CTRL+ALT+D** to access the Feather Selection dialog box.

CREATE A FEATHERED SELECTION USING A SELECTION TOOL

1. Select any of the **Lasso** or **Marquee** tools.

2. In the tool's Options bar, type a **Feather** value between 0.2 and 250 pixels. The larger the number, the more the edges of the selection will be blurred.

ANTI-ALIASING

Anti-aliasing smooths out the jagged edges of a selection by blending the colors of the pixels at the very edge of the selection with the background pixels. An element selected and copied without anti-aliasing and then pasted in front of a different-colored background will display an unsightly, ragged edge.

Without anti-aliasing   **With anti-aliasing**

You'll usually want to enable anti-aliasing on the Options bar of whatever selection tool you're using: Lasso, Marquee, or Magic Wand.

ENABLE ANTI-ALIASING

Click **Anti-Aliased** on the selection tool's Options bar.

TRANSFORM A SELECTION

You can transform a selection—making it larger or smaller, moving it, or even rotating it. To transform an existing selection:

1. From the Menu bar, click **Select** and then click **Transform Selection**.

2. Sizing handles appear at the sides and corners of the selection. Drag these handles, or the lines that connect them, to resize the selection.

3. Click within the selection and drag to move it to another position within your image.

4. Click outside of the selection, and drag to rotate the selection.

ADD TO A SELECTION

To add to an existing selection:

1. Choose any selection tool from the Toolbox palette.

2. Hold down the **SHIFT** key, and make another selection.

3. Change tools at any time, and hold down the **SHIFT** key to continue adding to the current selection.

MAKE MULTIPLE SELECTIONS

To make multiple selections using any combination of selection tools:

1. Choose a selection tool, such as the **Marquee** tool, from the Toolbox palette.

2. Make your first selection.

3. Hold down the **SHIFT** key, and then make another selection.

4. Change tools at any time, and hold down the **SHIFT** key to continue adding to the current selection.

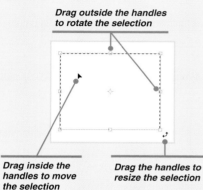

TIP

Holding down **SHIFT** while resizing will resize the selection proportionally.

Drag outside the handles to rotate the selection

Drag inside the handles to move the selection

Drag the handles to resize the selection

SUBTRACT FROM A SELECTION

To subtract from an existing selection:

1. Choose any selection tool from the Toolbox palette.
2. Hold down the **ALT** key, and drag with the selection tool over the area you want to subtract from the active selection.
3. Change tools at any time, and hold down the **ALT** key to continue subtracting from the current selection.

CONVERT A SELECTION TO A BORDER

You can create a border around the subject of an image without destroying the rest of the image. To convert an active selection into a border:

1. From the Menu bar, click **Select**, click **Modify**, and then click **Border**.
2. Type the size of the border in pixels, and click **OK**. Photoshop creates a new border selection centered on the original selection.

EXPAND OR CONTRACT A SELECTION

Sometimes, you might want a selection to be slightly larger overall. To expand a selection by a fixed number of pixels:

1. Click **Select**, click **Modify**, and click **Expand**.
2. Type the number of pixels by which to expand the selection.
3. Click **OK**.

To contract a selection:

1. Click **Select**, click **Modify**, and click **Contract**.
2. Type the number of pixels by which to contract the selection.
3. Click **OK**.

DESELECT OR RESELECT A SELECTION

To quickly deselect a selection, press **CTRL+D**. To quickly reselect a previous selection, press **CTRL+SHIFT+D**.

Crop to Fit a Selection

Cropping cuts off unwanted areas from the perimeter of an image. Photoshop has a Crop tool, but it is often easier to crop an image to fit a selection.

1. Choose a selection tool from the Toolbox.

2. Make your selection.

3. If necessary, move, resize, or rotate the selection by clicking **Select** and then clicking **Transform Selection**.

4. From the Menu bar, click **Image** and then click **Crop**. The crop will be rectangular to fit the dimensions of the selection.

Delete Using Selections

If a selection is active, pressing the DELETE key only deletes pixels within the selection. You can use selections to quickly erase large parts of an image.

1. Use one or more selection tools to select the area you want to delete.

2. Press **DELETE** (pressing **BACKSPACE** also works) to delete the selected area.

3. Click **Select** and click **Deselect** to remove the selection.

4. Use the **Eraser** tool to clean up the image.

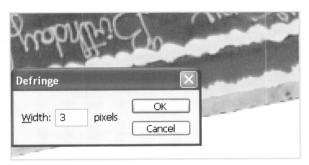

Remove Fringe Pixels

When you copy the contents of an anti-aliased selection to a new layer or document, a fringe of the original background color is often retained. The birthday cake in the illustration, for example, has a slight black fringe. The Defringe command replaces the color of edge pixels with the color of pixels farther away from the edge. To remove a fringe:

1. Click **Layer**, click **Matting**, and click **Defringe**. The Defringe dialog box appears.

2. Type the width in pixels of the colored halo to be replaced.

3. Click **OK**. The colored halo disappears.

If the Defringe command replaces the color on too many or too few pixels, press CTRL+Z to undo the Defringe command and try again, this time specifying a different width.

Save and Load Selections

You can save selections and then load them again later in the session, easily reselecting the same area. Keep in mind that saved selections will not be saved with your image in all image formats. If you want to load a selection the next time you open an image, save the document in Photoshop (PSD) format.

SAVE A SELECTION

With a selection active:

1. Click **Select** and click **Save Selection**. The Save Selection dialog box appears.

2. Type a name for your selection.

3. Leave the other settings alone, and click **OK** to save your selection.

LOAD A SELECTION

To reload a previously saved selection:

1. Click **Select** and click **Load Selection**. The Load Selection dialog box appears.

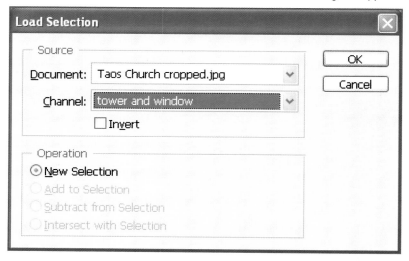

2. Click the **Channel** down arrow, and click your named selection.

3. Click **Invert** to invert, or reverse, the selection.

4. Leave the other settings alone, and click **OK** to load your selection.

Selections are saved in your Photoshop document as new *channels* (images that store information, such as color and image masks).

Extract Images from Backgrounds

Extracting, or subtracting, an area of an image from its background is another way to get the precise image you want. You can do it by copying to a new layer or to a new document or by using the Extract filter. In this case, you select the edges of the object—with many options for refining the area to be extracted—and then extract just the selected image.

QUICKSTEPS

COPYING LAYER STYLES

You can copy layer styles from one layer to another.

1. Click the layer in the layers palette containg the style to be copied.

2. Click **Layer**, click **Layer Style**, and then click **Copy Layer Style**.

3. Click the layer which will receive the **Layer Style**.

4. Click **Layer**, click **Layer Style**, and then click **Paste Layer Style**.

Copy to a New Layer

To copy a selection to a new layer:

1. Use any combination of selection tools to select the elements you want to extract from the background.

2. Press **CTRL+J** to copy the contents of the selection to a new layer. Since the copy will be positioned on a new layer directly above the original, the results of this process will not be apparent at first.

To see the copy by itself:

1. Open the Layers palette by clicking **Window** and clicking **Layers**. The Layers palette is displayed.

2. In the Layers palette, click the **eyeball** icon to the left of the background layer to hide the background layer. The new copy, without the background, becomes apparent.

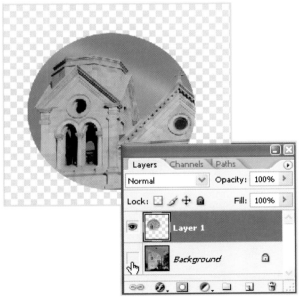

Layers are covered in more depth in Chapter 4.

Copy to a New Document

To copy a selection to a new document:

1. Use any combination of selection tools to select the elements you want to extract from the background.

2. Press **CTRL+C** to copy the contents of the selection to the Clipboard.

3. Click the **File** menu and click **New** to create a new document. By default, Photoshop sizes the new document to fit the contents of the Clipboard.

4. Press **CTRL+V** to paste the contents into the new document.

Extract Background Elements

While not exactly a selection tool, Photoshop's Extract filter automates the task of removing the background from around foreground elements in your image. To extract an element from its background using the Extract filter:

1. Click **Filter** and then click **Extract**. The Extract dialog box appears, seen in Figure 3-6.

2. Click the **Highlight** tool in the upper-left area of the Extract dialog box.

3. Drag with the Highlight tool to highlight the edge of the element you want to extract. This highlight shows Photoshop where to look for the edges of your elements:

   - If necessary, adjust the brush size. The smaller the brush, the better job Photoshop will usually do of finding the edges in your picture.

- If your element has a clearly defined border, make sure the highlight goes all the way around it.

- If your element doesn't have a clearly defined border, cover it completely with the Highlighter.

QUICKSTEPS

MOVING AND DUPLICATING

MOVE THE CONTENTS OF A SELECTION

With a selection active:

1. Select the **Move** tool from the Toolbox.
2. Drag within the selection to move the contents.

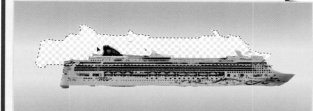

DUPLICATE THE CONTENTS OF A SELECTION

With a selection active:

1. Select the **Move** tool from the Toolbox.
2. Hold down the **ALT** key, and drag within the selection to duplicate the contents.

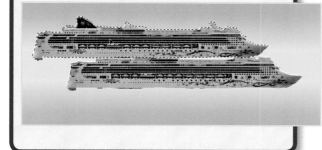

4. If your element has a clearly defined border, select the **Fill** tool in the upper-left area of the Extract dialog box, and click inside the area outlined by the Highlight tool to fill it. Pixels within the filled area will always be retained by the Extract filter.

5. Click **Preview** to preview the extraction.

If you don't like the results, change the settings and try again. To reset the Extract filter:

1. In the Preview section of the Extract dialog box, click the **Show Highlight** and **Show Fill** check boxes to redisplay your highlight and fill. Any errors will be more clearly revealed.

2. Click the **Show** down arrow, and click **Original**.

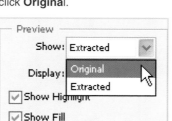
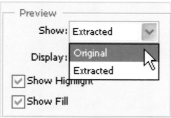

3. Make changes in your settings:

- Use a smaller **Highlighter** brush to make it easier for Photoshop to detect edges.
- Increase the **Smooth** setting to even out jagged edges. Too much smoothing will blur the outlines.
- If your element is against a textured background, click **Textured Image** to improve the extraction results.
- Change the **Highlight** and **Fill** colors to make them easier to see against your image.
- Preview and change the results as many times as you want. When finished, click **OK**.

If no amount of tweaking produces acceptable results using the Extract filter, you can manually touch up areas as described in the following sections.

Figure 3-6: You can extract an image using the Extract filter, which provides options that make it easy.

Use the Highlighter tool to mark the edge of the area to retain

Use the Fill tool to fill the area to be retained

Use the Edge Touchup tool to clean up edges

Click to enable more precise, smoother highlighting

Click when extracting from a textured background

Controls the size of the Extract tools

Use the Eraser tool to erase mistakes when marking the edge

Use the Eyedropper tool to select a new foreground color to extract

Use the Cleanup tool to erase parts of the image you don't want to retain

Click the Zoom tool to magnify edges

Use the Hand tool to move the image within the Extract window

Changes the highlight color

Changes the fill color

Smooths the outline of the extraction

Bases the outline on a saved selection

Foreground color

Switches between showing original image and extracted image

Forces extraction of highlighted pixels similar in color to foreground color

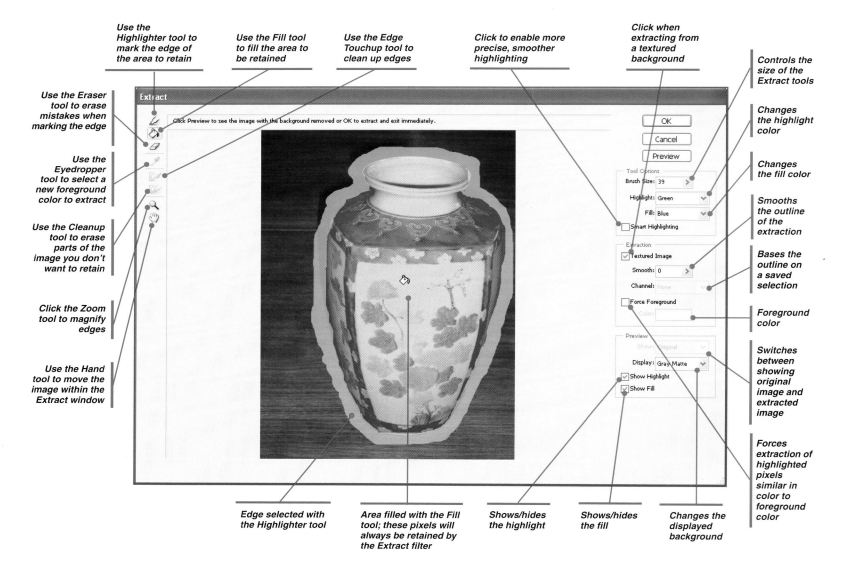

Edge selected with the Highlighter tool

Area filled with the Fill tool; these pixels will always be retained by the Extract filter

Shows/hides the highlight

Shows/hides the fill

Changes the displayed background

TIP

If your element has a well-defined edge, you can click the **Smart Highlighting** check box to have Photoshop automatically detect the edge as you paint.

☑ Smart Highlighting

CLEAN UP AN EXTRACTION USING THE CLEANUP TOOL

The Cleanup tool paints with transparency. To clean up problem areas:

1. With your preview visible in the Extract filter, select the **Cleanup** tool.

2. Paint using the Cleanup tool to erase any remaining extra pixels from the background.

3. Hold down **ALT** while painting to restore areas you want to extract.

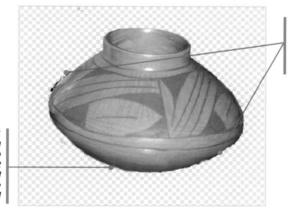

Use the Cleanup tool and the Edge Touchup tool to erase extra bits of the background and refine the edges

*Press **ALT** while using the Cleanup tool to repaint deleted parts of the foreground*

CLEAN UP AN EXTRACTION USING THE EDGE TOUCHUP TOOL

The Edge Touchup Tool erases ragged areas around the edges of extracted elements as you drag the tool over the areas.

1. With your preview visible in the Extract filter, select the **Edge Touchup** tool.

2. Drag the tool along the edges of your extracted image to clean them up.

3. When satisfied with the results displayed in Extract's preview pane, click **OK** to perform the extraction and return to your document.

EXPANDING SELECTIONS

The Grow and Similar commands expand the current selection, adding pixels of similar color to those pixels already selected.

Original selection

EXPAND A SELECTION WITH THE GROW COMMAND

The Grow command expands the selection to include only adjacent pixels that fall within the Tolerance range specified in the Magic Wand tool Options bar. With a selection active:

From the Menu bar, click **Select** and then click **Grow**. Similarly colored adjacent pixels are selected.

Selection expanded with the Grow command

EXPAND A SELECTION WITH THE SIMILAR COMMAND

The Similar command expands the selection to include any pixels throughout the image that fall within the Magic Wand's Tolerance range, whether those pixels are adjacent to the current selection or not.

With a selection active:

From the Menu bar, click **Select** and then click **Similar**. Similarly colored pixels are selected throughout the image.

Selection expanded with the Similar command

Use the Magic Eraser Tool

The Magic Eraser tool works like a combination of the Magic Wand tool and the DELETE key. It selects an area of similar color and deletes it.

1. If the Magic Eraser tool is not selected, click the current **Eraser** tool icon in the Toolbox palette, and hold down the mouse button. The Eraser tool pop-up menu appears.

2. Click the **Magic Eraser** tool.

3. You have these options on the Options bar:

   - **Tolerance**—The higher the value, the wider the range of colors erased. A good starting tolerance level is 32, which is also the default.

   - **Anti-Alias**—Click this check box to soften the edges of the selection.

   - **Contiguous**—Click this check box to erase only connected areas of the sampled color.

   - **Sample All Layers**—Click to sample the erased color in all visible layers of an image, not just the selected layer.

   - **Opacity**—Drag the slider to vary how much of the color will be erased. The higher the opacity, the more is erased.

4. Click a color in your image to delete all similar colors in the image.

Use the Background Eraser Tool

The Background Eraser tool erases areas of similar color. Use the Background Eraser tool to erase the background from around a foreground element. When you first click in the image using the Background Eraser tool, it samples the background color.

1. If the Background Eraser tool is not selected, click the current **Eraser** tool icon in the Toolbox palette, and hold down the mouse button. The Eraser tool pop-up menu is displayed.

2. Click the **Background Eraser** tool.

3. Click the **Limits** down arrow, and click **Contiguous**.

4. Click the **Sampling** down arrow, and click **Once**. This samples the background color each time you click with the tool.

5. Click in an area you want to erase to sample the background color.

6. Without releasing the mouse button, drag the tool over the background to erase pixels of similar color.

7. To erase multiple areas or multiple colors, repeat steps 5 and 6.

The Background Eraser tool has a number of options, which you can adjust for better results, as shown in Figure 3-7.

Figure 3-7: You will find many settings for working with the Background Eraser tool on the Options bar.

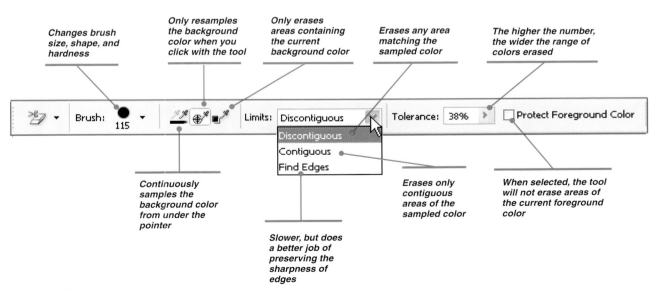

Changes brush size, shape, and hardness

Only resamples the background color when you click with the tool

Only erases areas containing the current background color

Erases any area matching the sampled color

The higher the number, the wider the range of colors erased

Continuously samples the background color from under the pointer

Slower, but does a better job of preserving the sharpness of edges

Erases only contiguous areas of the sampled color

When selected, the tool will not erase areas of the current foreground color

TIP

Switching to a soft-edged brush creates a soft edge for the selection, almost the equivalent of anti-aliasing.

Painting Selections with Quick Masks

A Quick Mask is a selection that you paint on, usually with the Brush tool (see Figures 3-8a and 3-8b).

Figure 3-8a: The mask defines the area to be protected; that is, the image not masked will be selected.

Figure 3-8b: The selection surrounds the image of Tank the cocker spaniel, which can be edited as with any selection.

Work with Quick Masks

To select an area using a Quick Mask:

1. Click the **Quick Mask** button [ ] in the Toolbox, or press **Q** to enter Quick Mask mode.

2. Click the **Brush** tool in the Toolbox.

3. Press **D** to set the foreground and background colors to black and white.

4. With the Brush tool, paint over the areas you do not want selected.

5. You can work with a Quick Mask in the following ways:

   - To remove some of the masked area from the selection, click the **Switch Foreground And Background Colors** button, or press **X**, and paint over the areas to be restored with white.

   - To add some additional area to the mask, press **D** to make the foreground color black, and paint over the areas to be added to the selection.

   - Switch back and forth between the **Edit In Standard Mode** button, to see the moving selection outline for a visual look-see, and the **Edit In Quick Mask Mode** button, to see the mask. You can press **Q** to quickly toggle between the two modes.

6. When you have the mask selection the way you want it, click **Edit In Standard Mode** to edit your selection in the usual manner.

TOUCH UP A SELECTION WITH QUICK MASK

You can use Quick Mask mode in combination with other selection tools to select images more easily.

1. Use a selection tool, such as the Magic Wand tool, to create a rough selection.

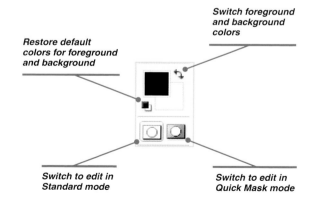

Switch foreground and background colors

Restore default colors for foreground and background

Switch to edit in Standard mode

Switch to edit in Quick Mask mode

3

TIP

Double-click the **Quick Mask icon** in the Toolbox palette to change the color and opacity of the Quick Mask.

TIP

Remember that the tinted parts of the image are the parts that are not selected.

2. Click the **Quick Mask** button in the Toolbox, or press **Q** to enter Quick Mask mode.

3. Press **D** to set the foreground and background colors to black and white.

4. Select the **Brush** tool from the Toolbox.

5. Right-click the image and adjust the brush's size and shape.

6. Paint with the **Brush** tool to touch up the mask, as shown here.

7. Press **X** to switch the foreground color between black and white. Black adds to the mask; white subtracts from the mask. Edit your mask as needed

8. When the mask is complete, press **Q** again to leave Quick Mask mode and view your selection in Standard mode. Here, too, you can edit the image with white and black brush strokes, finalizing your selection before you perform other editing tasks.

9. If necessary, flatten and save your image when the editing is complete.

Use the Pen Tool

You can create a selection by clicking a path with the Pen tool.

1. Select the **Pen** tool, from the Toolbox palette.

2. In the Pen tool Options bar, click the **Paths** icon.

3. Click repeatedly around the area you wish to select to create a path. Every time you click, the Pen creates a new anchor.

4. To close the path, click once on the anchor at the beginning of the path.

5. To add to the path, click the **Add To Shape Area** icon in the Options bar, and then click the new points to be added to the path. To subtract from the path, click the **Subtract From Shape Area** icon in the Options bar, and then click the area to be subtracted from the selection path.

6. Press **CTRL+ENTER** to select the area within the path.

You'll learn more about the Pen tool in Chapter 5.

How to...

- 🔲 *Hiding and Revealing Layers*
- • *Create New Layers*
- 🔲 *Linking and Unlinking Layers*
- • *Edit with Layers*
- 🔲 *Manipulating Layer Groups*
- • *Create a Layer Group*
- 🔲 *Flattening an Image*
- • *Merge a Layer with the Layer Beneath It*
- • *Merge Linked Layers*
- • *Merge Visible Layers*
- • *Create Layer Masks*
- 🔲 *Editing a Mask*
- 🔲 *Masking a Layer Group*
- • *Add Layer Drop Shadows*
- • *Create a Frame with Layer Effects*
- • *Save and Load Layer Styles*
- • *Work with Opacity and Fill*
- • *Use Blend Modes*
- • *Create a CD Label*

Chapter 4

Using Layers

Layers and layer masks are the key to creating advanced effects, such as collages. They allow you to build complex compositions while still maintaining control of the individual elements. Better yet, they allow you to keep all your assets intact so you can change how you use them later. Think of layers as a combination of photographs and overhead transparencies that can be stacked up, one on top of the other, almost indefinitely. You can use a layer mask to hide all or part of a layer and then vary a layer's opacity to achieve the desired effect. You can use layer styles to create drop shadows and other effects.

Work with Layers

Photoshop's Layers palette allows you to create, copy, delete, rearrange, and add special effects to your images. You'll do most of your manipulation of layers via the Layers palette, shown in Figure 4-1.

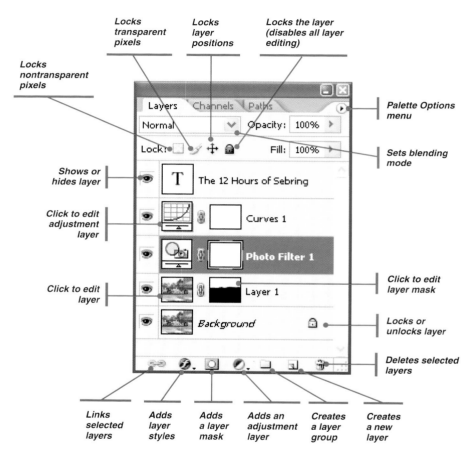

QUICKSTEPS

HIDING AND REVEALING LAYERS

In documents with multiple layers, you often need to temporarily hide individual layers. By doing so, you avoid having to sort through layers crucial to the document but that do not currently need editing.

TEMPORARILY HIDE A LAYER

Click the **eyeball** icon at the far left of the layer thumbnail in the Layers palette. The icon disappears and the layer is hidden.

REVEAL A HIDDEN LAYER

Click the empty space at the far left of the layer thumbnail in the Layers palette. The eyeball icon reappears and the layer is revealed.

Figure 4-1: You use the Layers palette to control image layers.

- Locks nontransparent pixels
- Locks transparent pixels
- Locks layer positions
- Locks the layer (disables all layer editing)
- Palette Options menu
- Sets blending mode
- Shows or hides layer
- Click to edit adjustment layer
- Click to edit layer
- Click to edit layer mask
- Locks or unlocks layer
- Deletes selected layers
- Links selected layers
- Adds layer styles
- Adds a layer mask
- Adds an adjustment layer
- Creates a layer group
- Creates a new layer

NOTE

Hidden layers cannot be modified or copied.

TIP

To rename a layer, double-click the layer's name in the Layers palette, and type a new name.

NOTE

If a selection is active, the Layer Via Copy command (**CTRL+J**) copies the selected portions to a new layer. If there is no selection, then the command copies the entire layer.

Create New Layers

You can create layers in a variety of ways: by clicking a button in the Layers palette, by using a keyboard shortcut, or by using a menu command. When you create a new blank layer using a menu command, the New Layer dialog box appears, which enables you to create a clipping mask (the transparent pixels of the underlying layers are used to mask the new layer), specify the blending mode, and set layer opacity.

CREATE A NEW BLANK LAYER

To create a new blank layer:

- Click the **Create New Layer** button at the bottom of the Layers palette.

  –Or–

- Click **Layer**, click **New**, and then click **Layer**.

  –Or–

- Press **SHIFT+CTRL+N**.

COPY AN EXISTING LAYER

You also can create a new layer by copying an existing layer.

- In the Layers palette, click the source layer. The cursor changes to a fist. Drag the layer to the **Create A New Layer** button at the bottom of the Layers palette.

  –Or–

- Click **Layer**, click **New**, and then click **Layer Via Copy**.

  –Or–

- Press **CTRL+J**.

Photoshop creates a new layer that is an exact copy of the original. The new layer appears immediately above the source layer in the Layers palette.

QUICKSTEPS

LINKING AND UNLINKING LAYERS

Layers that are linked move, rotate, and transform together. If you move the contents of a layer 50 pixels to the left, the contents of all layers linked to that layer will also move 50 pixels to the left.

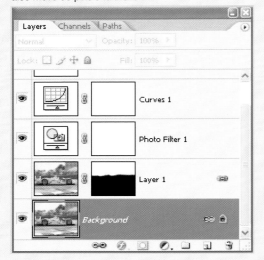

LINK LAYERS

To link another layer to the currently selected layer:

Select the layers you want to link, and then click the **Link Layers** button at the bottom of the Layers palette. A chain icon appears to the right of each layer's name.

UNLINK LAYERS

Select a linked layer and then click the **Link Layers** button at the bottom of the Layers palette. The chain icon disappears.

CREATE A NEW LAYER FROM A SELECTION

You can create a new layer by copying only the selected portions of an existing layer. This is a useful way to separate a selected element or elements from the background while leaving your original image intact.

1. Use any of the selection tools to select the portions of a layer that you want to copy.
2. Click **Layer**, click **New**, and then click **Layer Via Copy**.

   –Or–

   Press **CTRL+J**.

Edit with Layers

You can add as many layers to a document as needed. You can add layers using menu commands or by clicking icons in the Layers palette. You can also make the background layer editable. The sections that follow show you how to work with existing layers in the document, make the background layer editable, and add additional layers as needed.

UNLOCK THE BACKGROUND LAYER

The background layer in a Photoshop document is locked. You cannot erase it (other than painting over it with a background color). You cannot move, rotate, or resize it; nor can you create a mask for it. To make these kinds of changes on the background, you must first turn it into a normal layer. To do this:

Click **Layer**, click **New**, and then click **Layer From Background**. The background becomes a normal layer.

COPY MERGED LAYERS

You might want to copy a merged version of a layered document—a version that looks the same but does not contain multiple layers—to the Clipboard.

1. Select the entire document by clicking **Select** and clicking **All** or by pressing **CTRL+A**.
2. Click **Edit** and then click **Copy Merged**; or press **SHIFT+CTRL+C**. All layers in the document are copied to the Clipboard as a single layer.

TIP

Double-click the background layer lock icon to create a layer from the background.

When you copy the contents of the Clipboard to a new document, they appear as a new layer that comprises all layers from the parent document (see Figure 4-2 and Figure 4-3).

Figure 4-2: Before using the Copy Merged command, the document is comprised of many layers.

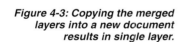

Figure 4-3: Copying the merged layers into a new document results in single layer.

Any time you paste something into a Photoshop document, it goes on a new layer located immediately above the currently selected layer.

COPY FROM ANOTHER APPLICATION TO A NEW LAYER

To copy an item from another application, for example, Microsoft Internet Explorer, to a Photoshop document:

1. Open an image in Photoshop.

2. Switch to another application, such as a web browser; and select and copy an image.

3. Return to Photoshop, click **Edit**, and then click **Paste**. The new image is pasted into the Photoshop document on a new layer.

COPY A LAYER FROM A PHOTOSHOP DOCUMENT

To copy a layer from one Photoshop document to another:

1. Open two images in Photoshop.

2. Click **Window**, click **Arrange**, and then click **Tile Horizontally** or **Tile Vertically** to display both images at once.

3. Select the **Move** tool from the Toolbox.

4. Click within the first document.

5. Click **Select** and then click **All**, or press CTRL+A, to select the entire image.

6. Click within the second document.

7. Click **Edit** and then click **Paste**, or press CTRL+V, to paste the first image into a new layer in the second document.

COPY A LAYER BY DRAGGING

You can drag layers directly from one Photoshop document to another.

1. With two documents and the Layers palette open in Photoshop, click the title bar of the source document.

2. In the Layers palette, drag the layer you want to copy, and place it anywhere in the target document. A copy of that layer appears in the target document.

TIP

When dragging a layer between documents, hold down SHIFT to center the new layer within the document. Remember to release the mouse button prior to releasing the SHIFT key; otherwise, the new layer will not be centered.

REARRANGE LAYER ORDER

The order of layers in the Layers palette usually determines the final result, as shown in Figures 4-4 and 4-5.

To change the order of layers:

1. Click a layer's name in the Layers palette.

2. Drag the layer up or down to a new position.

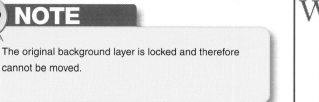

NOTE

The original background layer is locked and therefore cannot be moved.

Figure 4-4: The image of the white bird partially obscures the other layers when it is the top layer.

TIP

Before making changes, copy your work to a new layer. Make changes on the new layer, and if you don't like them, simply delete the layer.

Figure 4-5: When the white bird is moved to a lower layer, it is obscured by the layers above.

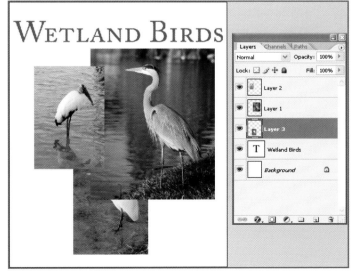

DELETE A LAYER

To delete a layer:

1. Click a layer's thumbnail in the Layers palette.

2. Drag the layer to the **Delete Layer** button at the bottom of the palette.

   –Or–

1. Right-click the layer's name in the Layers palette, and click **Delete Layer**.

2. Photoshop asks you to confirm the deletion. Click **Yes**.

Consolidate Layers into Layer Groups

Layers can be grouped together into folders called *layer groups*. Layer groups help you keep multilayer documents organized. Although you cannot paint on a layer group, in most other ways, they act the same as individual layers. You can reposition, resize, mask, and hide all layers in a layer group at the same time.

Create a Layer Group

When you create a new layer group, you are creating a blank folder into which you can drag other layers in the document. Creating layer groups when working with a multilayer document makes it easier for you to work within the Layers palette, since you can collapse any layer groups you are not currently editing to eliminate clutter and confusion in the Layers palette.

To create a new layer group:

Click the **Create A New Group** button at the bottom of the Layers palette.

–Or–

Click **Layers** and then click **Group Layers**.

MOVE A LAYER INTO A LAYER GROUP

To move a layer into a layer group:

1. In the Layers palette, click an existing layer.
2. Drag it to the desired layer group.

REMOVE A LAYER FROM A LAYER GROUP

To remove a layer from a layer group:

1. In the Layers palette, click the layer within the layer group that you want to remove.
2. Drag it to a position outside of the layer group.

Merge Layers

When you are finished editing several layers in a document, you can select them and then merge them into a single layer. When you merge selected layers, the other layers in the document are still editable. You can apply edits to the layer created by merging other layers. You can also select other layers in the document and merge them.

Merge a Layer with the Layer Beneath It

When you have edited two layers to your liking, you can select a layer and merge it with the underlying layer. This creates a new layer, which can be further edited.

1. In the Layers palette, select the topmost layer of the two layers you want to merge.
2. Click the **Options** button in the upper-right area of the Layers palette, and click **Merge Down** from the flyout menu.

   –Or–

   Press **CTRL+E**.

Merge Linked Layers

To merge all linked layers into a single layer:

1. In the Layers palette, click one of the linked layers to select it.
2. Click **Layer** and click **Select Linked Layers**.
3. Click **Layer** and click **Merge Layers**.

–Or–

1. Click the **Options** button in the upper-right area of the Layers palette. The palette Options menu appears.
2. Click **Select Linked Layers**.
3. Click the Layers palette **Options** button, and then click **Merge Layers**.

Merge Visible Layers

To merge visible layers into a single layer:

1. In the Layers palette, click the **eyeball** icon for any layers you want to hide.
2. Click a visible layer to select it.
3. Click the **Options** button in the upper-right area of the Layers palette. The palette Options menu appears.
4. Click **Merge Visible**.

–Or–

Press **CTRL+SHIFT+E**.

TIP

Mask, don't erase. When you erase a pixel, it's gone forever; but you can always change a mask if you change your mind later—nothing is ever lost.

Work with Layer Masks

A layer mask hides, or *masks*, part of a layer. Layer masks are black, white, and shades of gray. Where the layer mask is black, the masked layer is not visible. If the mask is a shade of gray, the underlying mask is partially visible. If the mask is white, the layer is completely visible. You can paint on the mask with shades of gray to partially reveal areas on underlying layers, or you can paint with black to completely reveal areas of the underlying layer.

TIP

If the mask is not perfect, press Q to revert to Quick Mask mode, and then paint white over the areas you do not want to mask.

Create Layer Masks

You create layer masks by painting them with the Brush tool, from a Quick Mask, or from a selected area of the image. The mask color can be controlled by the user. In Figure 4-5, the mask is white, which reveals all of the selected layer. Painting black hides, or masks, the pixels from the layer on which the mask resides.

PAINT A LAYER MASK

The most common way to create a layer mask is to paint one using the Brush tool.

Figure 4-6: Paint on a layer mask to reveal or conceal underlying layers.

1. In the Layers palette, select the layer to be masked.
2. Click the **Add Layer Mask** button at the bottom of the Layers palette to create a new blank mask for the selected layer. The icon to the immediate left of the layer thumbnail changes to a mask to show that you are editing a layer mask.
3. Select the **Brush** tool or other painting tool from the Toolbox.
4. By default, the foreground color is black. If you changed the default foreground color, reset it to black, white, or a shade of gray. Paint with black to mask parts of the image, as shown in Figure 4-6.

CREATE A LAYER MASK FROM A QUICK MASK

1. Press **Q** to switch to Quick Mask mode.
2. Select a painting or drawing tool from the Toolbox.
3. Set the foreground color to black, and paint on the areas of the image you want to mask.
4. Press **Q** again to leave Quick Mask mode. A border of what looks like marching ants signifies the area to be masked.
5. In the Layers palette, click the layer to be masked.
6. Click the **Add Layer Mask** button at the bottom of the Layers palette. Photoshop creates a new layer mask from the selection.

EDITING A MASK

The best thing about masks is that they aren't permanent. You can edit them at any time, hiding or revealing the underlying image.

EDIT A MASK WITH THE BRUSH TOOL

1. In the Layers palette, click the layer mask you want to edit.
2. Select the **Brush** tool or other painting tool from the Toolbox.
3. Select a foreground color: black to mask, white to reveal, or gray to partially reveal.
4. Paint to alter the mask.

ADD A SELECTION TO A MASK

You can expand a layer mask by selecting additional pixels to be masked and adding them to the layer mask.

1. In the Layers palette, click the layer mask you want to modify.
2. Use any selection tool to select an area you want to mask.
3. Press **D** to set the foreground and background colors to black and white.
4. Press **CTRL+BACKSPACE** to fill the selected area of the mask with black.

CREATE A NEW SELECTION FROM A MASK

In the Layers palette, press **CTRL** while you click the mask thumbnail. All unmasked pixels are selected.

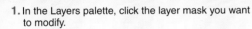

Click the layer thumbnail to edit the layer

Click the mask thumbnail to edit the mask.

NOTE

You cannot mask the original background layer.

CREATE A LAYER MASK FROM A SELECTED AREA

1. In the Layers palette, click the layer to be masked.
2. Use one or more of Photoshop's selection tools, such as the **Rectangular Marquee** or **Lasso** tool, to select the part of the image to be masked.
3. Click the **Add Layer Mask** button at the bottom of the Layers palette. Photoshop creates a new layer mask from the selection. Only pixels that were within the selection are now visible in this layer.

CREATE A NEW BLANK LAYER MASK

Click the **Add Layer Mask** button at the bottom of the Layers palette.

–Or–

Click **Layer**, click **Layer Mask**, and then click **Reveal All**.

You can now paint in the layer mask with black or shades of gray to hide parts of the layer.

HIDE A LAYER WITH A NEW LAYER MASK

Click **Layer**, click **Layer Mask**, and click **Hide All**.

You can now paint in the layer mask with white or shades of gray to reveal parts of the underlying layer.

CREATE A GRADIENT MASK

1. Press **D** to set the foreground and background colors to black and white.
2. In the Layers palette, click the layer to be masked.
3. Click **Add Layer Mask** at the bottom of the Layers palette to create a new blank layer mask.
4. Select the **Gradient** tool from the Toolbox.
5. Right-click within the image to bring up the Gradient context menu.
6. If you hover the pointer over a gradient, a Tool Tip appears showing you that gradient's name. Click **Foreground To Background** from the presets menu.

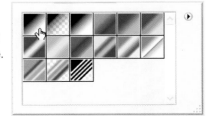

Figure 4-7: A linear gradient mask causes the top layer to fade in from left to right.

7. Drag in the image from left to right or from top to bottom to create the background gradient, as shown in Figure 4-7. The areas of the gradient that are white reveal the underlying layer; black reveals the entire masked layer; while shades of gray partially reveal the underlying layer.

In the same way, you can use any of Photoshop's other gradient settings—radial, angle, reflected, or diamond—to create different effects, as shown in Figure 4-7.

TURN MASKS OFF AND ON

To temporarily disable a layer mask:

In the Layers palette, right-click a layer mask and click **Disable Layer Mask**. A red X appears across the layer mask.

Disabling a mask does not delete it. To turn the mask on again:

In the Layers palette, right-click a layer mask and click **Enable Layer Mask**. The red X disappears from the layer mask.

DELETE A LAYER MASK

To delete a layer mask:

In the Layers palette, right-click a layer mask and click **Delete Layer Mask**.

APPLY A MASK

When you apply a mask, masked pixels are permanently deleted from the layer and the layer mask is discarded. Visually, the image will look the same, but the mask is no longer available for editing.

In the Layers palette, right-click a layer mask and click **Apply Layer Mask**.

Work with Layer Effects

Most layer effects are applied to the edges, so if you apply them to layers containing objects that are the same size as the document, you may not see any effect at all. Figure 4–9 shows a drop shadow applied to a layer object that is

QUICKSTEPS

MASKING A LAYER GROUP

Layer groups can be masked in the same way as can individual layers.

CREATE A LAYER GROUP MASK

1. In the Layers palette, click a layer group thumbnail.
2. Click the **Add Layer Mask** button at the bottom of the palette.
3. Use the **Brush** or **Gradient** tools to paint a new mask.

TIP

To see a mask full-screen while you edit it, press **ALT** while clicking the layer's mask thumbnail in the Layers palette. Press **ALT** and click the layer thumbnail again to return to layer view.

NOTE

Layer effects cannot be applied to the original background layer.

---

smaller than the object. Layer effects are usually, though not always, applied to layers that contain at least some areas of transparency. Figure 4–10 shows the layer effects.

Photoshop layer effects are almost infinitely malleable, and you can use them to create a wider variety of effects than would at first seem possible. Drop shadows are usually dark, but they can be colorful and lighter than the surrounding area. The Stroke effect is usually used to create a simple line around the outside of a shape, but you can also use it to create a realistic 3-D picture frame, as shown later in the chapter.

Figure 4-8: Drop shadows are visible when the contents of a layer are smaller than the document size.

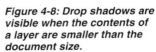

Figure 4-9: You use the Layer Styles menu to add effects to objects on a layer.

Add Layer Drop Shadows

Drop shadow is probably the most commonly used of all layer effects. You can apply a drop shadow to a text layer, a shape layer, or an image layer.

Figure 4-10: You add drop shadows and other effects from the Layer Style dialog box.

CREATE A SIMPLE DROP SHADOW

1. Create a Photoshop document with at least two layers. The top layer should not fill the entire canvas. A text layer or shape layer works well for this.

2. In the Layers palette, right-click the layer that will cast the shadow, and click **Blending Options**. The Layer Style dialog box appears, as shown in Figure 4-10.

3. On the left side of the Layer Style dialog box, click the **Drop Shadow** check box to reveal the Drop Shadow section.

4. Drag the **Distance** slider until the shadow falls the desired distance from the layer. The Distance slider controls how high the layer appears to be above the background.

5. Drag within the **Angle** circle to change the apparent direction of the light source and the direction the shadow falls.

6. Drag the **Size** slider until the shadow is the desired size. The Size slider controls the fuzziness of the shadow. The results should look something like Figure 4-11.

TIP

To create a new type layer, select one of the type tools from the Toolbox, and click anywhere on the image to begin typing. (See Chapter 7 for additional details on how to use the Type tool.)

Figure 4-11: You can add drop shadows to text and layer objects from the Layer Style dialog box.

Create a Frame with Layer Effects

You can combine any number of layer effects on a given layer; you are not limited to just a drop shadow or just a brush stroke. Let's look at an example that creates a realistic-looking picture frame from a simple rectangle using nothing but layer effects.

DEFINE THE FRAME AREA

1. Load a photo around which you want to put a frame.
2. In the Layers palette, click the **Add New Layer** button to create a new blank layer above the photo.
3. Select the **Rectangular Marquee** tool from the Toolbox.
4. Click in the photo and drag to create a marquee outline of your frame, as shown in Figure 4-12.

If you don't like your first outline:

Click and drag again with the Marquee tool to define a new outline.

–Or–

Click **Select**, click **Transform Selection**, and resize and reposition your outline.

Don't worry about getting it perfect; it will be easy to change things later.

CREATE THE FRAME

1. Press ALT+BACKSPACE to fill the selection with the foreground color; it doesn't matter what color that is. Alternatively, click **Edit** and then click **Fill** to open the Fill dialog box. Click the **Use** down arrow, and click **Foreground Color** from the drop-down menu.
2. Press CTRL+D to deselect the selection. This gets rid of the marquee around the edges of your rectangle.
3. In the Layers palette, set the Fill—not the Opacity—to **0**. This causes the rectangle fill to disappear, but all layer effects will still be visible.
4. In the Layers palette, right-click the new layer and click **Blending Options**. The Layer Styles dialog box appears.
5. Under Blending Options, at the left, click **Stroke**. Don't worry about the color.
6. Set the Position to **Inside**, set the Blend Mode to **Normal**, and leave Opacity at **100%**.

Figure 4-12: Create a rectangular marquee to define the frame area.

7. Drag the **Size** slider until the stroke is the desired size for your frame. Your frame should look something like Figure 4-13.

Figure 4-13: Add a stroke to the layer to define the thickness of the frame.

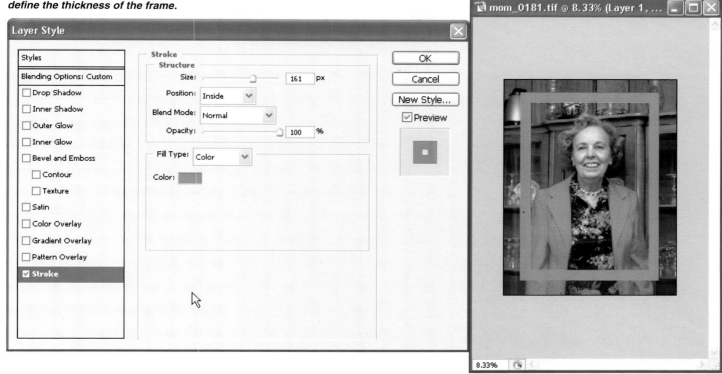

8. Under Fill Type, click **Pattern** and choose a pattern for your frame. A wood pattern works well, as shown in Figure 4-14.

9. Drag the **Scale** slider beneath the pattern thumbnail to adjust the fit of the pattern in the frame.

NOTE

You can edit existing layer effects at any time by right-clicking a layer in the Layers palette and clicking **Blending Options**.

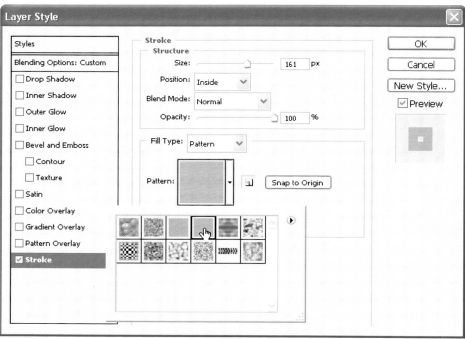

Figure 4-14: Replace the default stroke with a wood pattern to simulate a wooden frame.

BEVEL THE FRAME

The frame doesn't look very three-dimensional yet. Adding a bevel will fix that.

1. Double-click the layer to reveal the Layer Styles dialog box, and then click the **Bevel And Emboss** check box.

2. Set the Style to **Inner Bevel**, set the Technique to **Chisel Hard**, and set the Direction to **Up**.

3. Experiment with different settings for **Size** and **Depth** to find a combination you like.

4. Under Shading, drag in the **Angle** circle to adjust the height and angle of the light, as shown in Figure 4-15.

NOTE

By reducing a layer's fill to 0 percent, you can create layer effects, such as drop shadows, without showing the shapes that create them.

Figure 4-15: Add a bevel to the frame to give it a realistic 3-D effect.

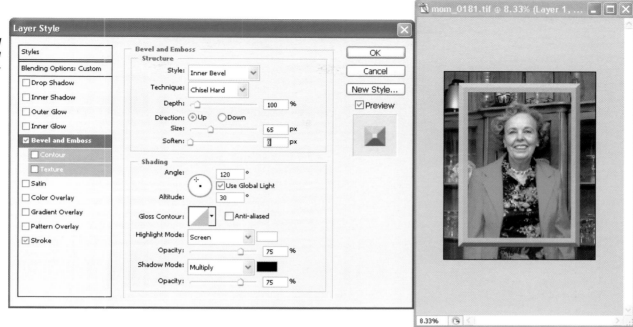

TIP

If you are combining multiple effects, click the **Use Global Light** check box, provided it is available for the effect you are adding. This guarantees that the same simulated light falls on each effect, creating a consistent look.

5. Under Shading, set the **Highlight** and **Shadow** modes. Multiply usually works best for shadows, but experiment with different modes, such as Vivid Light and Color Dodge for the highlights.

6. You can change the opacity of the shadows and highlights, as well as change the look of the simulated lighting. The higher the opacity, the brighter the simulated lighting will appear in the picture.

7. When finished, click **OK**.

POSITION THE FRAME AND CROP

You can resize, move, and transform layer contents to your heart's content; any layer effects will follow along.

1. With the frame layer still selected, press **CTRL+T** to invoke the Free Transform command, as shown in Figure 4-16.

2. Drag the handles to resize the frame.

Figure 4-16: Use the Free Transform command to move and resize the frame.

3. Drag within the frame to move the frame within the canvas.

4. Press **ENTER** to accept the changes.

To crop the image to fit the new frame:

1. Press **CTRL** while you click the frame layer's thumbnail in the Layers palette to select all visible pixels.

2. Click **Image** and then click **Crop** to crop the image to fit.

Save and Load Layer Styles

You needn't re-create a layer style every time you want to use it. You can save layer styles and recall them easily at any time.

1. If the Layer Style dialog box is not displayed, right-click the layer with the style you want to save, and click **Blending Options**.

2. In the Blending Options dialog box, click **New Style**.

3. Give your style a name, and click **OK** to save it.

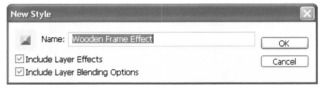

LOAD A STYLE

To load a saved style:

1. In the Layers palette, right-click the thumbnail of the layer you want to add layer effects to, and click **Blending Options**.

2. Click the **Styles** button in the upper-left area of the Layer Style dialog box. Thumbnails of the currently available styles are displayed to the right.

3. Click the style you want to apply to the layer.

LOAD A COLLECTION OF PRESET STYLES

Photoshop ships with several collections of preset styles for creating photographic effects, buttons, and so forth. To load a collection of presets:

1. Click the **Styles** icon at the bottom of the Layers palette. The Layer Styles dialog box is displayed.

2. Click **Styles** in the upper-left area.

3. Click the **triangular** button in the upper-right area of the style Thumbnails pane.

4. Choose a collection of styles from the pop-up menu. The Layer Style dialog box is displayed.

5. Replace the current styles with the new styles by clicking **OK**, or click **Append** to append the new styles to the bottom of the list of available styles.

Use Blending Modes and Transparency

Placing one layer on top of another layer and accepting the default Normal blending mode covers up the bottom layer. Sometimes, this is just what you want, but Photoshop's Layers palette allows you much more control than that. You can control the opacity (or transparency) of any layer. You can also change a layer's blending mode, which changes the way that layer interacts with any layers beneath it.

Work with Opacity and Fill

Each layer has two settings that control its transparency or lack thereof: Opacity and Fill. The difference between opacity and fill is not initially clear. A layer containing a photograph looks the same at 50 percent opacity as it does at 50 percent fill, as you can see in Figures 4-17 and 4-18. The difference is that the Fill setting affects the pixels in the layer; it does *not* affect any layer effects, such as drop shadows. Opacity, on the other hand, affects the pixels in the layer *and* any layer effects. See Figures 4-19 and 4-20 for a comparison. These show a text layer with a

NOTE

You can change the opacity and fill of layers in any blend mode, not just Normal.

stroke effect applied. As you can see, reducing the fill to 50 percent makes the actual text partially transparent while leaving the stroke effect entirely intact. On the other hand, reducing the opacity to 50 percent renders the entire layer, including the stroke effect, partially transparent.

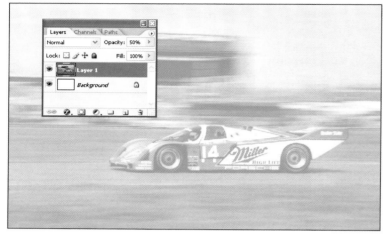

Figure 4-17: This is an example of an image layer at 50 percent opacity.

Figure 4-18: This is an example of an image layer at 50 percent fill.

Figure 4-19: This is an example of a text layer at 100 percent fill with a red stroke.

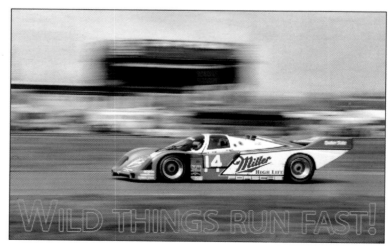

Figure 4-20: Reducing the text layer fill to 0 percent still preserves the red-stroke layer effect.

Figure 4-21: Reducing the layer opacity affects the fill and layer effects.

If you like the effect a blend mode produces but want to tone it down a bit, reduce the opacity of the layer.

NOTE

You cannot change the original background layer's blending mode.

ADJUST LAYER OPACITY

1. With an image open in Photoshop, create a second layer using any of the methods previously discussed.
2. In the Layers palette, click the thumbnail of the top layer.
3. Locate the **Opacity** control at the top of the Layers palette.
4. Click the arrow to the right of the current value, and use the drop-down slider to reduce the layer's opacity. The lower layer shows through, as shown in Figure 4-21.

Use Blend Modes

So far, we have only explored layers using the Normal blending mode; however, Photoshop has no fewer than 22 additional blend modes. Blend modes control the way Photoshop blends the selected image layer with the underlying layers.

CHANGE A LAYER'S BLEND MODE

You can change a layer's blend mode at any time.

1. In the Layers palette, locate the **Blending** mode drop-down list at the top. The default blending mode is Normal.
2. Click the **Blending** mode down arrow. A menu of blending modes is displayed.
3. Click a new blending mode, such as **Vivid Light**, and observe the effect.

USE COMMON BLENDING MODES

Although you can choose from more than 20 layer blend modes, a few of them are especially handy.

USE MULTIPLY MODE

A layer in Multiply mode *always* darkens the image (except where the layer is pure white or transparent, in which case Multiply has no effect). Creating a copy of the background layer, as shown in Figure 4-23 (Figure 4-22 shows the original picture)

| Normal |
| Dissolve |
| Darken |
| Multiply |
| Color Burn |
| Linear Burn |
| Lighten |
| Screen |
| Color Dodge |
| Linear Dodge |
| Overlay |
| Soft Light |
| Hard Light |
| Vivid Light |
| Linear Light |
| Pin Light |
| Hard Mix |
| Difference |
| Exclusion |
| Hue |
| Saturation |
| Color |
| Luminosity |

Figure 4-22: This is the original photograph of an exotic bird.

using the Multiply blend mode darkens the original everywhere except in areas of pure white. The lighter a pixel in the Multiply layer, the less it darkens the overall image.

Figure 4-23: Using the Multiply blend mode darkens pixels.

TIP

It's almost impossible to know in advance what a given blend mode will look like when applied to an image. When combining layers, try out the different blend modes to see how they look.

USE SCREEN MODE

Screen mode is the opposite of Multiply mode. A layer in Screen mode *always* lightens the image (except where the layer is pure black or transparent, in which case it has no effect). Copying an existing layer using the Screen blending mode lightens the original everywhere except in areas of pure black. The lighter a pixel in the Screen mode layer, the more it lightens the overall image.

Create a CD Label

A combination of layers and opacity is perfect for creating a label for a CD.

CREATE THE BACKGROUND

When creating a label for a CD, you can use an image as the basis for the collage, or you can generate a background, as shown in the procedure.

1. Create a new document, 4.75 inches x 4.75 inches, with a resolution of 300 dpi. Click **OK**.

2. Click **Filter**, click **Render**, and then click **Clouds**. Photoshop generates a random pattern of clouds. If you don't like the pattern, press **CTRL + F** to invoke the command a second time.

3. In the Layers palette, click the **Create New Layer** button.

4. Click the **Create New Fill Or Adjustment Layer** button at the bottom of the Layers palette, and then click **Solid Color**. The Color Picker dialog box appears.

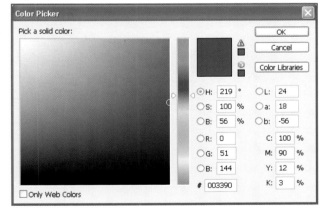

5. Choose the desired background color, and click **OK**.

6. Click the **Blending** arrow and click **Screen** from the drop-down menu. Your image should appear similar to Figure 4-24.

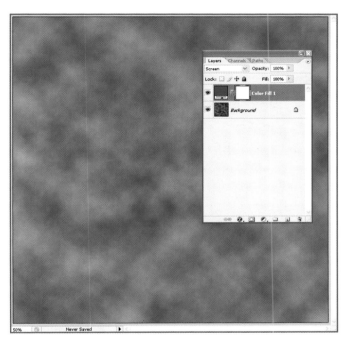

Figure 4-24: Adding a solid color layer using the Screen blend mode blends the clouds with the solid color layer.

NOTE

If you're not satisfied with how the color blends with the clouds, double-click the adjustment layer and choose a different color.

CREATE A CIRCULAR GUIDE

After you create the background, you can add other elements to your design. You can also add a circular guide to ensure that the contents appear within the CD label.

1. In the Layers palette, click the **Create New Layer** button.
2. Click the **Ellipse** tool.
3. In the Options bar, click the **Fill Pixels** button.
4. While pressing the **SHIFT** key, create a circle that goes from top to bottom and left to right. Press the **SPACEBAR** and drag to position the circle. Release the **SPACEBAR** to continue sizing the circle.
5. Click the layer where you just created the circle.
6. Click the **Fill** arrow and drag the slider to **0**.
7. From the Layers palette Options menu, click **Blending Options**. The Layer Styles dialog box appears.
8. Click **Stroke**.
9. Accept the default parameters for the stroke, but click **Inside** from the Position drop-down menu.

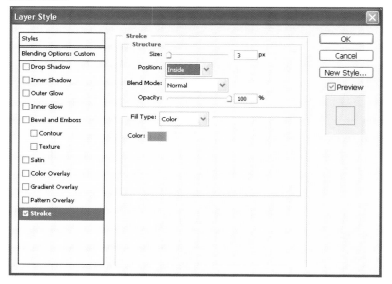

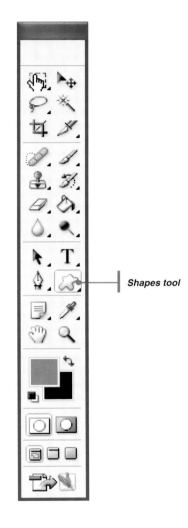

Shapes tool

ADD OTHER ELEMENTS TO YOUR DESIGN

Now that you've got a guide, it's time to add other elements.

1. Click the **Create New Layer** button at the bottom of the Layers palette.

2. Select a foreground color that's complimentary to your design.

3. Click the **Shapes** tool.

4. In the Options bar, click the **Shapes** down arrow, and click a shape from the drop-down menu. For the purpose of this exercise, click the **music note** shape.

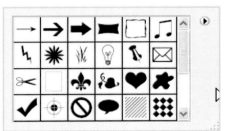

5. Drag inside the document to create the shape.

6. From the Layers palette Options menu, click **Blending Options**. The Layer Styles dialog box appears.

7. Click the **Bevel And Emboss** check box, and then click **Emboss** from the Style drop-down menu.

8. Click **OK** to exit the Layer Styles dialog box.

9. Open an image that you want to display on the CD label.

10. Drag the image into the CD label document. Photoshop creates a new layer for the image.

11. Press **CTRL+T** to invoke the Free Transform command, and then drag one of the outer handles while pressing the **SHIFT** key to resize the layer to fit your document. Remember to keep the important parts of the image inside the circular guide.

Figure 4-25: Paint on a layer mask to remove unwanted parts of the image.

Figure 4-26: Add text to the CD label for the finishing touch.

12. With the new image layer still selected, click the **Create Layer Mask** button.

13. Press **D** to revert to the default foreground and background colors.

14. Click the **Brush** tool.

15. In the Options bar, select a soft-edged brush.

16. Paint on the mask to mask out unwanted parts of the image, as shown in Figure 4-25.

ADD TEXT TO THE LABEL

To finish the design, add some text to the label.

1. Click the **Horizontal Text** tool.

2. In the Options bar, click the **Font** down arrow, and then click the desired font.

3. Click the **Font Size** down arrow, and then click the desired size.

4. Click the **Text Color** swatch, and select the desired color.

5. Type the desired text inside the document.

7. If necessary, use the **Move** tool to reposition the text.

8. From the Layers palette Options menu, click **Blending Options**. The Layer Styles dialog box appears.

9. Click the **Bevel And Emboss** check box, and then click **Emboss** from the Style drop-down menu.

10. Click **OK** to exit the Layer Styles dialog box.

11. Delete the layer on which you created the circular guide before printing the label. Your finished label should resemble Figure 4-26.

How to...

- *Use the Pen Tool*
- *Use the Magnetic Pen Tool*
- *Using the Freeform Pen Tool*
- *Understanding Paths*
- *Use Paths to Create Artwork*
- *Stroke and Fill Paths*
- *Converting Selections*
- *Use the Shape Tools*
- *Converting Paths*
- *Use the Brush Tool*
- *Editing Shapes*
- *Manage Brush Presets*
- *Using the Eraser Tool*
- *Erase Pixels*
- *Use the Gradient Tool*
- *Use the Paint Bucket Tool*
- *Create and Manage Patterns*
- *Use the Art History Brush*
- *Using the Preset Manager*
- *Use the Filter Gallery*
- *Use the Liquify Filter*

Chapter 5

Using Paths, Shapes, and Painting Tools

5

In addition to being one of the best image-editing applications around, Photoshop CS2 has a robust set of drawing tools. You can use these drawing tools to add vector-based graphics to your documents. With Photoshop, you can easily combine vector-based graphics with your bitmap images to create compelling illustrations, whether for commercial use or to spice up your holiday photos, by using shapes as borders for text captions.

Use the Pen Tool as a Drawing Tool

The pen may be mightier than the sword, but the Pen tool is not mightier than the bitmap image. The Pen tool can be used to add vector-based shapes to your documents as well as to add paths to them. You can align text to a temporary work path (which is not part of the final image). You can also use the Pen tool

NOTE

A selected node, or point, is represented by a solid square. An unselected node is represented by a hollow square.

NOTE

If you're creating a shape layer, you do not have to close the path to create a solid shape. However, you will not have a segment between the last point you create and the first point. The absence of a segment prevents you from adding points to the shape or otherwise modifying the shape between those points.

to create intricate shapes with pinpoint accuracy. You can use it to trace a shape from a bitmap on another layer and then use the shape as artwork for the illustration after deleting the bitmap.

Use the Pen Tool

You can use the Pen tool to create complex shapes and paths. You begin by clicking within the document where you want the shape or path to begin and then clicking to add additional points to define the shape. You use a combination of straight points and curve points to define the shape or path. Then, you can edit it point-by-point until you achieve the look you're after.

1. Select the **Pen** tool.

2. In the Options bar, click the **Shape Layers** button to create a shape with a fill, or click the **Paths** button to create a path.

3. Click the **color swatch** icon to open the Color Picker. This option determines the fill of a shape layer you create with the Pen tool.

4. Select a color.

5. Click inside the document to define the first point of the shape or path.

6. Click to add additional points to the shape or path. See Chapter 3 for additional information on using the Pen tool.

7. To create an open path (the end point does not connect to any part of the shape), either press CTRL while you click the last point or select another tool. To create a closed path (the end point connects to another point, often the first point), click the first point you created.

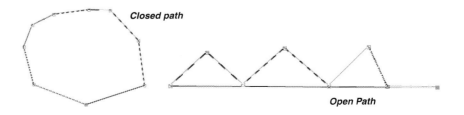

Closed path

Open Path

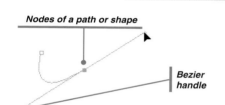

Nodes of a path or shape

Bezier handle

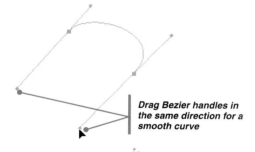

Drag Bezier handles in the same direction for a smooth curve

Drag bezier handles in opposite directions to create an "s" or figure 8 curve

DRAW A STRAIGHT PATH

The straightest distance between two points is a straight line, something you can easily create with the Pen tool.

1. Select the **Pen** tool.
2. Click inside the document to define the first point of the straight line.
3. Click elsewhere inside the document to create an anchor point for a straight-line segment.

DRAW A CURVED PATH

To create a complex shape or path, combine straight-line segments with curves.

1. Select the **Pen** tool.
2. Drag to create a curve point.
3. Click at the desired position to create a second curve point, and drag. As you drag, two Bezier handles emanate from the point. Drag the handles to shape the curve. You may have to experiment with it a bit before it becomes second nature.
4. Continue adding points to define the shape or path.
5. Click the first point to close the shape or path.

EDIT ANCHOR POINTS

Fine-tune a shape or path by moving, adding, deleting, or converting points.

1. Select the **Direct Selection** tool.
2. Click the layer shape or path whose points you want to edit. When you click a shape or path, the individual points that comprise the shape or path are displayed. You can then do any of these tasks:

   - Select a point with the Direct Selection tool, and drag it to a new location.
   - Select a curve point with the Direct Selection tool to display the curve's Bezier handles, and drag the handles to reshape the curved-line segment.
   - Click the **Pen** tool in the Toolbox, click the **Add Anchor Point** tool from the pop-up menu, and then click a location on the path where you want to add a point.

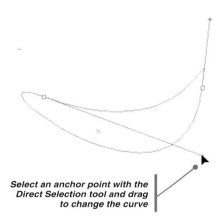

Select an anchor point with the Direct Selection tool and drag to change the curve

- Click the **Pen** tool in the Toolbox, click the **Delete Anchor Point** tool from the pop-up menu, and then click a point to delete it.

- As you drag a Bezier handle with the Direct Selection tool to reshape a curved segment, you can press **ALT** and then click a handle to modify only that handle, thereby reshaping one half of the line segment.

- From the Pen tool pop-up menu in the Toolbox, click the **Convert Point** tool, and click a curve point to convert it to a straight point.

- From the Pen tool pop-up menu in the Toolbox, click the **Convert Point** tool, and drag a straight point to convert it to a curve point. As you drag, two Bezier handles are displayed.

Use the Magnetic Pen Tool

The Magnetic Pen tool is a derivative of the Freeform Pen tool. This tool develops a magnetic attraction to object edges in your document. You can define the range and sensitivity of the tool's snapping behavior as well as the complexity of the resulting path.

1. Select the **Freeform Pen** tool.

2. In the Options bar, click the down arrow beneath the Help menu group to reveal the Freeform Pen tool Options dialog box, and set the parameters:

   - **Curve Fit** measures how tightly the curve is formed; that is, it determines how many anchor points will be created while forming the shape.

   - **Magnetic** transforms the Freeform Pen tool into the Magnetic Pen tool.

   - **Width** determines how far an edge must be from the pointer before the tool detects it. Type a value between 1 and 256.

Freeform Pen Options
Curve Fit: 2 px
☑ Magnetic
Width: 10 px
Contrast: 10%
Frequency: 57
☑ Pen Pressure

   - **Contrast** determines the percentage that the contrast between pixels must be before they are considered an edge. Type a value between 1 and 100. Use a higher value when you are using the tool to trace objects in a low-contrast image.

   - **Frequency** determines how quickly the tool creates points. Type a higher value, and the tool snaps the path to edges more quickly.

USING THE FREEFORM PEN TOOL

With the Freeform Pen tool, you can create shapes or paths that look like they were drawn with a pencil. If you use this tool with a digital tablet, you can create rather artistic shapes. As you move the tool about the document, Photoshop creates points to define the shape or path.

1. Select the **Freeform Pen** tool.

2. Click the **Shape Layer** or **Path** button in the Options bar.

3. Click the **Options** bar down arrow. The Freeform Pen Options dialog box appears.

4. Type a value between .5 and 10 in the **Curve Fit** box. Type a higher value to create a simpler path with fewer points.

Shape drawn with Curve Fit set to 10 contains fewer points

Shape drawn with Curve Fit set to 2 contains more points

5. Drag inside the document to define the shape or the path.

6. To complete the path, release the pointer. Drag to the beginning of the line to close the path.

- **Pen Pressure** varies the width of the path depending on the amount of pressure you apply when using a digital stylus and tablet. Deselect this option when using the tool with a mouse.

3. Drag the tool along the edges you want to trace. A shape will be created based on the traced outline.

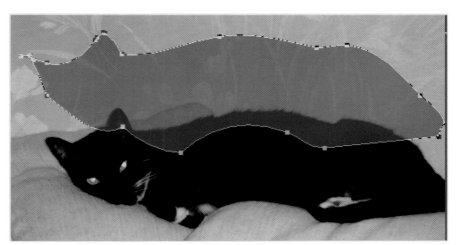

Figure 5-1: You can create art by tracing shapes and filling them with color.

Shape created by tracing the ship and filling it with a gradient

Bitmap layer can be deleted to retain just the new shape

Use Paths to Create Artwork

You can use paths to create vector-based artwork; for example, you can create logos or stylized versions of bitmap images. This process can be rather tedious, however, if you're attempting to create vector-based artwork from a complex bitmap image. An example is shown in Figure 5-1.

1. Open the bitmap image you want to use as the basis for your vector-based artwork.

2. In the Layers palette, click the **Create A New Layer** button.

3. Select the **Pen** tool.

4. Create the desired shapes, generating points as needed to create a reasonable facsimile of the shapes on the bitmap layer.

5. Fill the shapes as needed.

6. Delete the background layer.

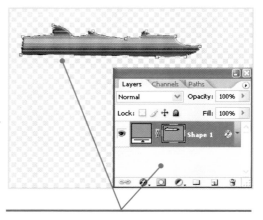

Deleted bitmap layer leaves shape to be used as needed

Figure 5-2: After drawing a path, you can either fill it or create a stroke effect.

TIP

If you are using more than one tool, you can duplicate stroke options from one tool to another. Select a path created by one tool to give it the attributes of a second tool. Click the **Use** down arrow, and select the options used by the second tool.

Stroke and Fill Paths

If you use the Pen tool to create a path and not a shape layer, the path has no stroke or fill until you add it. You add a stroke (outline) and/or fill (solid color or pattern) to a path by selecting the path and then using the options in the Paths palette (see Figure 5-2).

FILL A PATH

1. Select one of the **Pen** tools.
2. In the Options bar, click the **Paths** button.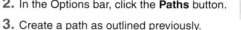
3. Create a path as outlined previously.
4. Select the **Path Selection** tool.
5. Select the path you want to use.
6. Click **Window** and click **Paths**. The Paths palette is displayed.
7. Click the right arrow in the upper-right corner of the palette, and, from the drop-down menu, click **Fill Path**. The Fill Path dialog box is displayed.
8. Click the **Use** down arrow, and select an option. The Use option determines the fill color.
9. Click **OK** to fill the path.

ADD A STROKE TO A PATH

1. Select one of the **Pen** tools.
2. In the Options bar, click the **Paths** button.
3. Create a path as outlined previously.
4. Click the **foreground color** swatch, and select a color for the stroke from the Color Picker.

QUICKSTEPS

CONVERTING SELECTIONS

If you create an intricate selection using the techniques outlined in Chapter 3, you can convert the selection to a path. After converting the selection to a path, add a stroke and fill it as the basis for vector-based artwork.

1. Create a selection using any of the techniques outlined in Chapter 3.

2. Click **Windows** and then click **Paths**. The Paths palette is displayed.

3. Click the right arrow in the upper-right corner of the Options palette, and click **Make Work Path**. The Make Work Path dialog box appears.

4. Type a value in the **Tolerance** text box, or accept the default value of 2.0 pixels. You can type a value between .50 and 10. This value determines the number of points used to create the path. Specify a high value for a smooth path with fewer points.

5. Click **OK** to convert the selection to a path.

TIP

When a path is selected with the Path Selection tool or Direct Selection tool, all anchor points are displayed.

5. Select the **Brush** tool.

6. Define the size and shape of the brush. This determines the look of the stroke. You can choose a wide brush that feathers gradually to blend with surrounding pixels or a hard-edged brush to create a high-contrast outline for the path.

7. Click the right arrow in the upper-right corner of the palette, and, from the drop-down menu, click **Stroke Path**. The Stroke Path dialog box appears.

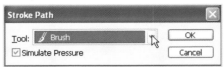

8. Accept the default **Pressure** option to simulate a stroke that was created with a digital stylus and tablet. Click the **Pressure** check box to deselect the option, and the stroke will be of uniform thickness.

9. Click **OK** to apply the stroke to the path.

Use the Shape Tools

You can use the Shape tools to add vector-based shapes to a document. You have six Shape tools from which to choose: Rectangle, Rounded Rectangle, Ellipse, Polygon, Line, and Custom Shape. You specify the settings for each tool in the Options bar (see Figure 5-3). For example, when you create a shape using the Rounded Rectangle tool, you can specify the radius of the rectangle's corners. When you select the Custom tool, you can select a preset shape.

1. Select one of the **Shape** tools.

2. In the Options bar, click one of the following buttons to define the type of shape:

   • **Shape Layers** creates a shape on its own layer. You can create shape layers with Shape tools or Pen tools. Shape layers are often used for creating graphics.

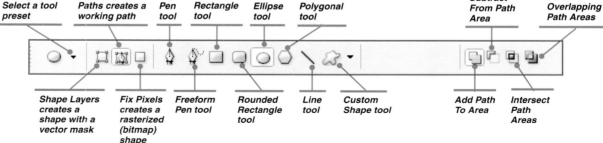

Figure 5-3: The Shape and Pen tools Options bar has some unique features.

Labels (top): Select a tool preset · Paths creates a working path · Pen tool · Rectangle tool · Ellipse tool · Polygonal tool · Subtract From Path Area · Exclude Overlapping Path Areas

Labels (bottom): Shape Layers creates a shape with a vector mask · Fix Pixels creates a rasterized (bitmap) shape · Freeform Pen tool · Rounded Rectangle tool · Line tool · Custom Shape tool · Add Path To Area · Intersect Path Areas

QUICKSTEPS

CONVERTING PATHS

You can create an intricate path with the Pen tool and then convert it to a selection. Trace the shape you want to select, and then convert it to a path.

1. Select the **Pen** tool from the Toolbox, and click it around the shape you want to select, creating a path.

2. Click **Window** and then click **Path**. The Path palette is displayed.

3. Click the **Options** button in the upper-right area of the Paths palette, and click **Make Selection From The Path**.

4. In the Make Selection dialog box, select these options:

- Create a feathered effect by entering the radius in pixels.

- Click **Anti-Alias** to smooth the selection edges.

- Click **New Selection** to create a new selection; click **Add To Selection** to add to an existing selection; click **Subtract From Selection** to decrease an existing selection by this new one being defined; or click **Intersect With Selection** to create one selection with the intersecting points on the new selection being defined.

5. Click **OK**.

If you look at a selected shape layer in the Paths palette, you'll find it contains both a fill layer with the shape color and a linked vector mask defining the shape path.

- **Paths** creates a working path that can be used to make a selection, create a vector mask, or fill or stroke the path with a color or a gradient. You can create raster graphics with paths, and they can be saved.

- **Fill Pixels** creates a rasterized (bitmap) shape. They are not vector-based, but as you paint, the pixels in the image are changed.

3. If you have selected the Fill Pixels option, specify the **Mode**, **Opacity**, and **Anti-Alias** options for the shape you are about to create. The Anti-Alias option prevents jagged edges at the border of the shape.

4. Specify other options for the shape.

5. Click the down arrow on the Options bar beneath **Help** to reveal a menu that enables you to specify geometry options for the tool. Here you can see the options for the Rounded Rectangle tool. Note that you can specify the exact size of the shape.

Rounded Rectangle Options
- ○ Unconstrained
- ○ Square
- ⦿ Fixed Size   W: [ ]   H: [ ]
- ○ Proportional   W: [ ]   H: [ ]
- ☐ From Center   ☐ Snap to Pixels

6. Drag diagonally inside the document to create the shape. If you've specified the size of the shape, click inside the document.

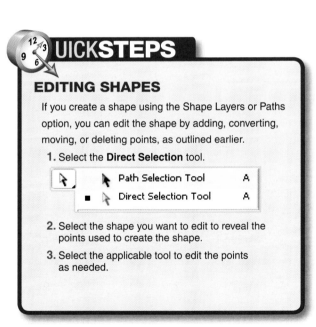

QUICKSTEPS

EDITING SHAPES

If you create a shape using the Shape Layers or Paths option, you can edit the shape by adding, converting, moving, or deleting points, as outlined earlier.

1. Select the **Direct Selection** tool.

	Path Selection Tool	A
■	Direct Selection Tool	A

2. Select the shape you want to edit to reveal the points used to create the shape.

3. Select the applicable tool to edit the points as needed.

Work with Paint

If you have a digital stylus or are adept at drawing with a mouse, you can use the Photoshop brushes to paint inside a document and add artistic splashes of color. You can also create a stylized work of art by painting on a separate layer with an underlying image as a template. You can add color to a document in the form of a gradient (a blend of two or more colors) or a pattern.

Use the Brush Tool

You use brushes in Photoshop for many things: creating selections, specifying the stroke for a path, and so on. You also use the Brush tool to create an artistic daub of color in a document or to paint stylized strokes of color in a document.

1. Click the **Set Foreground Color** swatch, and choose a color from the Color Picker.

2. Select the **Brush** tool.

3. In the Options bar, click the down arrow to the right of the current brush tip to reveal the Brush Options menu.

4. Drag the **Master Diameter** slider to specify the size of the brush tip in pixels.

5. Drag the **Hardness** slider to specify a value. Choose a low value for a soft-edged brush; choose a high value for a hard-edged brush.

6. Drag the scrollbar to reveal thumbnail images of available brush types. The thumbnail gives you an idea of the type of stroke you can expect to paint with the brush tip.

7. Click a brush tip thumbnail to replace the current tip.

8. In the Options bar, specify the **Mode**, **Opacity**, and **Flow** options for the brush.

9. Click the **Airbrush Capabilities** button to enable airbrush capabilities. Use this option if you're using a digital airbrush with a tablet.

10. Drag inside the document to create the desired brush strokes. You can also use a digital stylus and tablet to paint the desired brush strokes.

TIP

When you click either color swatch, an Eyedropper tool appears. Click the **Eyedropper** tool anywhere in the workspace to replace the current color in the Color Picker with the sampled color. Click **OK** to exit the Color Picker and apply the sampled color to the selected color swatch.

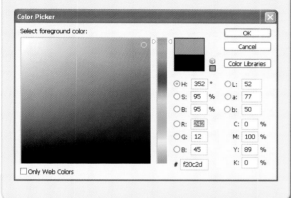

TIP

You can switch between foreground and background colors by clicking the curve-with-two-arrows icon or by pressing **X**.

TIP

You can restore the default foreground and background colors (black and white) by clicking the small icon ▪ at the left of the color swatches or by pressing **D**.

CHANGE BRUSH GROUPS

Photoshop has a wide variety of brushes you can use to create calligraphic brush strokes, watercolor brush strokes, and realistic facsimiles of objects like grass. The default brush group is powerful, but if you want more, you need look no further than the brush tip Options menu or the Preset Manager.

1. Select the **Brush** tool.
2. Click the down arrow to the right of the current brush tip to reveal the brush Options menu.
3. Click the right arrow in the upper-right corner of the Options menu, and select a brush group from the drop-down menu.

CREATE A CUSTOM BRUSH

If you like diversity, you can modify a brush preset. You can also create a brush from an image or from a portion of an image. After doing either, you can save the brush preset for future use.

1. Open an image that contains an area you want to use for a brush preset.
2. Using one of the Selection tools, select the area of the image you want to define as the brush tip.

3. Click **Edit** and then click **Define Brush Preset**. The Brush Name dialog box appears.
4. Type a name for the preset.
5. Click **OK** to add the preset to the Brushes palette using the selection area as the tip size.

New Brush Preset...

Rename Brush...
Delete Brush

Text Only
Small Thumbnail
Large Thumbnail
Small List
Large List
✔ Stroke Thumbnail

Preset Manager...

Reset Brushes...
Load Brushes...
Save Brushes...
Replace Brushes...

Assorted Brushes
Basic Brushes
Calligraphic Brushes
Drop Shadow Brushes
Dry Media Brushes
Faux Finish Brushes
Natural Brushes 2
Natural Brushes
Special Effect Brushes
Square Brushes
Thick Heavy Brushes
Wet Media Brushes

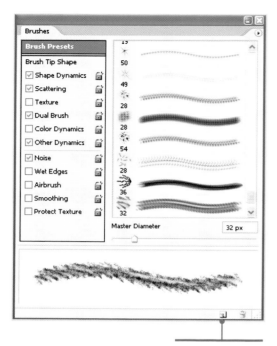

Create New Brush

CREATE A NEW DYNAMIC BRUSH

A brush with dynamic elements changes its tip as you paint. When you create a dynamic brush, you work with two elements: Jitter and Control. Jitter determines how much an element will vary as you paint with the brush. For example, you can vary the hue, saturation, and opacity of a brush tip. Control options are used to control dynamic attributes if you have a digital tablet, such as one manufactured by Wacom, attached to your system.

1. Create a new document with a white background. You will test your new brush on this blank canvas.

2. Select the **Brush** tool in the Options bar.

3. Select a brush preset.

4. Click **Window** and click **Brushes**. The Brushes palette is displayed.

5. Click the desired check box to select an option, and then click the option title to reveal the parameters for that option. This image shows the parameters for the Scattering option.

6. Adjust the parameters as desired.

7. Click the **Control** right arrow if you're using a digital tablet, and select one of the options from the drop-down list.

8. Test your new brush by painting on the canvas.

9. Click the **Create New Brush** button on the bottom of the Brushes palette. The Brush Name dialog box appears.

10. Type a name for the brush, and click **OK**.

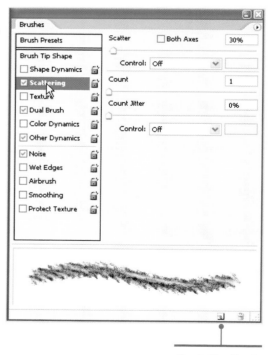

Create New Brush

TIP

From the Brush menu you can also rename brushes, change the manner in which brushes are displayed, and more.

TIP

To change the brush tip size on the fly, press the **RIGHT BRACKET** key (]) to increase the tip size; press the **LEFT BRACKET** key ([) to decrease the tip size. Hold down the applicable key until the brush is the desired size.

Figure 5-4: *You can create a library for brushes and then load it when you want to use those specific brushes.*

Manage Brush Presets

When you add several custom brushes to a library, the sheer volume may make finding a specific brush a difficult task. You can save a brush library as a custom library and manage the new library by deleting the presets that are duplicates of another library.

SAVE A BRUSH LIBRARY

1. Select a **Brush** tool.
2. Click the down arrow to the right of the current brush tip to reveal the Brush menu.
3. Click the right arrow in the upper-right corner of the Options menu, and click **Save Brushes**. The Save dialog box appears.
4. Type a file name for the new brush library.
5. Click **OK.**

LOAD A BRUSH LIBRARY

1. Select a **Brush** tool.
2. Click the down arrow to the right of the current brush tip to reveal the Brush menu.
3. Click the right arrow in the upper-right corner of the Options menu, and click **Load Brushes**. The Load dialog box appears, as seen in Figure 5-4.
4. Select the brush library you want to install, and then click **Load**.

DELETE A BRUSH

1. Select a **Brush** tool.
2. Click the down arrow to the right of the current brush tip to reveal the Brush menu, and select the thumbnail of the brush you want to delete.
3. Click the right arrow in the upper-right corner of the Options menu, and click **Delete Brush**. The Delete Brush dialog box appears.
4. Click **OK** to delete the brush.

TIP

To reset the brushes to the default set, click **Reset Brushes** from the Brush menu drop-down list.

USING THE ERASER TOOL

1. Select the **Eraser** tool.

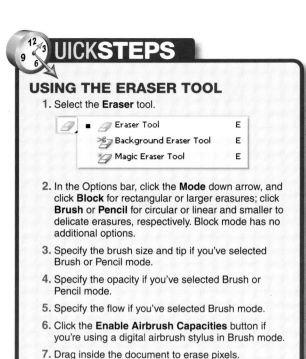

■	Eraser Tool	E
	Background Eraser Tool	E
	Magic Eraser Tool	E

2. In the Options bar, click the **Mode** down arrow, and click **Block** for rectangular or larger erasures; click **Brush** or **Pencil** for circular or linear and smaller to delicate erasures, respectively. Block mode has no additional options.

3. Specify the brush size and tip if you've selected Brush or Pencil mode.

4. Specify the opacity if you've selected Brush or Pencil mode.

5. Specify the flow if you've selected Brush mode.

6. Click the **Enable Airbrush Capacities** button if you're using a digital airbrush stylus in Brush mode.

7. Drag inside the document to erase pixels.

Erase Pixels

To err is human, which is why every graphics application has an erase tool. Photoshop designers have hedged all bets by giving you a choice of three erase tools: the Eraser tool erases unwanted pixels of color; the Background Eraser tool erases parts of a layer to transparency while preserving the edges of an object in the foreground; the Magic Eraser tool erases pixels similar in color to the background color.

USE THE BACKGROUND ERASER TOOL

1. Select the **Background Eraser** tool.

2. In the Options bar, click the down arrow to reveal the Background Eraser Settings dialog box.

	Eraser Tool	E
■	Background Eraser Tool	E
	Magic Eraser Tool	E

3. Specify the **Diameter** setting for the size of the eraser, the **Hardness** setting for the sharpness of the edge of the eraser, the **Spacing** setting for how close together each application of the eraser will erase the image (whether there will be spaces between the erasures), the **Angle** setting for the angle of the tip (this is only applicable when the Roundness is less than 100 percent), and the **Roundness** setting for the percent of roundness that the eraser shape holds.

4. If you're using a digital stylus, click the **Size** and **Tolerance** down arrows, and click **Pen Pressure** or **Stylus Wheel**, depending on the type of digital stylus you're using. Click **Off** if you're not using a digital stylus.

5. In the Options bar seen in Figure 5-5, click the **Limits** down arrow to select any of the following options:

   - **Discontiguous** erases pixels of the sampled color wherever they occur under the brush.

Figure 5-5: The Erase Background tool Options bar contains options for sampling color; defining limits of the erasure, tolerance, or selection ability of the erasure; and whether to preserve the foreground color during the erasure.

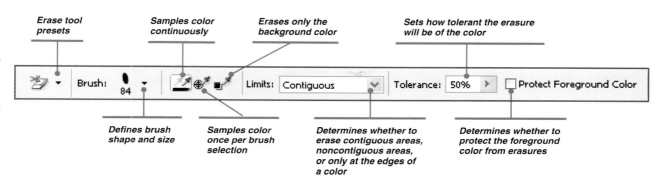

Erase tool presets

Samples color continuously

Erases only the background color

Sets how tolerant the erasure will be of the color

Defines brush shape and size

Samples color once per brush selection

Determines whether to erase contiguous areas, noncontiguous areas, or only at the edges of a color

Determines whether to protect the foreground color from erasures

- **Contiguous** erases pixels of the sampled color that are connected to each other.
- **Find Edges** erases pixels of the sampled color that are connected to each other while preserving the integrity of edges.

6. Type a value in the **Tolerance** text box. Specify a low value to erase areas similar to the sampled color; specify a high value to erase a broader range of colors.

7. Click the **Protect Foreground Color** option to prevent the tool from erasing pixels of the foreground color.

8. In the Options bar, choose one of the following options:

- **Once** erases only areas of the sampled color that you first click.
- **Continuous** samples colors under the Eraser tool continuously as you drag the tool across the document.
- **Background Swatch** erases only pixels of the current background color.

9. Drag the tool across the area you want to erase.

USE THE MAGIC ERASER TOOL

1. Select the **Magic Eraser** tool.

2. In the Options bar shown in Figure 5-6, type a value in the **Tolerance** text box. Specify a low tolerance to erase pixels similar in color to the first pixels you click with the tool; specify a high tolerance to erase a wider range of colors.

	Eraser Tool	E
■	Background Eraser Tool	E
	Magic Eraser Tool	E

TIP

To prevent erasing an area such as a silhouette of a building or a line of trees, click the foreground color swatch, and use the **Eyedropper** tool to sample the color you want to protect. Click the **Protect Foreground Color** option for the Background Eraser tool prior to dragging the tool along the border of the area you want to preserve.

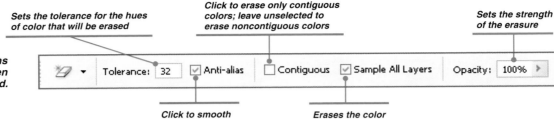

Sets the tolerance for the hues
of color that will be erased

Click to erase only contiguous
colors; leave unselected to
erase noncontiguous colors

Sets the strength
of the erasure

*Figure 5-6: The Magic Eraser tool Options
bar allows you to refine the tool when
selecting what will be erased.*

Click to smooth
erasure edges

Erases the color
in all layers

3. Click the **Anti-Alias** option (selected by default), and Photoshop smoothes the edges of areas you erase.

4. Click the **Contiguous** option (selected by default) to erase only areas of contiguous pixels containing the sampled color. Deselect the option to erase all areas of pixels of similar color as you erase.

5. Click the **Sample All Layers** option to erase similar colors on all visible layers in the document.

6. Type a value in the **Opacity** field. The default value of 100 percent erases pixels completely. Specify a lower value to partially erase pixels.

7. Drag the tool over the area you want to erase.

Use the Gradient Tool

Use the Gradient tool to apply a blend of two or more colors to a background layer or to a selection.

APPLY A GRADIENT FILL

1. Select the layer to which you want to apply the gradient fill. You can also use one of the Selection tools to select the area to which you want to apply the fill.

2. Select the **Gradient** tool.

Figure 5-7: The Gradient Options bar displays ways to vary the effects of a gradient fill.

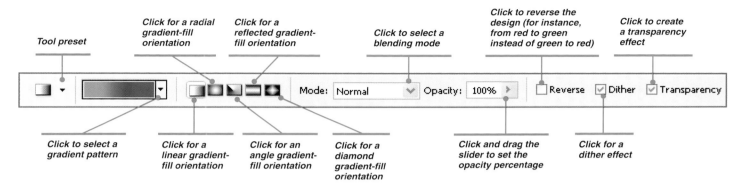

Tool preset

Click for a radial gradient-fill orientation

Click for a reflected gradient-fill orientation

Click to select a blending mode

Click to reverse the design (for instance, from red to green instead of green to red)

Click to create a transparency effect

Click to select a gradient pattern

Click for a linear gradient-fill orientation

Click for an angle gradient-fill orientation

Click for a diamond gradient-fill orientation

Click and drag the slider to set the opacity percentage

Click for a dither effect

3. In the Options bar shown in Figure 5-7, click the **Gradient Pattern** down arrow, and select one of the presets.

4. In the Options bar, click the appropriate options to select one of the following gradient types:

   ● **Linear** creates a fill that blends colors in a straight line from the starting point.

   ● **Radial** creates a circular fill that radiates from the starting point outward.

   ● **Angle** creates an angular fill in a counterclockwise direction from the starting point.

   ● **Reflected** creates symmetrical linear fills on either side of the starting point.

   ● **Diamond** creates a diamond-shaped fill that radiates from the starting point outward.

5. Specify a blending mode and an opacity.

6. Click the **Reverse** check box to reverse the order in which the gradient colors are applied.

7. Click the **Dither** check box to create a smoother blend of colors without bands.

8. Click the **Transparency** check box to create a transparency mask for the fill.

9. Click inside the document to specify the starting point for the fill, and then drag to create the fill.

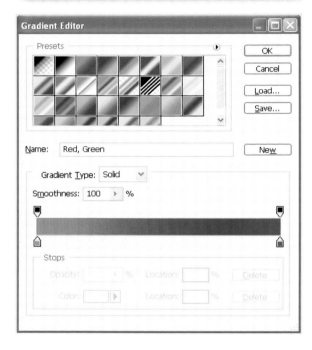

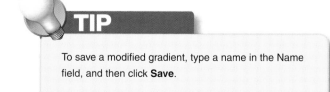

EDIT A GRADIENT

1. Select the **Gradient** tool and select a gradient, as outlined previously.

2. Double-click the **Gradient Preview** button (second button from the right) in the Options bar to open the Gradient Editor.

3. Click a preset thumbnail to set the values for the color bar.

4. Click the **Gradient Type** down arrow, and click either **Solid** or **Noise** to vary the concentration of color. If you choose Noise, new options will appear.

5. Click the **Roughness** down arrow, and drag the slider to set the percentage of distortion the color will have.

6. If you have chosen a gradient type of Solid, drag the sliders on the color bar above the Stops area:

   - Drag the **top** sliders to move the opacity stops. As you drag the stops, you determine where the opacity appears in the gradient. To add another opacity stop to the color bar, click the top edge of the color bar (the pointer will morph from an eyedropper to a hand, indicating you can insert a stop) where you want the stop inserted. Beneath the color bar, the opacity stops become available when you select or move an opacity stop.

   - Vary the opacity for a selected stop by clicking the stop, clicking the **Opacity** down arrow, and dragging the slider to the percentage you want. To delete an opacity stop, select the stop and click **Delete**.

   - Drag the **bottom** sliders to move the color stops. As you drag the stops, you determine where the color appears in the gradient. To add another color stop to the color bar, click the bottom edge of the color bar (the pointer will morph from an eyedropper to a hand, indicating you can insert a stop) where you want the stop inserted. Beneath the color bar, the color stops become available when you move or select a color stop.

   - Vary the color for a selected stop by clicking the stop, clicking the **Color** down arrow, and clicking **Foreground**, **Background**, or **User Color**. To delete a color stop, select the stop and click **Delete**.

7. If you have chosen a gradient type of noise, click the **Color Model** down arrow, and click **RGB**, **HSB**, or **LAB**. Beneath the color model, three smaller color bars will appear:

   - Drag the sliders on the color bars to determine where the color or opacity stops appear in the gradient.

- Click **Restrict Colors** to decrease the number of colors in a noise gradient.
- Click **Add Transparency** to make the gradient fill appear more transparent.
- Click **Randomize** to display another set of colors in the color bar.

8. Click **OK** to apply the changes.

Use the Paint Bucket Tool

Use the Paint Bucket tool to replace areas of color with a different color. You can determine the extent of the color replacement by specifying a tolerance value.

1. Click **Set Foreground Color** and select a color from the Color Picker.
2. Select the **Paint Bucket** tool.

	Gradient Tool	G
	Paint Bucket Tool	G

3. In the Options bar, click the **Tool Preset** down arrow, and click **Foreground** to fill the tool with the foreground color; or you can click **Pattern**. If you click **Pattern**, the Pattern field becomes available. Click the down arrow to the right of the current pattern preview, and select a preset.

4. Click the **Mode** down arrow to choose a blending mode, and click the **Opacity** down arrow to set the opacity for the Paint Bucket tool.
5. Type a value in the **Tolerance** text box. This value determines how closely pixels must match before they are filled. You can specify a value between 0 and 255. Type a low value to fill pixels that are similar in color; type a high value to fill pixels with a wider color range.
6. Leave the **Anti-Alias** check box selected to ensure smooth blending of adjacent pixels.
7. Leave the **Contiguous** check box selected to fill contiguous pixels of similar color. Deselect the option to fill all similar pixels within the image.
8. Place a check mark in the **All Layers** check box to apply the fill to pixels of similar color in all layers.
9. Click inside the area you want to fill.

Create and Manage Patterns

You can create patterns by sampling an area from within an image. After creating a pattern, you can apply it as a fill using the Paint Bucket tool. When creating your own patterns, you can use the tool to add patterns to the pattern library. The Pattern Maker is capable of generating up to 20 patterns from a selection. You select the patterns you want to add to the pattern library and delete the rest.

Figure 5-8: Create a pattern to add to your pattern library using the Pattern Maker dialog box.

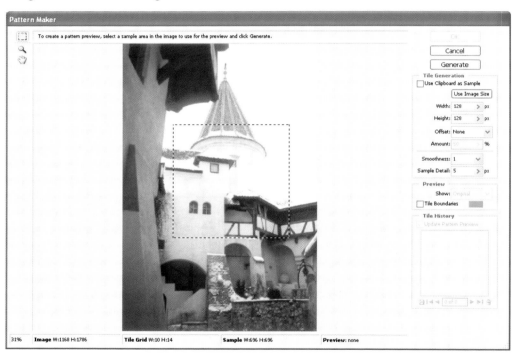

CREATE A PATTERN

1. Open the desired image.

2. Select the **Rectangular Marquee** tool, and select the pixels you want to use as the basis for your pattern. Hold down the **SHIFT** key while making the selection to constrain the selection bounding box to a square.

3. Click **Edit** and then click **Copy** to copy the selection to the Clipboard.

4. Click **Filter** and click **Pattern Maker**. The Pattern Maker dialog box appears.

5. Click the **Use Clipboard As Sample** check box.

6. Type equal values in the **Width** and **Height** fields to create a square pattern. You can also click the down arrow and drag the sliders to set the Width and Height fields. If you have a rectangular selection, click the **Use Image Size** button to force the Width and Height fields to be rectangular for the selection.

7. To offset the tiles, click the **Offset** down arrow, and click **Vertical** or **Horizontal**. After you select an offset option, the Amount field becomes available. Type the **Amount** by which you want the tiles offset. This value is a percentage of the dimension in the specified direction.

8. Click the **Smoothness** down arrow, and choose a value from the drop-down list. You can also type a value from 1 to 3 in the field. A higher value produces a more complex pattern and the pixel transitions are not as smooth.

9. Click the **Sample Detail** down arrow, and drag the slider to specify the sample size from within the selected area. Small values work better and often create more interesting patterns.

10. Click **Generate** to create a tiled preview of the pattern in the preview area.

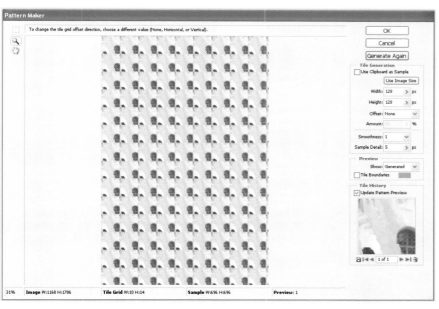

11. Click **Generate Again** to create additional patterns. You can generate up to 20 patterns. After generating patterns, you preview them and decide which ones you want to add to the pattern library.

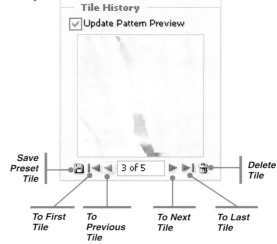

Save Preset Tile — To First Tile — To Previous Tile — To Next Tile — To Last Tile — Delete Tile

PREVIEW AND SAVE PATTERNS

1. In the Pattern Maker dialog box, after clicking the **Generate** and then **Generate Again** buttons, click the **Tile History**, **Next Tile**, and **Previous Tile** buttons to preview the patterns you've generated. You can also type the number of the pattern you want to view, and then press ENTER.

2. Click the **Trash** button to delete a tile.

3. Click the **Save Preset Tile** button. The Pattern Name dialog box appears.

4. Type a name for the pattern, and then click **OK**. After saving the pattern, it appears in the pattern library for future use.

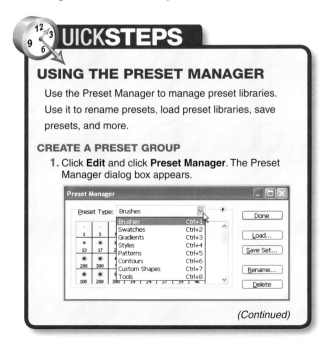

Use the Art History Brush

Find the image state you want to paint in the History palette

Click the set source for the History Brush

Figure 5-9: You can create stylized artwork by painting inside an image with the Art History Brush.

Use the Art History Brush

Use the Art History Brush tool to create stylized artwork by painting on an image using a history state. As a rule, you'll open an image, apply a filter to the image, and then use that history state as the basis for the Art History Brush. Figure 5-9 shows an example of how you can blur an image and then bring out the foreground.

1. Open the desired image.

2. Apply the desired filters to the image.

3. Select the **Art History Brush**.

4. In the Options bar, select a brush tip and diameter as described in the section "Use the Brush Tool."

5. Specify values for **Mode** and **Opacity**.

6. Click the **Style** down arrow, and choose an option from the drop-down list. Each option is a description of the type of brush stroke the tool will create.

7. Type a value in the **Area** text box. This value designates the area covered by a brush stroke with the tool. If you specify a large value, the tool covers a large area and creates numerous brush strokes.

8. Type a value in the **Tolerance** text box. Specify a low value to paint anywhere in the image; specify a high value to paint only in areas where the color of the history state varies greatly from the image's original color.

9. Click **Window** and click **History**. The History palette is displayed.

10. Click the **Open History** state. This returns the image to its original state; however, the history filter is still applied until you use the Art History Brush.

11. Click the blank square in the **Set Source For The History Brush**, located to the left of the image state that you want the Art History Brush to sample.

12. Drag inside the image to paint with the tool.

UICKSTEPS

USING THE PRESET MANAGER

Use the Preset Manager to manage preset libraries. Use it to rename presets, load preset libraries, save presets, and more.

CREATE A PRESET GROUP

1. Click **Edit** and click **Preset Manager**. The Preset Manager dialog box appears.

(Continued)

USING THE PRESET MANAGER

(Continued)

2. Click the **Preset Types** down arrow, and select the desired type from the drop-down list.

3. Click the preset thumbnails you want to combine as a group. Click the first preset and then press **CTRL** while clicking additional presets you want to add to the group.

4. Click **Save Set**. The Save dialog box appears. The file format will vary depending on the preset group you're editing. For example, the file format for styles is ASL.

5. Type a name for the preset group, and click **Save.**

SELECT A PRESET TYPE

1. Click **Edit** and click **Preset Manager**. The Preset Manager dialog box appears.

2. Click the **Preset Types** down arrow, and select the desired type from the drop-down list.

3. Click a preset thumbnail. After selecting a preset, you can do one of the following:

   • Click **Rename** to open the Rename dialog box and rename the preset.

   • Click **Delete** to delete the preset.

4. Click **Done** to exit the Preset Manager and apply your changes.

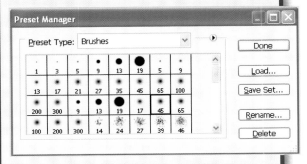

LOAD A PRESET GROUP

1. Click **Edit** and click **Preset Manager**. The Preset Manager dialog box appears.

2. Click the **Preset Types** down arrow, and select the desired type from the drop-down list.

3. Click **Load**. The Load dialog box appears.

4. Select the desired preset group.

5. Click **Load** to load the desired group.

Work with Filters

Photoshop has many filters that you can use to add artistic touches to images. If you've ever felt the need to unleash the repressed artist within you, the Filter Gallery is your source for artistic materials. You can apply a single filter to create an image that looks like a watercolor painting. If you're into distorting images for fun and profit, you'll love the Liquify filter: it's like virtual Silly Putty.

Use the Filter Gallery

You use the Filter Gallery to apply one or more filters to an image to achieve a desired look. Each filter has parameters that you can modify to suit your individual taste. When you apply multiple filters to an image, you can arrange the order in which they are applied to the image. An example of working with the Filter Gallery is shown in Figure 5-10.

APPLY FILTERS INDIVIDUALLY

1. Select the desired image.

2. Click **Filter** and click **Filter Gallery** to display the image in the Filter Gallery.

3. Select the desired filter from one of the filter groups. To display the contents of a filter group, click the right arrow.

4. Adjust the filter parameters to suit your taste.

5. Click **OK** to apply the filter.

NOTE

You can apply a filter to part of an image by selecting the desired part with one of the selection tools.

Figure 5-10: You can achieve a desired effect by applying filters to an image.

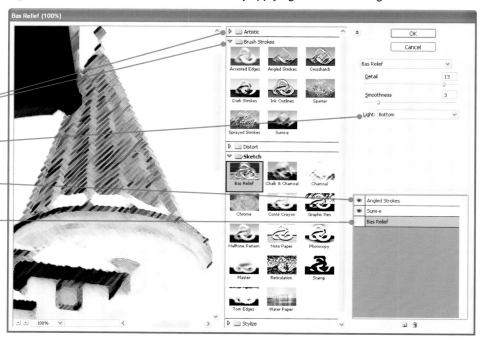

Click to open the filter presets

Options will vary depending on the preset selected

Multiple filters are listed here

Click the eyeball icon to hide the filter's effects

NOTE

To edit filter parameters after applying the filter, click **Filter** and then click **Filter Gallery** to reopen the image in the Filter Gallery. If you're using a third-party filter, it cannot be edited from within the Filter Gallery.

TIP

Certain filters, such as Rough Pastel, have a right-pointing-arrow icon you can click to load a grayscale image that will be used to determine the texture applied to the image. The image must be a Photoshop PSD file.

APPLY MULTIPLE FILTERS WITH THE FILTER GALLERY

1. Select the desired image

2. Click **Filter** and click **Filter Gallery**.

3. Apply a filter as described in "Apply Filters Individually."

4. Press the **ALT** key while clicking another filter.

5. After applying multiple filters, you can do the following:

   - Click the **eyeball** icon to the left of a filter's name to temporarily hide it.

   - Drag a filter to a different position in the hierarchy. Drag it up the list to apply it before filters beneath it, or drag it down the list to apply it after other filters.

   - Select a filter and click the **Delete Effect Layer** button to remove the filter.

6. Click **OK** to apply the filters to the image.

Use the Liquify Filter

If you like Salvador Dali's painting with the melting watches, *The Persistence of Memory*, you'll love the Liquify filter. The Liquify filter is a great tool that you can use to achieve surreal effects.

1. Select the image you want to liquify.

2. Click **Filter** and click **Liquify**. The Liquify dialog box appears.

3. Click the tool from the Toolbox that you want to use (see Figure 5-11).

Figure 5-11: The Liquify filter provides some interesting and far-out possibilities for artistically changing an image.

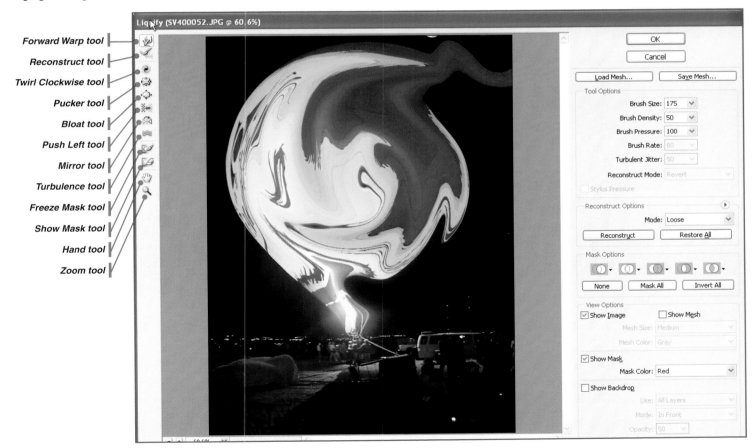

- Forward Warp tool
- Reconstruct tool
- Twirl Clockwise tool
- Pucker tool
- Bloat tool
- Push Left tool
- Mirror tool
- Turbulence tool
- Freeze Mask tool
- Show Mask tool
- Hand tool
- Zoom tool

NOTE

To protect areas of the image you don't want to distort with the Liquify filter, select the **Freeze Mask** tool, and drag it over areas of the image you want to protect. This creates a red mask over the protected area. You can also use this tool to protect areas of the image you have already distorted with the Liquify filter, thereby protecting them from further distortion.

TIP

To distort an area of an image, define the area by creating a mask or using one of the Selection tools. You can then select one of the options in the Mask section to determine how the tool alters the mask or selection.

TIP

With a steady hand, you can use the Liquify filter to remove love handles from a slightly overweight subject.

TIP

Click the **Reconstruct** button to undo the last transformation you applied using the current reconstruct mode. Click the **Restore All** button to undo all transformations using the current reconstruct mode. If you click the **Revert** reconstruct mode, the image will be restored to its original state.

4. In the Tool Options section, the options available depend on the tool you have selected from the Toolbox. Type values in the applicable boxes to set the following parameters:

- **Brush Size** sets the size of the brush you'll use to distort the image.
- **Brush Density** determines the range of the brush from the center point. Specify a low value, and the transformations occur at the center of the brush without radiating outward; specify a high value, and the tool distorts pixels at a greater distance from the center.
- **Brush Pressure** sets the rate at which the transformations occur when you drag the brush across an image. Specify a low value, and the transformations occur at a slower rate; specify a high value, and the transformations occur at a faster rate.
- **Brush Rate** determines how quickly transformations occur when a tool such as Twirl Clockwise is held stationary in the image. Specify a low value, and transformations occur slowly; specify a high value, and transformations occur more rapidly.
- **Turbulent Jitter** determines how tightly the Turbulence tool scrambles pixels.

5. Click the **Reconstruct Mode** down arrow, and select an option to determine how the Reconstruct tool reconstructs the area of the preview image you drag the tool across. Your options are:

- **Revert** returns the area of the image over which you use the Reconstruct tool to its original state without any smoothing of pixels.
- **Rigid** restores the reconstructed area to its original state while maintaining the right angles between frozen and unfrozen areas.
- **Stiff** configures the Reconstruct tool to act as a weak magnet between frozen and unfrozen edges, thus reconstructing the edge area without disturbing any distortions in the frozen areas.
- **Smooth** causes pixels between edges of distortions and edges between frozen and unfrozen areas to be smoothed while reconstructed.
- **Loose** is similar to the Smooth option, reconstructing the edges between frozen and unfrozen areas with even greater continuity.

6. Select and drag a **Liquify** tool across the image in the preview window. Use as many tools as often as needed to achieve the desired distortion level.

7. Select the **Reconstruct** tool to selectively reconstruct areas of the image using the current Reconstruct mode.

8. Click **OK** to apply the Liquify filter to the image.

How to...

- *Rotate and Flip Images*

- *Straighten a Photo with Free Transform*

- *Straightening a Photo*

- *Resize and Trim Images*

- *Use a Histogram to View the Tonal Range of an Image*

- *Manually Adjust Levels*

- *Use the Curves Command*

- *Color-Correct Images*

- *Using Color Balance*

- *Change Hue and Saturation*

- *Working with Adjustment Layers*

- *Edit in 16-Bit Mode*

- *Sharpen and Blur Images*

- *Editing in 32-Bit Mode*

- *Fine-Tuning with the Sharpen, Blur, and Smudge Tools*

- *Retouch and Repair Images*

- *Changing Image Colors*

- *Use Dust & Scratches Filter*

- *Creating a Sepia-Tone Photo*

Chapter 6

Color Correcting, Retouching, and Repairing Images

This chapter shows you how to use powerful Photoshop menu commands and tools to resample and resize images. You'll also learn how to repair defective images and how to use the Photoshop Toolbox to sharpen photos and add pizzazz to images.

Perform Simple Image Corrections

Simple image corrections make it possible for you to correct faults, such as skewed images resulting from originals being incorrectly placed in a scanner. If you shoot images with a digital camera and rotate the camera to take a portrait, the image may come into your computer in landscape (horizontal) format. You can rotate these images so they are properly displayed. You can also use the Crop command to remove unwanted material from around your center of interest.

Rotate and Flip Images

If an image is not properly oriented, you can rectify this by rotating the image. You can rotate an image 90 degrees in a clockwise or counterclockwise direction, or you can rotate an image 180 degrees. You can also flip an image horizontally or vertically.

1. Open the image you need to reorient.
2. Click **Image**, click **Rotate Canvas**, and click one of the following options:

   - **180°** rotates the image 180 degrees.

   - **90° CW** rotates the image 90 degrees in a clockwise direction.

   - **90° CCW** rotates the image 90 degrees in a counterclockwise direction.

   - **Arbitrary** opens a dialog box in which you can enter the number of degrees to rotate the canvas. Click the **CW** button to rotate the image clockwise, or click the **CCW** button to rotate the image counterclockwise.

   - **Flip Canvas Horizontal** flips the canvas horizontally (from left to right).

   - **Flip Canvas Vertical** flips the canvas vertically (from top to bottom).

Straighten a Photo with Free Transform

If an image is slightly skewed, you can easily straighten it using the Free Transform command. First display a grid, which provides a visual reference in the form of vertical and horizontal lines. After selecting the Free Transform command, you can rotate the image and align a feature, such as the edge of a building that should be vertical or horizontal to the grid.

1. Open the image you want to straighten.
2. Click **View**, click **Show**, and click **Grid** to display the grid, shown in Figure 6-1.
3. Click **Edit** and click **Free Transform**. You can also press **CTRL+T**. After invoking the Free Transform command, eight sizing handles appear around the image perimeter. If you cannot see the handles, maximize the image.
4. Move your pointer beyond the border of the image until it becomes a curved line with two arrowheads.

QUICKSTEPS

STRAIGHTENING A PHOTO

If you have an image that is askew and has a straight edge, such as the edge of a roof or side of a building, you can quickly straighten the image using the Measure tool and a menu command. If you need to straighten a photo quickly, this is the ideal method to use.

1. Open the image you want to straighten.

2. Click the **Measure** tool.

Eyedropper Tool	I
Color Sampler Tool	I
Measure Tool	I

3. Drag the tool along an edge that should be vertical or horizontal.

4. Click **Image**, click **Rotate Canvas**, and then click **Arbitrary**. The Rotate Canvas dialog box appears. Notice that a value is already entered and a rotation direction has been selected by default. Based on your use of the Measure tool in step 2, Photoshop has determined that rotating the image this number of degrees will straighten it.

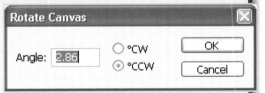

Rotate Canvas

Angle: 2.86   ○ °CW   [OK]
             ⊙ °CCW   [Cancel]

5. Click **OK**. Figure 6-2 shows an image after straightening it.

6. Use the Crop tool to remove the non-image areas at the edge of the canvas. See "Crop a Photo with the Crop Tool" later in this chapter.

Figure 6-2: You can straighten an image using the Measure tool.

Figure 6-1: Use the grid to straighten an image.

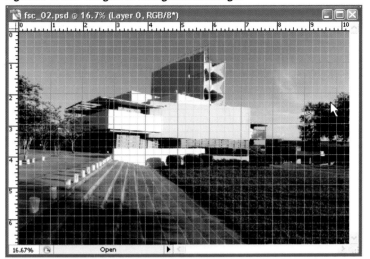

5. Drag left or right to rotate the image, releasing the mouse button when the image is straightened as desired.

6. Press **ENTER** to apply the transformation.

7. Use the **Crop** tool to remove non-image areas at the edge of the canvas. See "Crop a Photo with the Crop Tool" later in this chapter.

8. Click **File** and click **Save**.

Resize and Trim Images

When you edit images, you often have more information than you need. An image may have unwanted objects that detract from your center of interest, or it may simply be too large for the intended destination. After all, you don't post a 4-MB image on a web site. Other times you may need additional canvas area to add text and other elements. Photoshop has a plethora of tools that you can use to resize and trim images.

CROP A PHOTO WITH THE CROP TOOL

Use the Crop tool to trim an image to the desired size. You can make a freehand selection, or you can specify the resolution and size of the area to which the tool will crop.

1. Open the image you want to crop.
2. Click the **Crop** tool.
3. Drag diagonally inside the image to define the size of the cropped image. Photoshop displays a cropping rectangle inside the image. Eight sizing handles appear on the perimeter of the rectangle, as shown in Figure 6-3.
4. If the cropping rectangle is not sized as desired, do one of the following:

   - **Drag a corner handle** to resize the width and height of the cropping rectangle. Hold down the **SHIFT** key to resize proportionately.

   - **Drag the middle handle** on the left or right border to change the width of the cropping rectangle.

   - **Drag the center handle** on the top or bottom border to change the height of the cropping rectangle.

   - **Drag inside the cropping rectangle** to move it to a different position.

   - **Drag outside the cropping rectangle** to rotate it in a free-form manner.

5. Press **ENTER** or click the **Commit** button on the Options bar to crop the image.

RESIZE AN IMAGE

You can use menu commands to resize an image to specific dimensions. You can also change the image resolution to suit the intended destination. For example,

Figure 6-3: Adjust the cropping rectangle to the desired size.

NOTE

You can resize an image by a percentage by clicking the down arrow to the right of the unit of measure field (which by default reads "pixels") and clicking **Percent** from the drop-down menu.

TIP

If you want to increase the size of an image, never increase the size of the image by more than 10 percent, otherwise image degradation will occur. If you're upsizing a high-resolution image, you can increase it by 10 percent several times until the image is the desired size. When upsizing by 10 percent, always use the Bicubic interpolation method.

if you're going to print the image, select a resolution between 150 and 300 pixels per inch.

1. Open the image you want to resize.

2. Click **Image** and click **Image Size**. The Image Size dialog box appears.

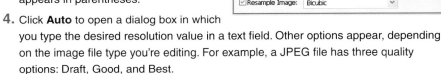

3. In the Pixel Dimensions area, type values for the **Width** and **Height** fields. Alternatively, you can enter values in the Document Size area to size an image for a printer. After you enter new values, the document file size is updated near the top of the dialog box. The old file size appears in parentheses.

4. Click **Auto** to open a dialog box in which you type the desired resolution value in a text field. Other options appear, depending on the image file type you're editing. For example, a JPEG file has three quality options: Draft, Good, and Best.

5. If you have layers with styles applied, accept the default **Scale Styles** option; otherwise, click the **Scale Styles** check box to deselect the option.

6. Accept the default **Constrain** option, and Photoshop will resize the height based on the width you enter or vice-versa. If you deselect this option, you can enter values for the width and height; however, the image will be distorted if the values you enter are not the same ratio as the original image.

7. Accept the default **Resample Image** option, and click one of the following interpolation options from the drop-down menu:

   ● **Nearest Neighbor** is the quickest, yet least precise, method of interpolation. Use this method when resizing illustrations with no embedded bitmaps (full-color images), as this method of interpolation does not apply anti-aliasing to edges. This interpolation method results in the smallest file size.

   ● **Bilinear** is acceptable for bitmaps and produces a medium-quality image.

   ● **Bicubic** is a more precise method of interpolation, resulting in smooth gradations between tones.

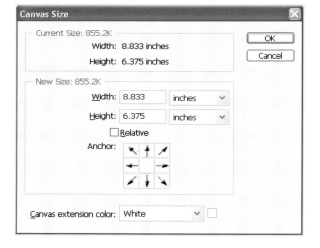

- **Bicubic Smoother** should be used when you're increasing the size of an image. This method smoothes the pixels in an attempt to avoid the blocky, pixilated look that sometimes occurs when an image is upsized.

- **Bicubic Sharper** should be used when you decrease the size of an image. This method of interpolation sharpens the image to maintain detail. If the resized image is too sharp, select the Bicubic method instead.

8. Click **OK**.

CHANGE THE CANVAS SIZE

When you open an image in Photoshop, the canvas size and the image size are the same. You can, however, increase the size of the canvas, which gives you more working area around the image. You can also change the canvas size to display a color border around your image. When you change the canvas size, you can specify where the additional canvas is to be added to the document.

1. Click **Image** and then click **Canvas Size**. The Canvas Size dialog box appears. The current canvas dimensions are listed in the Width and Height fields.

2. Type new values in the **Width** and **Height** fields. Alternatively, you can click the **Relative** check box, and type values that will be added to the current canvas width and height.

3. In the Anchor section, click the direction from which you want the canvas extended. If you accept the default option, the canvas will be extended equally from the middle of the image, as shown in Figure 6-4. The additional canvas appears around the perimeter of the image.

4. Click the **Canvas Extension Color** down arrow, and click one of the following options:

- **Foreground** uses the current foreground color as the canvas extension color.

- **Background** uses the current background color as the canvas extension color.

- **White** uses white as the canvas extension color.

- **Black** uses black as the canvas extension color.

- **Gray** uses gray as the canvas extension color.

- **Other** gives you the option of specifying a color from the Color Picker.

NOTE

You can select a different unit of measure by which to resize the canvas by clicking the down arrow to the right of the unit of measure field and clicking a different option from the drop-down menu.

Figure 6-4: You can modify the canvas size to add additional area to the image.

You can use the Eyedropper tool to match the foreground or background color to a color in the image you are working on. Click the **Eyedropper** tool, and then click inside the image to set the foreground color, press **ALT** + click inside the image to set the background color.

Press **ALT** to temporarily select the Eyedropper tool while using any of the painting tools.

TRIM A PHOTO WITH THE TRIM COMMAND

When you increase the canvas size, you add solid areas of color around the image (or images, if you're working on a multilayer collage). Typically, you use the extra canvas area to add text to identify an image or to add shapes created with one of the drawing tools (the Brush, Pencil, or Pen tool). When you are ready to save the image, you may find that you have more canvas than you need. You can easily remove excess canvas with the Trim command while preserving text and other items you have added to the document.

1. Click **Image** and click **Trim**. The Trim dialog box is displayed.

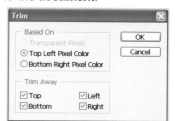

2. Select the method by which the image is trimmed:

   • **Transparent Pixels** trims the image by removing transparent pixels from the specified trim area.

   • **Top Left Pixel Color** trims the image by removing all pixels matching the color of the top-left pixel from the specified trim area.

   • **Bottom Right Pixel Color** trims the image by removing all pixels matching the color of the bottom-right pixel from the specified trim area.

3. Click one or more of the Trim Away options: **Top**, **Bottom**, **Left**, or **Right**.

4. Click **OK** to trim the image.

Color-Correct with Curves and Levels

Whether you acquire your images directly from a digital camera, scan them into Photoshop, or acquire them from clip art CDs, you'll probably need to do some color correction. Sometimes you might be dealing with a slight color cast; for example, the image may have a bluish tint; while other times the image is too dark or too light. You can manually perform sophisticated corrections to your images using the Curves and Levels commands, or you can let Photoshop take the reins with the Auto Color and Auto Levels commands.

Use a Histogram to View the Tonal Range of an Image

A *histogram* is a graph that shows the distribution of color pixels at each color level. There are 256 color levels ranging from 0 to 255. The distribution is in three ranges: shadows, which are on the left side of the histogram; midtones, which occupy the middle of the histogram; and highlights, which are on the right side of the histogram.

ANALYZE AN IMAGE'S HISTOGRAM

The distribution of pixels on a histogram consists of peaks and valleys. Whenever you see a large peak, there are a large number of pixels in that tonal range. If the histogram graph is flat or has very few pixels in the shadows tonal range, the image is overexposed. If the histogram graph is flat or has very few pixels in the highlights tonal range, the image is underexposed. If you have peaks that extend beyond the right side of the histogram, the image is badly overexposed and highlight details are clipped to white. If you have peaks that extend beyond the left side of the histogram, the image is badly underexposed and areas of shadow details are clipped to black. When details are clipped to white or black, the image details cannot be restored in Photoshop.

1. Open the image you want to color-correct.
2. Click **Window** and then click **Histogram**. The top illustration shows the histogram of a properly exposed image.
3. Click the right arrow in the upper-right corner of the palette to reveal the Histogram palette menu. Click one of these options:
   - **Compact view** displays the histogram of the image with no statistical information, as shown in the bottom illustration.

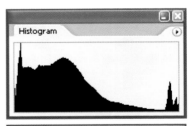

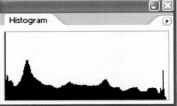

Compact view

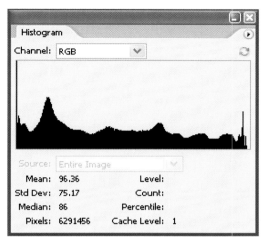

Expanded view

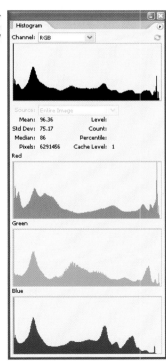

All Channels view with Show Channels In Color selected

- **Expanded view** displays the histogram of the image along with statistical information, as shown at left.

- **All Channels view** displays the histogram of the entire image, plus one for each channel. Note that the channels will be different depending on the color model used for the image. The histogram in the lower-left illustration shows the color channels for an RGB image.

- **Show Statistics** displays the statistical information for the histogram.

- **Show Channels In Color** displays the color channel histograms in the appropriate color. For example, if you're viewing a histogram for an RGB image, the color channel histograms will be red, green, and blue.

USE THE HISTOGRAM CHANNELS MENU

When you're viewing a histogram in Expanded or All Channels view, you can view the histogram for a specific channel by clicking the **Channels** down arrow and clicking one of these options:

- Click **RGB**, **CMYK**, or **Composite**, depending on the color model for the image whose histogram you are viewing.

- Select a specific **color channel** to view a histogram for that channel. Again, your choices will vary depending on the color model for the image you are analyzing.

- Click **Luminosity** if the image is RGB (Red, Green, Blue) or CMYK (Cyan, Magenta, Yellow, Black) to view a histogram displaying the luminance (intensity) values in the composite channel.

- Click **Colors** if the image is RGB or CMYK to view a composite histogram of all channels. Each channel is displayed in its native color.

VIEW STATISTICAL INFORMATION

If you view a histogram in Expanded or All Channels view, you can view statistical information. Certain information, such as level or count, changes depending on where you position your pointer in the histogram channels. The following statistical information is listed in a window below the histogram:

- **Mean** shows the average intensity value.

- **Std Dev** (Standard Deviation) shows the variance of intensity values.

- **Median** shows the middle value in the intensity range exhibited by the image.

- **Pixels** shows the number of pixels used to calculate the histogram.

- **Level** shows the intensity level of the histogram area underneath the pointer.

- **Count** shows the number of pixels corresponding to the intensity level underneath the pointer.

- **Percentile** shows the cumulative number of pixels below the level currently under the pointer. This value is expressed as a percentage of pixels in the image, ranging from 0 at the far left of the histogram to 100 at the far right.

- **Cache Level** shows the current image cache used to display the histogram. The original cache is Level 1. Each subsequent cache level uses the average of four adjacent pixels as a single pixel, effectively halving the dimension of each cache level. By default, Photoshop has six levels of memory cache.

Manually Adjust Levels

You can manually adjust levels using the sliders in the Levels dialog box. It's helpful if you view the histogram for the image while you're adjusting levels.

1. Click **Window** and click **Histogram**.

2. Click **Image**, click **Adjustments**, and then click **Levels**. The Levels dialog box appears.

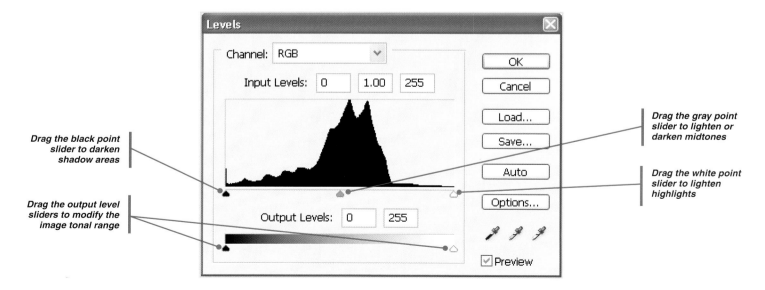

Drag the black point slider to darken shadow areas

Drag the output level sliders to modify the image tonal range

Drag the gray point slider to lighten or darken midtones

Drag the white point slider to lighten highlights

TIP

You can quickly toggle through the channels by pressing **CTRL** plus a number. For example, if you're working with an RGB image, press **CTRL+1** to adjust the Red channel, press **CTRL+2** to adjust the Green channel, and press **CTRL+3** to adjust the Blue channel. Press **CTRL+ ~** to return to the composite channel.

TIP

Hold down the **ALT** key while dragging the black point or white point slider. As you drag the slider, any clipped colors will be revealed in the image.

NOTE

Avoid flattening the top or bottom of the curve. When you flatten the curve in these areas, you clip colors from highlights and shadows of the image.

3. Click the **Channel** down arrow, and, from the drop-down menu, click the channel for which you want to adjust levels. Your choices will vary depending on the type of image you're editing; for example, for an RGB image, your choices are Red, Green, and Blue.

4. Drag the **black point** slider to the edge of where the pixels start to leave the bottom of the histogram.

5. Drag the **white point** slider to the edge of where the pixels start to leave the bottom of the histogram.

6. Drag the **gray point** slider to change the gamma of the image (*gamma* refers to the brightness and contrast of image midtones produced when the image is displayed on a device such as a computer monitor). Move the slider to the left to lighten the image; move it to the right to darken the image.

7. Drag the **output level black point** and **white point** sliders to set new shadow and highlight values. As you adjust levels, a gray band appears in the Histogram palette showing you how the histogram will look when the new levels are applied.

8. Click **OK** to apply the new levels settings. After you apply the settings, an information icon appears in the Histogram palette. This signifies that the histogram has changed.

9. Click the **Information** icon (the triangle with the exclamation point on it) in the Histogram palette to update the histogram.

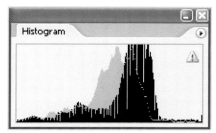

Use the Curves Command

Use the Curves command to alter the tonality and color of an image. You can modify the curve for the composite of all image channels or modify an individual channel to change the characteristics of that color in an image. The default curve in the Curves dialog box is a diagonal line running from left to right starting at the bottom. You alter the curve by adding points. When you add or move a point, you modify the pixels at a specific level. When you add points near the top of the curve, you modify the highlights of the image; points in the middle of the curve modify the midtones; points near the bottom of the curve modify shadows. Drag a point up to lighten pixels at the level; drag down to darken them.

1. Open the image you want to color-correct.

2. Click **Image**, click **Adjustments**, and then click **Curves**. The Curves dialog box is displayed.

3. Click the **Channel** down arrow, and select the channel or channels you want to modify. The default option modifies the curves for the entire image.

4. Click the curve to add a point. Alternatively, with an RGB image, you press **CTRL** while you click a pixel in the image to add a point to the curve. You can add as many as 16 points to a curve. Points are anchored until you move them.

5. To move a point, drag it to a new position in the dialog box. The following illustration shows a curve with several points.

6. Click **OK** to apply the changes. The illustration shows a before and after of an image with a blue color cast that was corrected using the Levels command.

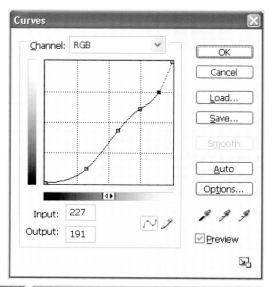

TIP

You can modify a small part of the tonal range by creating three neighboring points. Move the middle point to affect only a small part of the tonal range.

TIP

Click the **pencil** icon in the lower-right corner of the Curves dialog box to draw a curve. Click the **Smooth** button to smooth the curve. You can click the Smooth button as often as needed to smooth the curve.

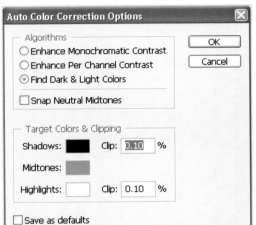

CHANGE AUTO COLOR AND AUTO LEVELS OPTIONS

When you select the Auto Color, Auto Contrast, or Auto Levels commands or the Auto option in the Levels or Curves dialog boxes, the black, gray, and white points are mapped to default levels of 0, 128, and 255, respectively. The gray point is perfect for removing color casts; however, the black and white default values may be too dark or too light depending on the type of images you're editing and personal taste. You can change the default to suit your tastes.

1. Click **Image**, click **Adjustments**, and then click **Levels**.

2. Click the **Options** button to open the Auto Color Correction Options dialog box.

3. Click one of these options:

   - **Enhance Monochromatic Contrast** lightens highlights and darkens shadows to improve overall contrast.

   - **Enhance Per Channel Contrast** maximizes contrast in each channel to greatly enhance image contrast. As this algorithm changes color values in each channel, the image may introduce a color cast. The Auto Levels command uses this algorithm.

   - **Find Dark & Light Colors** finds the average darkest and lightest pixels in an image and maps these values to the black and white points. The Auto Color command uses this algorithm.

4. Click the **Snap Neutral Midtones** option if you want the gamma values of the image snapped to a neutral midtone. The Auto Color command uses this option.

5. Click the **Shadows** color swatch to open the Color Picker.

6. Enter the desired values. Note that you must enter identical values in the R, G, and B fields to create a neutral highlight color. The values you enter are a matter of personal taste. This determines the value to which the darkest areas of the image will be mapped. Settings of 8, 8, and 8, respectively, should produce satisfactory shadows that are not obtrusively dark.

NOTE

The color in the Midtones setting is used for removing color casts from images; therefore, you should leave it at the default color.

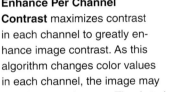

7. Click the **Highlights** color swatch to open the Color Picker.

8. Enter the desired values. Enter identical values in the R, G, and B fields to specify a neutral highlight color. Again, these values are a matter of personal taste. Settings of 245, 245, and 245, respectively, should produce satisfactory highlights.

9. In the Shadows and Highlights Clip fields, accept the default values or enter different values. The values you specify determine to what extent white and black pixels are clipped. A value between 0.0 percent and 1.0 percent is recommended.

10. Click **Save As Defaults** to save these settings as your default color corrections settings.

MANUALLY ADJUST LEVELS AND CURVES WITH THE EYEDROPPERS

Within the Levels and Curves dialog boxes are three Eyedropper tools: Black Point, Gray Point, and White Point. You select each Eyedropper tool, and then click inside the image to map the sampled image colors to black, gray, and white. When used in conjunction with the Info palette and a threshold adjustment layer, you can accurately select the colors to map to the black, gray, and white points.

1. Open the image you want to color-correct with the Levels or Curves command.

2. Click **Window** and then click **Info**. The Info palette is displayed.

3. Click the **triangle** to the left of the Eyedropper tool in the upper-left quadrant, and click **Total Ink** from the drop-down list. When the Info palette is in Total Ink mode, the palette displays the intensity of the color value of the pixel you sample using the Color Sampler tool.

4. Click **Window** and then click **Layers**. The Layers palette is displayed.

5. Click the **Create New Fill Or Adjustment Layer** button to display the Fill And Adjustment Layer list.

6. Click **Threshold** to open the Threshold dialog box. The image you are color correcting is displayed as a black-and-white image.

Create New Fill Or Adjustment Layer button

Threshold Level slider

Set the Color Sampler tool sample size to **Point Sample** in order to sample the color directly under the pointer.

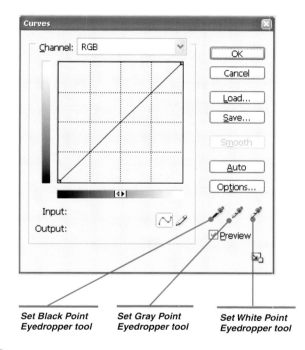

Set Black Point
Eyedropper tool

Set Gray Point
Eyedropper tool

Set White Point
Eyedropper tool

The Levels and Curves dialog boxes have the same Eyedropper tools. You'll get the same results using either command.

7. Drag the **Threshold Level** slider to the left until there are only a few black areas in the image. These are the image's darkest parts, which you will map to the black point.

8. Click **OK** to exit the Threshold dialog box.

9. Select the **Color Sampler** tool.

10. Click inside one of the dark areas to position a crosshair pointer with the number 1 at that spot in the image.

11. In the Layers palette, double-click the **Threshold** layer. The Threshold dialog box is displayed.

12. Drag the **Threshold Level** slider to the right until only a few white areas remain. These are the image's lightest areas, which you will map to the white point.

13. Click inside one of the light areas to position a crosshair pointer with the number 2 at that spot in the image.

14. Click **OK**.

15. Select the **Threshold** layer and drag it to the **trash can** icon in the Layers palette.

16. Select the **Color Sampler** tool.

17. Drag inside the image while viewing the Info palette. Your goal is to locate an area in the image with the value 128, the same value as the gray point. This removes any color cast from the image.

18. Click the area of the image with a value of 128 or thereabouts.

19. Click **Image**, click **Adjustments**, and then click **Curves**. The Curves dialog box is displayed.

20. Click the **Set Black Point Eyedropper** tool, and click inside the first point you created with the Color Sampler tool. The point will be mapped to the black point value, and all values in the image are adjusted accordingly.

21. Click the **Set Gray Point Eyedropper** tool, and click inside the third point you created with the Color Sampler tool. The point will be mapped to the gray point value, and all values in the image are updated to reflect the change.

23. Click the **Set White Point Eyedropper** tool, and click inside the second point you created with the Color Sampler tool. The point will be mapped to the white point value, and all values in the image are updated to reflect the change.

24. Click **OK** to exit the Curves or Levels dialog box. Figure 6-5 shows an image before and after color correction.

Figure 6-5: You can color-correct an image using Eyedropper tools.

Color-Correct Images

Another task you can accomplish with Photoshop is color correcting images. Using Photoshop tools and menu commands, you can remove red eye, adjust the hue and saturation of an image, adjust color balance, and more. If the Levels and Curves commands intimidate you, you can eyeball color corrections using the Variations command. If you're editing a digital photograph in which the subject is in heavy shadow but the rest of the image is properly exposed, you can easily fix this using the Shadow/Highlight command.

USE THE RED EYE TOOL

When you take a portrait of a person with a standard flash, the flash bounces off the person's retina, producing a reddish glow in the person's eyes known as red eye. Red eye can ruin an otherwise interesting portrait. You can easily remove red eye with the Red Eye tool.

1. Open the image you want to repair.

2. Zoom in on the eyes.

3. Click the **Red Eye** tool.

	Spot Healing Brush Tool	J
	Healing Brush Tool	J
	Patch Tool	J
	Red Eye Tool	J

4. In the Options bar, click the **Pupil Size** right arrow, and drag the slider to set the size of the pupil. Use a higher value if you're repairing an image in which the eyes are a large portion of the image; use a smaller value if the eyes are not predominant in the image but the red eye is still apparent.

5. Accept the default darken amount of **50** percent; or click the **Darken Amount** arrow, and drag the slider to specify a different value. Lower values darken the pupil less, while higher values darken the pupil more.

6. Set the **foreground** color to black or a very dark gray.

7. Click inside the pupil to repair the image.

8. Repeat for the other eye. These images show the before and after of an eye that was repaired with the Red Eye tool. If the first use of the tool doesn't remove the red eye, click the pupil again.

USING COLOR BALANCE

Yet another tool in your color-correction arsenal is the Color Balance command. Use this command when you need to balance the mix of colors in an image.

1. Open the image you want to color-correct.

2. Click **Image**, click **Adjustments**, and then click **Color Balance**. The Color Balance dialog box is displayed.

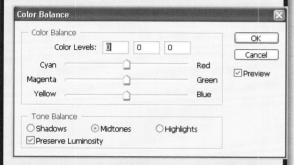

3. In the Tone Balance section, select the tonal range for which you want to balance color. Your choices are **Shadows**, **Midtones**, or **Highlights**.

4. Click **Preserve Luminosity** (the default) to prevent changing the tonal balance in the image.

5. Drag the sliders to balance the color. Drag a slider away from a color you want to decrease; drag it towards a color you want to increase. As you make adjustments, the values above the color sliders update to show the increase or decrease for the red, green, and blue values. If you're working with an image with the Lab color model, you balance greens and blues, which changes the balance in the A and B channels.

6. Click **OK** to apply the changes.

REMOVE UNWANTED COLOR CAST

You can use the Set Gray Point Eyedropper tool in either the Levels or Curves dialog box to remove a color cast from an image. You do so by identifying the area of the image that should be a neutral tone and then mapping it to the gray point.

1. Open the image from which you want to remove the color cast.

2. Click **Image**, click **Adjustments**, and click **Levels** or **Curves**.

3. Click the **Set Gray Point Eyedropper** tool, and then click an area inside the image that should be a neutral gray. This should correct the color cast for the entire image. If the color cast is predominantly in the shadow areas of the image, click the **Set Black Point Eyedropper** tool, and then click an area inside the image that should be black. If the color cast is predominately in the highlight areas, click the **Set White Point Eyedropper** tool, and then click an area inside the image that should be white.

USE THE VARIATIONS COMMAND

If you're visually oriented and don't like dealing with curves, histograms, or levels, Photoshop has a wonderful command that lets you eyeball a color correction. This gem is an image-adjustment command known as Variations. With the Variations command, you can remove a color cast or highlight by clicking a variation of the original image and then comparing the original to the modified version.

1. Open the image you want to edit.

2. Click **Image**, click **Adjustments**, and then click **Variations**. The Variations dialog box appears, shown in Figure 6-6. The **Show Clipping** option is selected by default. This option identifies areas of the applied-variation image that will be out-of-gamut with a neon-like overlay.

3. Select the type of adjustments you'd like to make:

   - **Shadows**, **Midtones**, and **Highlights** adjust the dark, middle, and light tones in your image, respectively.

   - **Saturation** increases or decreases the hue of the image.

4. Drag the **Fine/Coarse** slider to determine the degree of correction you want to apply. As you drag the slider, the variation thumbnails change. Fine settings produce subtle changes, while coarse settings produce pronounced changes.

TIP

Start with the default Fine/Coarse setting to make your initial adjustments; then drag the slider all the way to Fine to make your final adjustments.

TIP

To restore the current selection to the original image, click the **Original Image** thumbnail.

6. To adjust the image, do one of the following:

- To adjust the brightness of the image, click a thumbnail in the right window.

- To add a color to an image, click the appropriate variation thumbnail.

- To remove a color cast from an image, click the opposite variation thumbnail. For example, if the image has a green cast, click the **Yellow** variation thumbnail.

7. Click **OK** to apply the changes.

Figure 6-6: You can use the Variations command to color-correct an image.

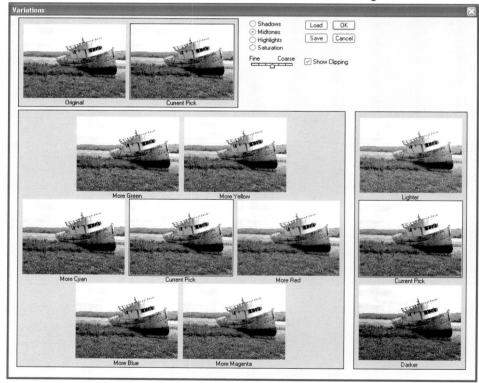

Change Hue and Saturation

Use the Hue/Saturation command to adjust the hue and saturation for an entire image or for a specific color component. This command is an excellent tool to correct color deficiencies. You can also use this command to change the hue of specific colors and achieve special effects.

CHANGE HUE AND SATURATION FOR THE ENTIRE IMAGE

1. Open the image for which you want to adjust hue and saturation.

2. Click **Image**, click **Adjustments**, and then click **Hue/Saturation**. The Hue/Saturation dialog box appears.

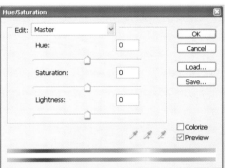

3. Accept the default Edit option of **Master**.

4. Drag the **Hue** slider until the colors appear as desired. Alternatively, you can type a value from −180 to 180 in the Hue field.

5. Drag the **Saturation** slider to achieve the desired result. Drag to the right to increase saturation; drag to the left to decrease saturation. Alternatively, you can type a value from −180 to 180 in the Saturation field.

6. Drag the **Lightness** slider to darken or lighten the image. Alternatively, you can type a value from −180 to 180 in the Lightness field.

7. Press **OK** to apply the settings.

CHANGE HUE AND SATURATION FOR A SPECIFIC COLOR

1. Open the image for which you want to adjust hue and saturation.

2. Click **Image**, click **Adjustments**, and then click **Hue/Saturation**. The Hue/Saturation dialog box appears.

3. Click the **Edit** down arrow, and select the color for which you want to adjust hue and saturation. The Hue/Saturation dialog box changes to the configuration shown here. Notice that a range of color has been selected in the dialog box.

4. Modify the range of colors by doing one of the following:

   • Drag the **inner vertical** sliders to change the range of colors.

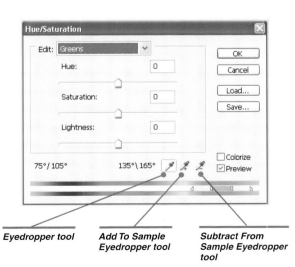

Eyedropper tool **Add To Sample Eyedropper tool** **Subtract From Sample Eyedropper tool**

TIP

Press **CTRL**, click in the color range selected, and drag the color bar to select a different range of color.

TIP

With the Eyedropper tool selected, press **SHIFT** and click colors inside the image to add colors to the range, or press **ALT** and click colors inside the image to decrease the range of color.

TIP

If you can't find a color filter to suit your needs, click the **Color** option, click the color swatch, and select the desired color from the Color Picker.

• Drag the **outer triangular** sliders to increase or decrease the range falloff. This setting determines how many similar colors will be affected by your edits.

• Click the **Eyedropper** tool and click inside the image to define the color.

• Click the **Add To Sample Eyedropper** tool, and click inside the image to add colors to the range.

• Click the **Subtract From Sample Eyedropper** tool, and click inside the image to remove colors from the range.

5. Drag the **Hue** slider to change the range of color. If needed, drag the **Saturation** and/ or **Lightness** sliders to change the lightness and/or saturation of the color range.

6. Click **OK** to apply your changes, or modify additional colors as needed.

USE PHOTO FILTERS

If you're an avid 35-mm photographer, you may have used photo filters to warm or cool an image. Another popular photo filter you may have used is a color filter to tint an image. In Photoshop, you can apply the same filters digitally to cool, warm, or tint an image.

1. Open the image to which you want to apply a photo filter.

2. Click **Image**, click **Adjustments**, and then click **Photo Filter**. The Photo Filter dialog box appears.

3. Click the **Filter** down arrow, and click one of the following options:

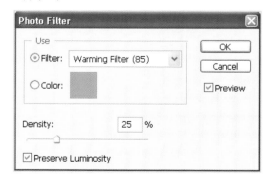

• **Warming Filter (85)** warms up the color tones in a cool image that has a bluish color cast.

• **Cooling Filter (80)** cools an image that has a yellowish cast by making the colors bluer.

• **Warming Filter (81)** warms the color tones of a bluish image by making them more yellow.

• **Cooling Filter (85)** cools an image with a yellow cast by making the colors bluer.

NOTE

The Preserve Luminosity check box is selected by default. Leave this unless you want the image to be darkened by the filter.

NOTE

If the source image has multiple layers, you can select the layer you want to use for matching purposes by clicking the **Layer** down arrow and then clicking the desired layer from the drop-down list.

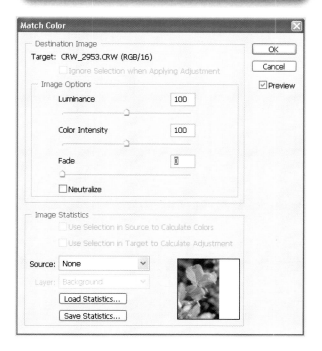

- **Warming Filter (LBA)** warms up the color tones in a cool image that has a bluish color cast.

- **Cooling Filter (LBB)** cools an image that has a yellowish cast by making the colors bluer.

- **Color Filters** tint an image. You can remove a color cast from an image by selecting a filter with a complimentary color. You can also use a color filter for special effects.

4. Drag the **Density** slider to determine how much color is applied to the image. Alternatively, you can type a value in the Percentage field. Select a higher density for a more pronounced effect.

5. Click **OK** to apply the filter.

USE THE MATCH COLOR COMMAND

If you have two images of the same subject that were photographed in different lighting conditions, you can use the Match Color command to make it appear as if the images were shot with the same lighting conditions. This command is especially useful if consistency is important when preparing a portfolio of several images.

1. Open the images you want to match.

2. Select the image whose colors you want to match to other open images.

3. Click **Images**, click **Adjustments**, and then click **Match Color**. The Match Color dialog box appears.

4. Click the **Source** down arrow, and select the image to which the selected image will be matched.

5. Click the **Neutralize** check box to remove any color cast in the target image.

6. Drag the **Luminance** slider to increase or decrease brightness in the target image. Alternatively, you can type a value between 1 and 200 in the Luminance field.

7. Drag the **Color Intensity** slider to modify color saturation in the target image. Alternatively, you can type a value between 1 (desaturated, which converts the image to grayscale) and 200 (maximum saturation). The default setting is 100, which is the original saturation of the image.

8. Drag the **Fade** slider to determine how much the target image is changed. Drag the slider to the right to reduce the effect the command has on the target image.

9. Click **OK** to apply the changes.

QUICKSTEPS

WORKING WITH ADJUSTMENT LAYERS

When you edit an image and apply a command, pixels are modified. When you apply other commands, additional pixels are modified. If, after applying several commands, you decide that you applied a command in error, you can use the History palette to restore the image to the step prior to the command you applied in error. When you do this, however, you lose all edits from that point forward. You can alleviate this problem by using adjustment layers. When you apply an adjustment layer to an image, you can use many of the commands previously discussed in this chapter. If you decide that you need to tweak a command, you can easily do so by activating the applicable adjustment layer and modifying the parameters.

1. Open the image you want to modify.
2. Click **View** and then click **Layers**. The Layers palette is displayed.
3. Click the **Adjustment Layers** button, and click the desired option from the pop-up menu.

   Solid Color...
   Gradient...
   Pattern...

   Levels...
   Curves...
   Color Balance...
   Brightness/Contrast...

   Hue/Saturation...
   Selective Color...
   Channel Mixer...
   Gradient Map...
   Photo Filter...

   Invert
   Threshold...
   Posterize...

Continued...

ADJUST SHADOWS AND HIGHLIGHTS

If you've ever tried to correct an image in which the subject was in deep shade or backlit, you know what a difficult process it can be. Fortunately, Photoshop has a command to adjust shadows and highlights. Figure 6-7 shows an image before and after the Shadow/Highlight command was used.

1. Open the image you want to adjust.
2. Click **Image**, click **Adjustments**, and then click **Shadow/Highlight**. The Shadow/Highlight dialog box is displayed.
3. Drag the **Amount** sliders to determine how correction is applied to shadow and highlight areas. As you drag the sliders, your image updates to reflect the new settings.
4. Click **OK** to apply the changes. Click the **Show More Options** button to adjust additional parameters and fine-tune the process.

Figure 6-7: You can use the Shadow/Highlight command to brighten subjects that are in shadow.

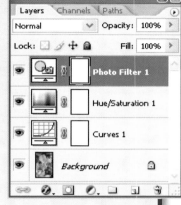
Edit in 16-Bit Mode

When you perform extensive editing on an image, you may notice that the histogram starts looking a little ragged, with gaps in the tonal curve. This is because of the limited number of values available with the default 8-bit mode. Each pixel in an 8-bit image has 256 possible values. By contrast, a pixel in a 16-bit image has roughly 24 million possible values. This means that a 16-bit image has more color information, which ensures a smoother blending of adjacent pixels. You achieve better results when you edit an image in 16-bit mode, especially when working with curves and levels. The additional color information safeguards against clipping colors.

1. Open the image you want to edit.

2. Click **Image**, click **Mode**, and then click **16 Bits/Channel**.

3. Edit the image as needed using the techniques discussed previously in this chapter.

4. If desired, print the image. When you print a 16-bit image, the results are stunning.

5. Save the image in a format that supports 16-bit mode, such as Photoshop's native PSD format.

Sharpen and Blur Images

Sharpening and blurring—the yang and the yin. If you have a blurry image, you can sharpen it in Photoshop. On the other hand, you can blur a perfectly sharp image for artistic purposes. You control the amount of sharpening or blurring applied. You can take the Zen approach—that less is more—or lavishly apply these effects.

SHARPEN WITH THE UNSHARP MASK FILTER

Photoshop has many filters that you can use to sharpen an image. The Unsharp Mask filter is undoubtedly the best of the lot. This filter controls the amount of sharpening applied to "unsharp" edges.

1. Open the image you want to sharpen.

2. Click **Filter**, click **Sharpen**, and then click **Unsharp Mask**. The Unsharp Mask dialog box appears.

QUICK**FACTS**

EDITING IN 32-BIT MODE

New to Photoshop CS2 is the ability to edit in 32-bit mode. When you edit in 32-bit mode, you can create an HDR (High Dynamic Range) image. HDR images exceed the dynamic range of shadows and highlights available to display devices and cameras. HDR images mimic the luminance values in a real-world scene as viewed through the human eye. When working with HDR images, you can create realistic blurs and lighting effects. Current technology uses HDR images in motion pictures, 3-D work, and high-end photography. To edit an image in 32-bit mode, click **Image**, click **Mode**, and then click **32-Bits/Channel**. When you edit in 32-bit mode, you do not have access to all of the filters you enjoy when editing in 8-bit or 16-bit mode. You cannot add layers to an image when editing in 32-bit mode, and you must flatten any layers in an image before converting it to 32-bit mode. You are also limited to saving a 32-bit/channel file in the following formats: Photoshop (PSD or PDD), Large Document Format (PSB), Radiance (HDR), Portable Bitmap (PFM), OpenEXR, and TIFF.

3. Drag the **Amount** slider to determine the amount of sharpening to be applied to the image. A value between 150 and 200 is an excellent choice for an image that will be printed; otherwise, select a value between 85 and 150.

4. Drag the **Radius** slider to determine the number of pixels surrounding an edge that will be sharpened. Experiment with values from 2 to 4.

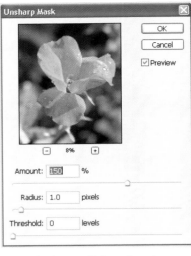

5. Drag the **Threshold** slider to determine how different edge-pixels must be from surrounding pixels before they are actually considered edge-pixels. Alternatively, you can enter a value in the Threshold field. As you experiment with different values, pay close attention to the image. If the edges become posterized, lower the value. Experiment with values from 1 to 12.

6. Click **OK** to sharpen the image.

USE THE GAUSSIAN BLUR FILTER

You can apply an artistic blur to an image to achieve a dreamlike effect with the Gaussian Blur filter. When you apply this blur to an image, you determine the extent of the blur by specifying the radius beyond each pixel that is blurred.

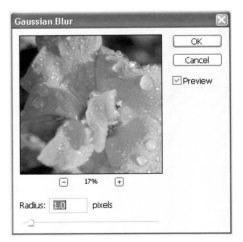

1. Open the image you want to blur.

2. Click **Filter**, click **Blur**, and then click **Gaussian Blur**. The Gaussian Blur dialog box appears.

3. Drag the **Radius** slider to determine the extent of the blur.

4. Click **OK** to blur the image.

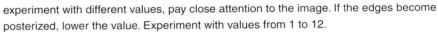

QUICKSTEPS

FINE-TUNING WITH THE SHARPEN, BLUR, AND SMUDGE TOOLS

When you edit an image, you often want to touch up small areas. For example, you can draw attention to a subject's eyes with the Sharpen tool. You can also smudge or blur an area that you want to de-emphasize. With these tools, you brush on the effect; hence, you can control the opacity of the brush, size, and so on.

1. Select the **Sharpen**, **Blur**, or **Smudge** tool from the Toolbox.

◊	Blur Tool	R
△	Sharpen Tool	R
✋	Smudge Tool	R

2. In the Options bar, specify the values in the **Brush Size**, **Brush Tip**, **Mode**, and **Strength** fields.

3. Drag the tool over the area you want to touch up.

USE THE MOTION BLUR FILTER

With the Motion Blur filter, you can make a photograph of a stationary object appear as if it were moving at high speed when the picture was taken. You can use the filter to add a sense of realism to an object, such as a car or a truck that was photographed at a high shutter speed and appears to be parked instead of moving.

1. Open the image you want to blur.

2. Click **Filter**, click **Blur**, and then click **Motion Blur**. The Motion Blur dialog box appears.

3. Drag the **Angle** slider to determine the direction in which the subject in the image will appear to be traveling. Alternatively, you can enter a value from 0 to 360.

4. Drag the **Distance** slider to determine the intensity of the blur.

5. Click **OK** to apply the motion blur to the image.

Retouch and Repair Images

If you need to retouch a small area of an image, you can do so using a myriad of Photoshop tools. With the Clone Stamp tool, you can copy pixels from one area to another. This tool works wonders on scanned images with small tears. It's also a great tool for a digital face-lift. You can repair large areas of an image using the Patch tool.

USE THE CLONE STAMP TOOL

The Clone Stamp tool makes it possible to copy pixels from one part of an image to another or from one image to another (as long as the images are both the same color model). You can control the size of the brush for the tool and, therefore, control the size of the area you clone.

1. Open the image from which you want to clone.

2. Click the **Clone Stamp** tool.

🖊	Clone Stamp Tool	S
🖊	Pattern Stamp Tool	S

Figure 6-8: Use the Clone Stamp tool to copy pixels from one area to another.

QUICKSTEPS

CHANGING IMAGE COLORS

You can change an image from color to grayscale easily in Photoshop.

CREATE A GRAYSCALE PHOTO FROM A COLOR PHOTO

One way to create a grayscale photo from a color image is to change the mode to grayscale. You can also convert from color to grayscale using a layer adjustment. This is the preferred method to control the transformation, plus the image is still in RGB mode, which means you'll get a more accurate print from your printer since all color nozzles will fire to print the image.

Continued...

3. In the Options bar, select the **Brush Size**, **Mode**, **Opacity**, and **Flow**. The brush size you specify is the diameter of the area that the brush will clone as you click the tool within the image.

4. Click **Aligned** (the default) to sample pixels from the current sampling point. If you deselect this option, you sample pixels from the original sampling point each time you resume painting. With this option, the current sampling point is equidistant from your brush, as the original sampling point was from the first stroke you took with the tool.

5. Click **Sample All Layers** to sample pixels from all layers in the image. If you deselect this option, pixels are only sampled from the currently selected layer.

6. Press **ALT** while you click the desired area inside the image to set the anchor point for sampling.

7. Drag inside the selected image or inside another image to clone pixels from the anchor point, as shown in Figure 6-8.

USE THE SPOT HEALING BRUSH TOOL

The Spot Healing Brush tool makes it possible for you to repair small areas of an image without selecting a source. This tool works wonders for removing blemishes from a subject's face or removing other unwanted items, such as freckles or crow's feet.

1. Open the image you want to repair.

2. Click the **Spot Healing Brush** tool.

3. In the Options bar, set the **Brush Diameter**, **Hardness**, **Spacing**, **Angle**, and **Roundness** options. If you're using a digital tablet, click an option from the **Size** drop-down menu. Click **Pen Pressure** to vary the size of the stroke based on pen pressure; click **Stylus Wheel** to vary the brush size according to the position of the pen thumbwheel; or use neither of these to create strokes that don't vary in size.

4. In the Options bar, click an option from the **Mode** drop-down list to determine how the pixels are blended.

CHANGING IMAGE COLORS
(Continued)

1. Open the image you want to convert to grayscale mode.

2. Click **Layer**, click **New Adjustment Layer**, and then click **Channel Mixer**. The Channel Mixer dialog box is displayed.

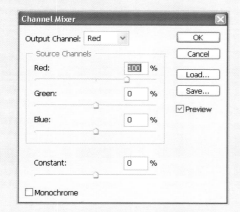

3. Type a name for the new layer, and click **OK**. Alternatively, you can accept the default name and click **OK**.

4. Click the **Monochrome** check box. The image is converted to grayscale, and the Red channel value is 100 percent. If this is acceptable, click **OK**.

5. Adjust the channel mix as desired. You can mix the channels to achieve a slightly different-looking grayscale image. For example, use a value of 60 for the Red channel, 20 for the Green channel, and 20 for the Blue channel. As long as the total value of all three channels equals 100, you're good to go.

6. Click **OK** to exit the Channel Mixer dialog box.

7. Flatten the image.

---

5. Click one of the following options:

- **Proximity Match** uses the surrounding pixels to patch the area you drag the tool across. If the repair is not satisfactory, click **Edit**, click **Undo**, click the **Create Texture** option, and perform the repair again.

- **Create Texture** uses the surrounding pixels to create a texture for the pixels you drag the tool across. You may have to use the tool a second time to achieve the desired repair effect.

6. Click **Sample All Layers** if you want the tool to sample pixels from all layers in the document.

7. Click the area you want to repair. The following image shows a before and after shot of a photograph in which slight blemishes around the subject's eyes and on her cheek were removed with the Spot Healing Brush tool.

USE THE HEALING BRUSH TOOL TO FIX SMALL AREAS

The Healing Brush tool makes it possible for you to touch up small areas. If you need to remove minor imperfections in an image or features such as crow's feet from a subject's face, this is the ideal tool. When you use this tool, you specify the area from which to sample, whereas the Spot Healing Brush tool samples pixels from the area surrounding the tool.

1. Open the image you want to repair.

2. Click the **Healing Brush** tool.

3. In the Options bar, set the **Brush Diameter**, **Hardness**, **Spacing**, **Angle**, and **Roundness** options. If you're using a digital tablet, click an option from the **Size** drop-down menu. Click **Pen Pressure** to vary the size of the stroke based on pen pressure; click **Stylus Wheel** to vary the brush size according to the position of the pen thumbwheel; or use neither of these to create strokes that don't vary in size.

4. In the Options bar, click an option from the **Mode** drop-down list to determine how the pixels are blended.

5. In the Options bar, click **Aligned** to align sampled pixels to the current pointer position. Deselect this option to paint from the initial anchor point.

6. In the Options bar, click **All Layers** to sample pixels from all layers. Deselect this option to sample pixels from the currently selected layer.

7. In the Options bar, select a source option. Click **Sampled** to sample pixels from the image, or click **Pattern** to sample pixels from a pattern. If you select Pattern, select a pattern from the Pattern drop-down list.

8. Press **ALT** while you click to set the anchor point.

9. Drag the **Healing Brush** tool across the area you want to repair. The following image shows fine lines around a subject's eyes repaired using the Healing Brush tool.

USE THE PATCH TOOL TO FIX LARGE AREAS

The Patch tool works like the Healing Brush tool in that it copies pixels and textures from one source to another. The Patch tool, however, lets you define the size of the area that you want to repair. You can use the tool to clone pixels or a pattern.

1. Open the image you want to repair.

2. Click the **Patch** tool.

3. In the Options bar, click one of the following:

- **Source** copies pixels from the destination to the source.

- **Destination** copies pixels from the source to the destination.

4. Drag inside the image to define the source area or the destination area, depending on the option you chose in step 3.

5. Drag to the destination or source from which you want to sample pixels to patch the selected area, and release the mouse button. For example, if you had selected puffy flesh under a subject's eyes, you'd drag the tool to an unblemished area of the face.

USE THE PATTERN STAMP TOOL

TIP

Click **Pattern** to copy pixels from a pattern to the source or destination file.

With the Pattern Stamp tool, you can paint patterns on an image. You can select a preset pattern from the pattern library.

1. Click the **Pattern Stamp** tool.

	Clone Stamp Tool	S
	Pattern Stamp Tool	S

2. In the Options bar, select a **Brush Tip** and specify **Brush Size**, **Mode**, **Opacity**, and **Flow**.

3. Click the **Pattern** icon and select a pattern.

4. In the Options bar, click **Aligned** to align pixels sampled from the pattern to the current sampling point, even if you release the mouse button. Deselect **Aligned**, and pixels will be sampled from the pattern at the initial sampling point.

5. In the Options bar, click **Impressionist** to paint patterns in an Impressionist style.

6. Drag inside the image to paint the pattern.

Use the Dust & Scratches Filter

If you're working with old photos that have damage in the form of dust specks or scratches, you can easily remove them using the Dust & Scratches filter. The filter performs its magic by blurring dissimilar pixels.

1. Open the image you want to repair.

2. Click **Filter**, click **Noise**, and then click **Dust & Scratches**. The Dust & Scratches dialog box appears.

CREATING A SEPIA-TONE PHOTO

When you convert a color or grayscale photo to a sepia-tone photo, it has a warm brown tone reminiscent of old photos. People pay good money to have sepia-tone photos taken in mall kiosks. You can quickly create a sepia-tone photo in Photoshop without breaking a sweat.

1. Open the image you want to convert to sepia tone.

2. Click **Window** and then click **Actions**. The Actions palette is displayed.

3. Click the **Options** arrow to display the Options menu.

4. Click **Sample Actions**. Photoshop loads sample actions into the Actions palette.

5. Click the **Sample Actions** down arrow to display all of the sample actions.

6. Scroll to the **Sepia Toning** title, and click it.

7. Click the **Play** button in the Actions palette. The image is converted to sepia tone.

Play button

---

3. Drag the **Radius** slider to the right until the "noise" begins to disappear. Alternatively, you can enter a value between 1 and 16 in the Radius field. Don't select a value higher than needed, as you'll excessively blur the image.

4. Drag the **Threshold** slider to the right to specify the highest possible value that eliminates the dust marks and scratches. This setting determines how dissimilar pixels must be before the filter eliminates them.

5. Click **OK** to apply the repair.

USE THE HISTORY BRUSH FOR TOUCH-UPS

If you use Photoshop to edit images of people, you end up using a variety of filters to bring out the best in your subject. For example, to smooth out the skin of a subject, you can apply a slight Gaussian blur. However, you don't want to blur the fine details of your subject's hair, mouth, or eyes. You can restore detail to these areas using the History Brush tool.

1. Open the image you want to retouch.

2. Apply the desired filters.

3. Click **Window** and then click **History**. The History palette is displayed. The illustration on the right shows the History palette after a Gaussian blur has been applied to an image.

Set Source For The History Brush column

4. Click the blank square in the **Set Source For The History Brush** column to the left of the image state that you want to selectively restore. For example, if you want to selectively restore a Gaussian blur to parts of the image, click the blank square to the left of **Gaussian Blur** in the History palette. After selecting an image state, the History Brush icon appears in the Set Source For The History Brush column.

5. Click the **History Brush** tool.

6. In the Options bar, set the **Brush Size**; select the **Brush Tip**; and then specify **Mode**, **Opacity**, and **Flow**.

7. Paint over the areas of the image you want to restore to a previous state.

How to...

- Create Text
- Committing Type
- Edit Type
- Hyphenating and Justifying Type
- Use the Spelling Checker
- Find and Replace Text
- Transforming Type
- Warp Text
- Create Text on a Path
- Edit Text on a Path
- Create Text within a Closed Path
- Add Special Type Effects with Layer Styles
- Finding and Using Layer Styles
- Create Text Masks

Chapter 7

Using Type and Type Effects

When working in Photoshop, you can make your type as effective and dramatic as possible using the myriad effects you can create with images. In this chapter you will discover how to create and edit type on images using typical formatting techniques, hyphenation, and justification. You will see how to perform the commonly needed tasks of checking spelling and finding and replacing text. Then, with the mundane but critical tasks out of the way, you will see how to play with your type: warping it, transforming it by rotating, skewing it, and resizing it. You will find out how to use layer styles that let you create special effects like drop shadows, beveling and embossing, inside and outside glows, and gradient fills. Finally, you will learn how to mask your type, thereby enabling you to copy images as fill for type, and how to make a *selection* of type, which can then be manipulated just like any other selection.

Create and Edit Text

When you use the Text tool to type text, it creates its own text layer, which can be edited until you *rasterize* it. Initially, text is vector-based; however, when you rasterize it, it becomes a bitmap object. At this point, it can no longer be accessed as editable text. Some of the special tools and effects, such as the Paint tools and filter effects, can be used to enhance text once it is rasterized. See Chapter 1 for additional information on the differences between bitmaps and vector-based graphics.

When you select the Type tool, the Options toolbar becomes a Formatting toolbar. Figure 7-1 shows the tools available for creating and editing text.

Figure 7-1: The Options toolbar contains formatting tools when you select the Type tool.

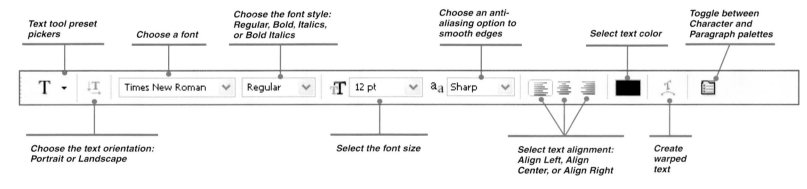

Text tool preset pickers

Choose a font

Choose the font style: Regular, Bold, Italics, or Bold Italics

Choose an anti-aliasing option to smooth edges

Select text color

Toggle between Character and Paragraph palettes

Choose the text orientation: Portrait or Landscape

Select the font size

Select text alignment: Align Left, Align Center, or Align Right

Create warped text

Create Text

You can enter text in two ways: as point type or as paragraph type. Use point type when you have only a few words to enter. Use paragraph type when you are working with more than a few words.

ENTER POINT TYPE

Point type becomes a new text layer. As you are entering text, it doesn't wrap to the next line; rather, it continues on the same line.

QUICKSTEPS

COMMITTING TYPE

After your text has been entered and you are satisfied with the results, you *commit* the text to accept the changes. Do one of these to accept, or commit, the changes:

- Click **Commit** in the Options toolbar. ✔
- On the numeric keyboard, press **ENTER**.
- On the main keyboard, press **CTRL+ENTER**.
- Select another tool or select a menu option.

NOTE

You can change from point type to paragraph type or vice versa. Select the type layer (not the text itself), click **Layer**, click **Type**, and click **Convert To Point Text** or **Convert To Paragraph Text**.

1. Open an image and set attributes for the text (see the section "Format Type with the Character Palette").

2. Select either the **Horizontal Type** tool or the **Vertical Type** tool.

	T Horizontal Type Tool	T
	T Vertical Type Tool	T
	T Horizontal Type Mask Tool	T
	T Vertical Type Mask Tool	T

3. Click in the image area, and the pointer morphs into an I-beam pointer. Click where you want the text to begin. For horizontal type, the small intersecting line marks where the bottom of the type will appear. For vertical type, the intersecting line identifies the center of the type. Figure 7-2 shows horizontal text on a photo.

4. Select any formatting you want from the type options in the Options bar, the Character palette, or the Paragraph palette (see "Edit Type" later in this chapter).

5. Type your characters. Press **ENTER** to begin a new line.

6. Click **Commit** on the Options bar (see "Committing Type"). ✔

Figure 7-2: Point type entered using the Horizontal Type tool creates a useful label for photos.

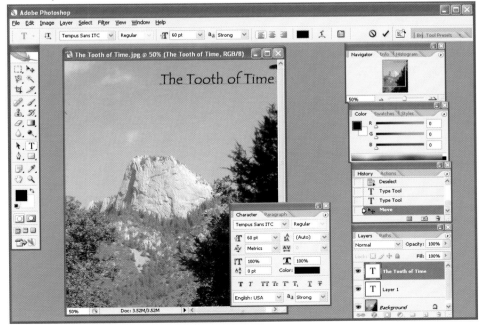

NOTE

You can resize the bounding box using the handles on its perimeter. If you press **ALT** as you drag to form a bounding box for paragraph text, the Paragraph Text Size dialog box will appear. Type values in points in the **Height** and **Width** text boxes for the bounding box, and click **OK**.

TIP

You can tell when you are in Edit mode by looking for the Commit and Cancel Transform buttons in the Option toolbar. If these buttons are there, you are in Edit mode.

ENTER PARAGRAPH TYPE

You type a paragraph of text into a *bounding box* that contains the text and creates a separate text object on its own layer. Then set attributes for the paragraph (see "Format Paragraphs with the Paragraph Palette").

1. Select either the **Horizontal Type** tool or the **Vertical Type** tool.

2. Drag the pointer diagonally so that a bounding box is created.

3. Select any formatting you want from the type options in the Options bar, the Character palette, or the Paragraph palette (see "Format Type with the Character Palette" later in this chapter).

4. Type your characters. To break to a new line, press **ENTER**. The text will automatically wrap to the next line when it reaches the end of the bounding box.

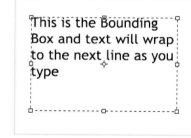

5. Click **Commit** on the Options bar (see "Committing Type").

Edit Type

You can edit your text by changing the font, text color, font size and style, leading, and kerning. This is most easily done using the Character or Paragraph palettes.

FORMAT TYPE WITH THE CHARACTER PALETTE

You can use the Character palette to edit the most common text attributes.

1. If it is not already showing, display the Character palette by clicking **Window** and then clicking **Character**. The Character palette is displayed, as shown in Figure 7-3.

2. Click the text layer in the Layers palette, and then select the text in the text box in the document by highlighting it with the appropriate text tool.

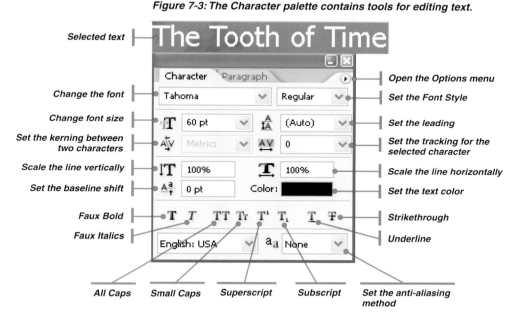

Figure 7-3: The Character palette contains tools for editing text.

Selected text — The Tooth of Time

Change the font — Tahoma | Regular — Set the Font Style
Change font size — 60 pt | (Auto) — Set the leading
Set the kerning between two characters — Metrics | 0 — Set the tracking for the selected character
Scale the line vertically — 100% | 100% — Scale the line horizontally
Set the baseline shift — 0 pt | Color: — Set the text color
Faux Bold — T T TT Tr T¹ T₁ T F — Strikethrough
Faux Italics — English: USA | aₐ None — Underline

Open the Options menu

All Caps   Small Caps   Superscript   Subscript   Set the anti-aliasing method

.This is Times Roman, regular style, 14 points

This is Palace Script M.T.
Faux Bold, 24 points

This is Trebuchet MS,
Bold-Italics style, 24 points

3. Select from among these options:

- **Font** changes the font used.

- **Font Style** changes the look of the font. The options will vary depending on the font used.

- **Font Size** changes the point size of the characters.

- **Leading** changes the space between lines of text. Auto is the default. You usually want to select a leading larger than the size of the text. For example, if the point size is 20 points, you might use a leading of 24 or larger. Leading can be used to overlap lines of text for special effects.

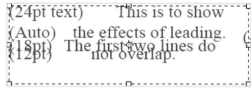

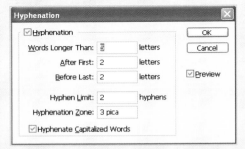

QUICKSTEPS

HYPHENATING AND JUSTIFYING TYPE

HYPHENATE WORDS

On the Paragraph palette, click the **Hyphenate** check box to have Photoshop automatically hyphenate words.

SET HYPHENATION RULES

1. Click the Paragraph palette **Options** button in the upper-right corner, and click **Hyphenation**. The Hyphenation dialog box appears.

Hyphenation		
☑ Hyphenation		OK
Words Longer Than:	5 letters	Cancel
After First:	2 letters	
Before Last:	2 letters	☑ Preview
Hyphen Limit:	2 hyphens	
Hyphenation Zone:	3 pica	
☑ Hyphenate Capitalized Words		

2. Accept the defaults or change the following options:

- **Words Longer Than __ Letters** hyphenates only words longer than the given number of letters; the default is five letters.

- **After First __ Letters** requires a given number of letters to be typed before hyphenating.

- **Before Last __ Letters** requires hyphenation to occur at least that many letters from the end.

- **Hyphenate Limit __ Hyphens** limits the number of hyphens in adjoining lines; 0 provides no limit.

- **Hyphenation Zone** defines the distance (the default is 3 picas) from the end of the line within the bounding box that hyphenation will occur.

- **Hyphenate Capitalized Words** restricts the hyphenation of capitalized words.

3. Click **OK**.

Continued...

- **Kerning** changes the space between two characters. Place the pointer between the two characters you want  to manipulate. You can move characters closer together or set them farther apart.

- **Tracking** changes the spacing for a selected line of characters. Using a higher number increases space; a negative number decreases spacing.

- **Scale Vertically** adjusts the height of selected text.

- **Scale Horizontally** adjusts the width of selected text.

- **Baseline Shift** moves the selected characters above or below the baseline, such as in subscripts and superscripts.

- **Text Color** sets the color of text.

- Several character attributes can be chosen for selected characters: **Faux Bold** (when your font has no bold typeface), **Faux Italics** (when your font has no italics), **All Caps**, **Small Caps**, **Superscript**, **Subscript**, **Underlining**, and **Strikethrough**.

- **Language** establishes the language being typed.

- **Anti-Aliasing** adjusts the smoothness of the letters, from None to Smooth.

FORMAT PARAGRAPHS WITH THE PARAGRAPH PALETTE

When you type a paragraph into a bounding box, you have a Paragraph palette available for formatting line and paragraph spacing. Figure 7-4 shows the tools available with the Paragraph palette.

1. If the Paragraph palette is not displayed, click **Window** and then click **Paragraph**.

2. Set your paragraph parameters before typing text by clicking the attribute or filling in a text box (see step 5).

7

1 2 3 4 5 6 8 9 10

HYPHENATING AND JUSTIFYING TYPE *(Continued)*

SPECIFY NO BREAKS

To prevent a group of letters from being broken during word wrap:

1. Select the letters that are not to be broken.
2. Click the Character palette **Options** button in the upper-right corner, and click **No Break**.

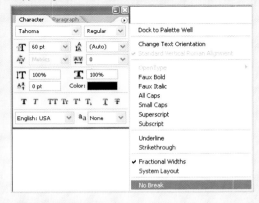

SET JUSTIFY RULES

You can set the spacing between words, letters, and glyphs (any characters or symbols in a font, including non-text characters, such as Wingdings font characters).

1. Click the Paragraph palette **Options** button in the upper-right corner, and click **Justification**. The Justification dialog box appears.
2. Set the values to define the spacing between words, letters, and glyphs, as described in Table 7-1.
3. Click **OK**.

Justification

	Minimum	Desired	Maximum	
Word Spacing:	80%	100%	133%	OK
Letter Spacing:	0%	0%	0%	Cancel
Glyph Scaling:	100%	100%	100%	Preview
Auto Leading:	120%			

Left Align Text, Center Text, or Right Align Text

Justify Last Left, Justify Last Centered, Justify Last Right, or Justify All

Indent Left Margin

Indent First Line

Add Space Before Paragraph

Hyphenate For Word Wrap

Indent Right Margin

Add Space After Paragraph

Figure 7-4: Use the Paragraph palette to define paragraph attributes, such as alignment, spacing, and indentation.

3. Create paragraph text by selecting the **Horizontal Type** tool or the **Vertical Type** tool and then dragging a bounding box.
4. Begin to type the paragraph.
5. To change paragraph settings, select the paragraph and move your pointer over the option, such as **Indent Left Margin**. When your pointer becomes a pointing hand with a two-headed arrow, drag to change the value. (Dragging horizontally seems to work better than dragging vertically.)

Element	Minimum	Maximum	No Effect
Word Spacing	0%	1000%	100%
Letter Spacing	–100%	500%	0%
Glyph Spacing	50%	200%	100%

TABLE 7-1: DEFINES JUSTIFICATION RULES

Use the Spelling Checker

To check whether the words in your paragraph are correct, use the Spelling Checker feature.

1. Select the text to be examined.

2. Click **Edit** and then click **Check Spelling**.

3. If a word cannot be found in the Photoshop dictionary, the Check Spelling dialog box will appear, as shown in Figure 7-5. If the word is not in its dictionary, Photoshop thinks the word has been misspelled. Choose from among these options:

   - **Ignore** skips the word identified as a potential mistake.

   - **Ignore All** skips all occurrences of this word.

     - **Change** replaces the word in the Not In Dictionary text box with the one in the Change To text box.

     - **Change All** replaces all occurrences of the identified word with the one in the Change To text box.

     - **Add** adds the word in the Not In Dictionary text box to Photoshop's dictionary.

4. Click **Done** to close the dialog box. If the Spelling Checker finds no more misspelled words, it will display a message that the spelling check is complete.

Figure 7-5: The Spelling Checker feature identifies all words that are not in the Photoshop dictionary as potential misspellings.

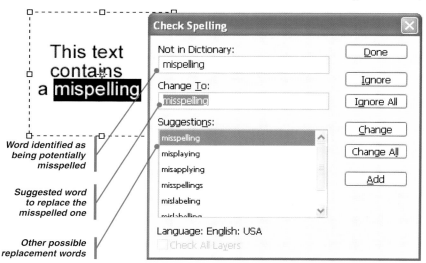

Word identified as being potentially misspelled

Suggested word to replace the misspelled one

Other possible replacement words

Find and Replace Text

To find text and replace it with other text:

1. Click **Edit** and then click **Find And Replace Text**. The Find And Replace Text dialog box appears.

2. Under Find What, type the text to be searched for and replaced.

3. Under Change To, type the new text.

4. Select any of the following options:

   - **Search All Layers** searches for the text in all layers of an image.

   - **Forward** searches forward from one text object to another.

   - **Case Sensitive** restricts the search to the case of the text in the Find What text box.

TRANSFORMING TYPE

You can transform type by manipulating the bounding box surrounding it.

SELECT A BOUNDING BOX

To display the bounding box with handles for rotating and resizing, select your text layer and press **CTRL+T,** or click **Edit** and click **Free Transform.**

RESIZE A BOUNDING BOX

1. Place your pointer over the bounding-box handles until you see a double-headed arrow.

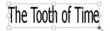

2. Drag the handles until the bounding box is the size you want.

3. To change the size proportionally, press **SHIFT** while you drag.

ROTATE A BOUNDING BOX

1. Place the pointer outside the bounding box until the pointer morphs into a curved double-headed arrow.

2. Drag the pointer in the direction the box is to be rotated.

3. Press **SHIFT** while you drag to change the rotation in 15-degree increments.

4. Press **CTRL** while you drag the center point to another place, even outside the bounding box. The new location of the center point becomes the center of rotation for the text. Then you can rotate the bounding box around a wider circle.

Continued...

- **Whole Word Only** searches only for whole words that match the text in the Find What text box.

- **Find Next** searches for the next occurrence of the word in the text.

- **Change** changes the selected text to the text in the Change To text box.

- **Change All** changes all occurrences of the text in the Find What text box.

- **Change/Find** changes the selected text to the text in the Change To text box and then continues the search.

5. Click **Done**.

Warp Text

You can create interesting effects on text by warping it.

1. In the Layers palette, double-click the **T** icon on the layer containing the text to be warped. The text is highlighted.

2. Right-click the highlighted text and click **Warp Text** from the context menu. The Warp Text dialog box, shown in Figure 7-6, is displayed.

3. Click the **Style** down arrow, and select a warp style.

4. Click **Horizontal** or **Vertical** to orient the text horizontally or vertically.

5. Drag the **Bend** slider to exaggerate or lessen the warp of the text. You can also type a percentage in the Bend text box to set the degree of warp.

6. Drag the **Horizontal Distortion** slider to increase or decrease the horizontal warp, or you can type a percentage in the text box.

7. Drag the **Vertical Distortion** slider to increase or decrease the vertical warp, or type a percentage in the text box.

8. Click **OK** when the warp effect is as you want.

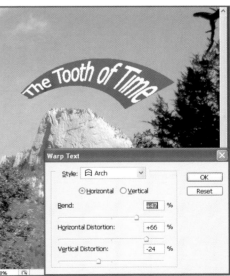

Figure 7-6: The Warp Text dialog box presents options for the style of warp you want.

TRANSFORMING TYPE (Continued)

USE THE OPTIONS BAR TO TRANSFORM TEXT

You can also use the Options bar, shown in Figure 7-7, to make changes to text. When the text is selected and the transform bounding box is displayed:

- Click a point on the **Reference Point Position** icon to locate the reference point within the text box.
- Click **X** (for Set Horizontal Position Of The Reference Point), **Y** (for Set Vertical Position Of The Reference Point), or **W** (for Set Horizontal Scale), and drag to expand or decrease the horizontal, vertical, and left and right sides of the bounding box relative to where the reference point is located.
- Click **Set Vertical Scale** and drag to expand or decrease the text vertically.
- Click **Rotate** and drag to rotate the text.
- Click **Set Horizontal Skew** or **Set Vertical Skew** to skew the text horizontally or vertically.

SKEW TEXT IN A BOUNDING BOX

1. Select the text layer that you want to skew.
2. Click **Edit**, click **Transform**, and click **Skew**. The pointer morphs into an arrow

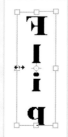

that you can use to drag the handles, thus skewing the shape of the bounding box.

FLIP THE TEXT

To flip the text, drag the bounding box across itself to the other side. For example, click the right handle and drag it to the left until the text flips.

Figure 7-7: Use the Options bar to skew text within the bounding box.

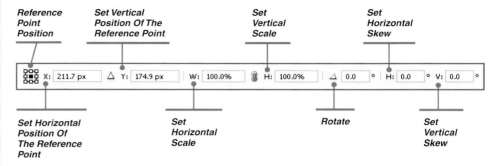

Reference Point Position · Set Vertical Position Of The Reference Point · Set Vertical Scale · Set Horizontal Skew

Set Horizontal Position Of The Reference Point · Set Horizontal Scale · Rotate · Set Vertical Skew

Create Text on a Path

You can type text along a path, such as that seen in Figure 7-8. First you create a path and then you type text, pulling it along the path.

1. Create a layer for your path and text.
2. Select a tool, such as the **Pen** tool or the **Freeform Pen** tool, to create a path. (See Chapter 5 for additional information on creating paths.)
3. Click **Paths** on the Options toolbar, and draw the path.
4. Select the **Horizontal Type** tool for text parallel to the path, or select the **Vertical Type** tool for text perpendicular to the path.
5. Place the pointer above the path until it morphs into an I-beam. Click the path, and an insertion point appears.
6. Type your text.

Figure 7-8: Type text on a path for special effects.

Edit Text on a Path

To edit the text on a path by inserting and deleting letters and making formatting changes:

1. Select the text layer containing the text to be edited.
2. Click either the **Horizontal Type** tool or the **Vertical Type** tool.
3. Click the text string to place the insertion point, or highlight the text to select it.
4. Make your changes.

Create Text within a Closed Path

To type text within a closed path, such as a circle or ellipse, create a path around a shape and type text, dragging the text where you want it.

1. Select a shape tool, and draw a shape, such as the oval seen in Figure 7-9.
2. Click **Path** on the Options bar to make the shape into a path.
3. Click the **Horizontal Type** tool or the **Vertical Type** tool, and place the insertion point on the path.
4. Type the text.
5. Adjust the positioning using the **Path Selection** tool or the **Direct Selection** tool to pull the text string one way or the other. You may also want to rotate the text, format it, or apply layer styles to it before you finish.

NOTE

If your letters seem to disappear as you type, you may need to *pull* the text string along the path. Select the **Path Selection** tool, and where the text disappears, drag an anchor point along the path in the direction the text is to flow. As you release the Path Selection tool, the missing letters will appear.

TIP

Text will appear in the direction that a path is drawn, so if you draw a line from left to right, that is how letters will be inserted. If a path is too short or the text comes to the end of the path before all the letters are on the path, the letters will follow the path and curve around the end of it.

Figure 7-9: You can type text around a closed path to create unusual effects.

TIP

To move text along a path or to flip it to the opposite side of a path, select the **Direct Selection** tool or the **Path Selection** tool. Hold the tool over the type until it changes to an I-beam with an arrow. To move the text along the path, drag the I-beam along the path, which drags the type, taking care not to cross the path. To flip the text to the opposite side of the path, drag the I-beam across the path.

TIP

To move text on the other side of a path but not flip it, select the text. On the Character palette, set the **Baseline Shift** option to a negative number. To move whole characters across the path, enter a number equal to the point size of the type.

TIP

To open the Layer Style dialog box, click the **Layer Style** button at the bottom of the Layers palette.

Add Special Type Effects with Layer Styles

You can apply special effects to your text using options from the Layer Styles dialog box. Photoshop has several predefined, or preset, styles that can be used to create drop shadows, embossing or beveling, inside and outside glows, gradient coloring, patterns, and more. Figure 7-10 shows examples of some effects described in this section. Three commonly used styles are described next.

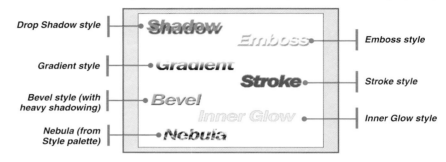

Figure 7-10: Examples of effects you can create using layer styles.

Drop Shadow style — Shadow   Emboss — Emboss style

Gradient style — Gradient   Stroke — Stroke style

Bevel style (with heavy shadowing) — Bevel   Inner Glow — Inner Glow style

Nebula (from Style palette) — Nebula

CREATE DROP SHADOWS

To create a slight shadow on selected type:

1. Select the text to which you want to apply the effect.

2. Click **Layer**, click **Layer Style**, and then click **Drop Shadow**. The Layer Style dialog box appears with the Drop Shadow options displayed, as shown in Figure 7-11. (You can also click the **Add A Layer Style** button on the Layers palette, and then click **Drop Shadow** to display the relevant options in the Layer Style dialog box.)

3. Experiment with the options and view the results in the preview box (refer to Chapters 4 and 6 for additional information on the options):

   • **Blend Mode**—By default, this is set to **Multiply**, and the default color is black. (You can change the color by clicking the color preview and selecting a color from the Color Picker dialog box.)

   • **Opacity**—The Blend Mode determines how much of the image underlying the shadow is visible. At a value of 100, the shadow obscures anything underneath it.

FINDING AND USING LAYER STYLES

Preset layer styles can be found in a couple of places in Photoshop CS2.

USE THE STYLES PALETTE

1. Click **Windows** and click **Styles**. The Styles palette is displayed. This contains thumbnails showing what the style effects will look like.

2. Select the text layer to which the layer style will be applied.

3. Click the style, or drag the style to the selected text.

4. Press **SHIFT** while you drag to add the selected style to those already applied to the selected text. Without pressing **SHIFT**, the selected style replaces any styles currently applied.

USE THE LAYER STYLE DIALOG BOX

1. Select the text layer to which the style will be applied.

2. Click the **Layer** menu, click **Layer Style**, and click an option to display the dialog box for layer styles. (An example of the dialog box is shown under "Create Drop Shadows.")

3. Choose the settings for the option you selected. The choices will vary, depending on which style you picked. See "Add Special Type Effects with Layer Styles" for specifics on the common styles used.

4. Click **OK**.

Figure 7-11: Use the Drop Shadow options to precisely control the shadowing.

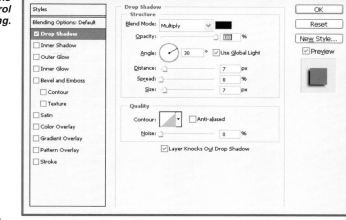

- **Angle**—This directs the source of the light. **Global Light** places a fixed light source on the type. Because it is global in nature, if you apply a drop shadow to the text, for example, at different parts of the document, the light source will reflect its fixed location.

- **Distance**—This is how far the shadow is offset from the type.

- **Spread**—This relates to the percentage of thickness a shadow has, and it is related to the Size option.

- **Size**—This is how sharp or fuzzy the shadow is.

- **Contour**—This opens a submenu of shadow curves or shapes.

- **Anti-Aliased**—This blends the edges of the letters with the surrounding pixels of color to eliminate jagged edges.

- **Noise**—This makes the shadow smoother, clumpier, or noisier. Drag the slider to add noise to the shadow.

- **Layer Knocks Out Drop Shadow**—This determines whether the shadow will be visible on a semitransparent layer. When the check box is selected, the type layer knocks out the shadow, so if you turn the layer-fill down, you can still see where the type cuts the shadow. If the check box is unselected and you turn the layer-fill down, as the type disappears, the shadow still shows fully—a shadow with no type. It is similar to a stencil.

4. When you are satisfied, click **OK**.

BEVEL AND EMBOSS TYPE

To create either beveling or embossing on type:

1. Select the layer containing the text to which you want to apply the effect.

2. Click **Layer**, click **Layer Style**, and then click **Bevel And Emboss**. The Layer Style dialog box appears. (You can also click the **Add A Layer Style** button  on the Layers palette and click **Bevel And Emboss** to display the Layer Style dialog box.)

3. The options for controlling the beveling and embossing are displayed in the dialog box, as shown in Figure 7-12. As you select options, you can view the results in the preview box (refer to Chapters 4 and 6 for additional information on the options):

- **Style** displays a menu of styles you can use: **Outer Bevel** forms the bevel beyond the edge of the original type; **Inner Bevel** forms the bevel from the edge of the text inwards; **Emboss** makes the type look as if it were stamped, or standing apart from the background; **Pillow Emboss** is a more rounded look; **Stroke Emboss** adds an edge to the outline.

- **Technique** displays three options: **Smooth** blurs the edges; **Chisel Hard** makes it look crisp and defined; **Chisel Soft** is less sharp than Chisel Hard but more defined than Smooth.

- **Depth** sets the depth of the bevel or embossing.

- **Direction** determines whether the surface of the type is up and rounded or down and indented.

- **Size** determines the size of the shading, that is, how deep into the text it is.

- **Soften** blurs the shaded part of the bevel or embossing.

- **Angle** establishes the degree of the light source and whether all the type has the same light source.

- **Altitude** determines how high the light source is.

- **Gloss Contour** displays a menu of options for the shape, or contour, of the bevel.

- **Anti-Aliased** smoothes the edges of the contour.

- **Highlight Mode** is applied to the highlights of the bevel or embossing. By default, this is set to **Screen**, and the default color is white.

Figure 7-12: The Bevel and Emboss effects can give your text depth and a more professional look.

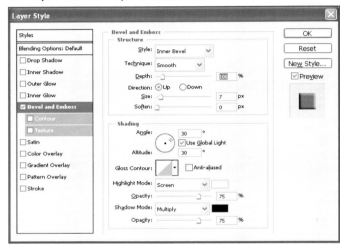

TIP

To copy an effect from one layer to another, arrange both layers in the Layers palette so that you can see them. Select the layer containing the desired effect. Click the **Layer Style** icon on the right side of the layer, press **ALT**, and drag the icon to the other layer in the Layers palette. If you don't press **ALT**, the effects will be moved from one layer to the other.

If your text does not conform to the path or if the path disappears, make sure you are on the right layer.

Figure 7-13: The inner glow effect makes your type look as if there were an inside source of light.

- **Opacity** is connected to Highlight mode and varies it. Drag the sliders to set the values.

- **Shadow Mode** is applied to the shadows of the bevel or embossing. By default, this is set to **Multiply**, and the default color is black.

- **Opacity** can be varied for the Shadow Mode. Drag the slider to set the values.

4. When you are satisfied, click **OK**.

MAKE TYPE GLOW INSIDE AND OUT

The inside glow and outside glow effects make your type look as if there were a light source either inside or behind the type.

1. Select the layer containing the text to which you want to apply the effect.

2. Click **Layer**, click **Layer Style**, and then click **Inner Glow**. The Layer Style dialog box appears. (You can also click the **Add A Layer Style** button ⬡ on the Layers palette, and then click **Inner Glow** to display its options on the Layer Style dialog box.)

3. The options for controlling the inside and outside glows are displayed on the dialog box, as shown in Figure 7-13. As you select options, you can view the results in the preview box. You can see that many of options are the same as with the drop shadow or bevel and emboss effects. Figure 7-13 shows the options unique to inner glow:

- **Noise** makes the glow harsher and clunkier. Drag the **Noise** slider to add more noise to the glow. Specify a value between 0 (no noise) and 100 (maximum noise).

- **Fill** for the glow can be solid, or you can select a graduated color scheme from the drop-down list. Click the color swatch to determine the color for the glow.

- **Technique** determines whether the effect is blurry or sharp.

- **Source** determines whether the light source is coming from the center of the type or from the inside edges.

- **Choke** increases or decreases the perimeter of the matte of the glow.

- **Size** defines the size of the glow.

- **Contour** pertains to the pattern of the fading of the glow.

- **Range** describes where the contour will be applied to the glow.

- **Jitter** increases or decreases the variations around the layer.

4. When you are satisfied, click **OK**.

Create Text Masks

You can use a text mask either to create a selection of type or to fill type with the background from one image or layer that you want to use on another image or layer. It is like making a cutout of one image to use in another.

1. In the Layers palette, select the layer that contains the image you want to use.

2. Select the **Horizontal Mask Type** tool or the **Vertical Mask Type** tool.

3. Set your formatting the way you want, as described previously in this chapter. Click the image to set the insertion point. The canvas will be filled with a protective red masking layer, as shown in Figure 7-14.

4. Type the words you want to mask, and then click **Commit**. You will see a selection of the text.

5. You can do several tasks, although you cannot edit the type as text at this point:

   ● Copy and paste the masked type to place it on its own layer without removing the type from the background image.

   ● While the copied type is selected, it can be dragged to another position, copied, filled, or treated like another selection.

The text shown in Figure 7-15 has been surrounded with a transform bounding box so that it can be enlarged or reshaped.

How to...

- 🔵 *Resizing an Image for Printing*
- *Print Images with a Desktop Printer*
- 🔵 *Printing a Single Copy of a Page*
- *Print Vector-Based Graphics*
- *Use Color Management when Printing*
- 🔵 *Printing a Part of an Image*
- 🔵 *Using a Proof Setup*
- *Create a Contact Sheet*
- *Create a Picture Package*
- 🔵 *Creating a Digital QuickMat*
- *Use the Save As Command*
- 🔵 *Saving a Document*
- *Save a Layered File*
- *Add File Information and Metadata*
- *Create a Digital Copyright*
- *Save Document Metadata as a Template*
- *Import Document Metadata*
- *Create a PDF Presentation*

Chapter 8
Printing and Exporting Images

After you use the Photoshop CS2 toolset to hone your image to perfection, you're ready to print your image or save it for future use. In this chapter you'll learn valuable information about printing and saving images. You'll learn to save your images as uncompressed files and as Photoshop (PSD) files.

You'll also learn to save a document while preserving layers. You'll learn to print your images on a desktop inkjet printer and use the powerful Print With Preview command to resize the document and set other parameters within a single dialog box.

Print Your Work

Editing your image and applying special effects puts your creative muse to work. However, Photoshop also lets you be creative on the print end. You can print your image to your local printer or create a picture package that includes several different sizes of the same image on a single sheet.

QUICKSTEPS

RESIZING AN IMAGE FOR PRINTING

You can resize an image prior to printing. If the image is already at the desired aspect ratio, however, you can save yourself some time by using the Print With Preview command (see "Use the Print With Preview command").

1. Click **Image** and click **Image Size**. The Image Size dialog box appears.

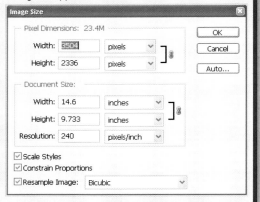

2. In the Document Size section, type the desired values for the **Width** and **Height** fields. As a rule, you'll type a value matching the document size to the paper size in your printer's paper tray.

3. Accept the default document resolution or enter a different value in the **Resolution** field. You should not exceed the current document resolution; otherwise, pixelation (the image appears to be small blocks of color rather than a smooth continuous blend of colors) may occur when Photoshop resamples the image. You can select a lower resolution to match your desktop printer.

4. Click **OK** to size the image.

When you print an image from within Photoshop, you can print a single image, print multiple images, preview an image prior to printing, and more. From within the Page Setup dialog box, you can specify the size and orientation of the printed image. If you prefer to set all parameters for printing within a single dialog box, however, you can do so using the Print With Preview command.

Print Images with a Desktop Printer

One of the easiest ways to see the fruits of your creative labor in Photoshop is to print a copy of the image on your local printer. If you own a printer that is capable of using photo-quality paper, you can create an image suitable for framing on glossy or matte paper. The results can be stunning, especially if you own one of the new six-, seven-, or eight-color inkjet printers. These gems are capable of mixing about any color you can throw at them. If your monitor is properly calibrated, what you see on the screen is what you'll take out of the printer tray.

USE THE PAGE SETUP COMMAND

1. Click **File** and click **Page Setup**. The Page Setup dialog box appears.

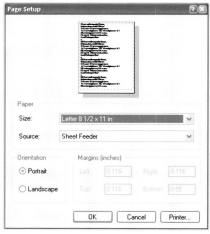

2. Click the **Size** down arrow, and select the desired paper size from the drop-down list.

3. Click the **Source** down arrow, and select the paper source from the drop-down list.

When you enter a different resolution, deselect the **Resample Image** check box. If you don't, Photoshop will change the pixel dimensions of the image, which involves interpolation when redrawing the image. When Photoshop redraws pixels, image degradation may occur and the file size will increase. When you deselect the Resample Image check box and change image resolution, the image print-size is changed accordingly. For example, if you have an 800 × 600-pixel image at 72 ppi (pixels per inch), the document will print at 11.111 × 8.333 inches. If you change the resolution with the Resample Image check box deselected and change the image resolution to 300 ppi, the pixel dimensions are still 800 × 600, but the document will print at 2.66 × 2 inches.

TIP

If you're printing an image on photo-size paper with perforations, you can set the Crop tool's width, height, and resolution to match the paper size. Resize the image to the approximate size of the paper, and then use the Crop tool to crop the image to the exact paper size. See Chapter 6 for more information on the Crop tool.

4. In the Orientation section, click **Portrait** or **Landscape**. This determines how your image will be mapped to the printed page. Click **Portrait** if your image is taller than it is wide; click **Landscape** if your image is wider than it is tall.

5. Click **Printer** to open the second Page Setup dialog box.

6. Click the **Name** down arrow, and select the desired printer from the drop-down list.

7. Click **Network** to select a printer on your network.

8. Click **Properties** to set properties for the selected printer. This opens a dialog box from which you specify settings for the selected printer. The illustration shows the Epson Stylus Photo 1280 Properties dialog box.

9. Specify the settings for your printer.

10. Click **OK** to exit the second Page Setup dialog box, and then click **OK** again to exit the first Page Setup dialog box.

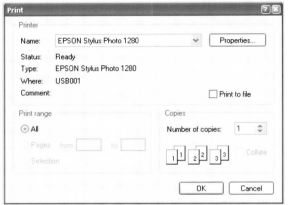

PRINT AN IMAGE

After setting up the page, you're ready to print the image.

1. Click **File** and click **Print**. The Print dialog box appears.

2. If needed, click the **Name** down arrow, and select the desired printer from the drop-down list. This step is not necessary if you've already invoked the Page Setup command.

3. Click **Properties** to reveal the dialog box for the selected printer's properties. This step is not necessary if you've already invoked the Page Setup command.

4. In the Copies area, type the number of copies you want to print. Alternatively, you can click the spinner buttons to set the value.

5. Click **OK** to print the document.

USE THE PRINT WITH PREVIEW COMMAND

When you use the Print With Preview command, the dialog box provides you with a visual display of what the printed image will look like on the selected media. You can also resize or reposition your image, add a border, and more when using this command.

1. Click **File** and click **Print With Preview**. The Print With Preview dialog box appears.

2. Drag one of the corner handles of the image preview to rescale the image. The white area around the image thumbnail represents the printer media size.

NOTE

The Print dialog box shows a Page Range section and a Collate check box. Photoshop does not support multipage documents. These items are carryovers from the generic Windows Print dialog box.

NOTE

If the image is bigger than the currently selected printer media, the handles will not be visible. Click the **Center Image** option to deselect it (it is selected by default), and then drag the image into the window until you can see the top or bottom border. Move your pointer over the top or bottom border of the bounding box. When the pointer becomes a vertical line with a dual-headed arrow, drag to resize the image.

NOTE

The options in the Show More Options section are discussed in the "Use Color Management When Printing" section later in the chapter.

TIP

When you have an image such as a panoramic landscape with subtle colors, consider using one of the third-party fine art papers, such as those manufactured by Moab Paper Company (www.moabpaper.com). Images printed on fine art paper often resemble paintings. As an added bonus, most fine art papers are acid-free, which means they have a much longer life than conventional papers.

3. Accept the default **Position** options, or click the **Center Image** check box to deselect the option. If you deselect this option, the Top and Left text fields become available, enabling you to enter the value you want the image offset from the top and left borders of the page. Alternatively, with Center Image deselected, you can drag the thumbnail preview to determine where the image will appear on the printed page.

4. In the Scaled Print Size area, accept the default value, which is **100** percent; or type a different value if you manually scaled the image preview. Alternatively, you can select from the following options:

   - **Scale** enables you to type a value to which you want the image scaled. This is a percentage of the image's original size.

   - **Scale To Fit Media** scales the document to fit the printer media.

   - **Width** enables you to enter a value to which you want the width of the document sized. After entering a value, the height of the document is scaled proportionately.

   - **Height** enables you to enter a value to which you want the height of the document sized. After entering a value, the width of the document is scaled proportionately.

   - **Show Bounding Box** (selected by default) displays a bounding box around the image thumbnail with four handles that you use to resize the document.

   - **Print Selected Area** becomes available if you select a region of the document with one of the marquee select tools. This technique will be covered in the section "Printing Part of an Image" later in this chapter.

5. After setting print options, do one of the following:

   - Click **Print** to print the image.

   - Click **Cancel** to cancel printing.

   - Click **Done** to exit the dialog box and preserve the current options.

   - Press **ALT** and click **Print One** to print one copy of the image with the current settings.

   - Press **ALT** and click **Reset** to reset the dialog box to the default settings for the image.

   - Press **ALT** and click **Remember** to save the current print options without exiting the dialog box.

TIP

Often, what you see on the screen isn't what you get from the printer. You can ensure better results if you calibrate your monitor. You can use the Adobe Gamma utility, which is shipped with Photoshop, to calibrate your monitor or purchase third-party calibration software and hardware. The hardware—a device called a colorimeter—is attached to your monitor and analyzes the colors generated by the software. The software then creates a profile, which ensures that what you see in Photoshop is what you get when you print your images.

NOTE

You can also include vector data when you save an image with vector-based objects in EPS (Encapsulated PostScript) format.

Print Vector-Based Graphics

When you create a document with vector-based graphics, such as shapes or text, you can print the image to a PostScript printer, such as an Adobe Acrobat PDF file. When you print to a PostScript printer, Photoshop sends the vector information in the form of separate images for each type layer and each vector shape. This enables the vector-based graphics to be printed at full resolution regardless of the resolution of the background image.

1. Click **File** and click **Page Setup**. The Page Setup dialog box appears.
2. Click **Printer** to select a PostScript printer and specify other print options.
3. Click **OK** to exit the Page Setup dialog box.
4. Click **File** and click **Print With Preview**. The Print dialog box appears.
5. Click the **More Options** button.
6. Open the drop-down list beneath the thumbnail image, and click **Output**.
7. Click the **Include Vector Data** check box.
8. If necessary, click the **Encoding** down arrow, and click a PostScript encoding option.
9. Click **Print**.

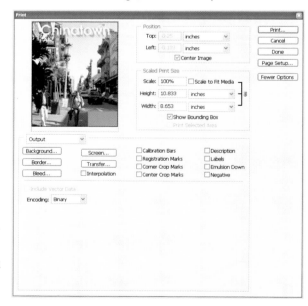

Use Color Management When Printing

When you print an image, you can let the printer take the reins and perform color management, or you can override the printer's color management by specifying a color management profile. A color management profile describes the color space of a device, such as a monitor or

PRINTING PART OF AN IMAGE

At times, you may want to print part of an image without altering the original using the Crop tool. You can easily print the desired portion of an image by selecting the area and then invoking the Print With Preview command.

PRINT A SELECTION

1. Click the **Rectangular Marquee** tool, and drag inside the image to define the area you want to print.

2. Click **File** and click **Print With Preview**. The Print dialog box appears.
3. Click the **Print Selected Area** check box.
4. Click **Print**.

printer, and the color space of the actual document. Color management profiles are also created by third-party paper manufacturers for the color characteristics of popular printers to ensure accurate color output of the printed image.

A color management profile is embedded with the document. You decide whether to accept the embedded color profile or to use the specified Photoshop color profile. A device color profile does not change the document color values; it is merely a method used by the device to properly interpret color values in the document.

1. Click **File** and click **Print With Preview**. The Print dialog box appears.
2. If the drop-down list below the thumbnail image doesn't read "Color Management," click the down arrow and click **Color Management**. (If this option is not available, click the **More Options** button.)
3. In the Print area, located beneath the Color Management drop-down list, accept the default **Document** option to print the document with the color profile currently assigned to the document.
4. If necessary, click **Page Setup** to access the Page Setup dialog box; and select a printer, media size, image orientation, and so on.
5. Click the **Color Handling** down arrow, and click **Let Photoshop Determine Colors**.
6. Click the **Printer Profile** down arrow, and click an option as shown in the illustration. Your list will vary depending on the devices you have attached to your system.

Working RGB - sRGB IEC61966-2.1
Working CMYK - U.S. Web Coated (SWOP) v2
Working Gray - Dot Gain 20%
Lab Color
Adobe RGB (1998)
Apple RGB
ColorMatch RGB
sRGB IEC61966-2.1
Europe ISO Coated FOGRA27
Euroscale Coated v2
Euroscale Uncoated v2
Japan Color 2001 Coated
Japan Color 2001 Uncoated
Japan Color 2002 Newspaper
Japan Standard v2
Japan Web Coated (Ad)
U.S. Sheetfed Coated v2
U.S. Sheetfed Uncoated v2
U.S. Web Coated (SWOP) v2
U.S. Web Uncoated v2
Dot Gain 10%
Dot Gain 15%
Dot Gain 20%
Dot Gain 25%
Dot Gain 30%
Gray Gamma 1.8

TIP

Open a digital image, click **File**, and click **Print Online** to order prints online using Adobe Services. You can order prints as large as 30 x 20 inches, provided the image you want printed contains sufficient resolution.

QUICK**FACTS**

USING A PROOF SETUP

You can simulate how the image will look when printed with the International Color Consortium (ICC) profiles.

To view a soft proof on your computer monitor:

1. Click **View** and click **Proof Setup**.
2. Click the **Proof Setup** down arrow, and select a profile.
3. Click **Custom** to use a profile other than the presets.
4. To view your image with the profile you selected, click **View** and click **Proof Colors**. The monitor will change to show how the image will look when printed with the selected profile. If the colors differ greatly, you can use adjustment layers until the soft proof and the image appear the same.

NOTE

Print a hard proof by following the "Use Color Management When Printing" section of this chapter. In the Proof area, click **Proof**. The profile to the right of the option is the same profile you clicked from the Proof Setup drop-down list. Click **Print**.

7. Accept the default **Rendering Intent** option. Alternatively, click the **Rendering Intent** down arrow, and click one of the following options:

- **Perceptual** attempts to preserve color values to produce a print with colors that appear natural to the human eye. This rendering option may change color values; it is useful for photographic images that may contain out-of-gamut colors.

- **Saturation** renders a print with vivid saturated colors. This rendering option will change color values; it is especially useful for documents that contain graphics, such as graphs or bar charts, where visual impact is more important than preserving the relationship between colors.

- **Relative Colormetric** renders an image by comparing the extreme highlight of the image's color space to the color space of the selected color profile. This option shifts out-of-gamut colors to the closest reproducible color in the destination color space; it preserves more of the image's original colors than the Perceptual option does.

- **Absolute Colormetric** does not alter image colors that fall within the destination gamut. This rendering option clips out-of-gamut colors and does not scale colors to the destination white point. Use this color option to maintain color accuracy while creating a proof to simulate the output of a particular device. Note that this rendering option may not preserve the color relationship between colors.

8. Click the **Black Point Compensation** check box (selected by default) to deselect this option. This option preserves the shadow detail in your image by mimicking the full dynamic range of your printer.

9. Click **Print** to print the document.

Create a Contact Sheet

If you're a digital photographer, you need to download your pictures from a media card to your hard drive before editing them in Photoshop. Many digital photographers archive their original images to CD or DVD for future use. Before archiving the images to disk, you can create a contact sheet, which can be used to identify the images stored on the disk. Figure 8-1 shows a sample contact sheet.

Figure 8-1: Create a contact sheet of images stored in a folder.

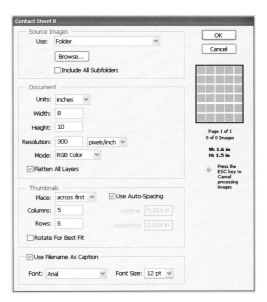

1. Click **File**, click **Automate**, and click **Contact Sheet II**. The Contact Sheet II dialog box appears.

2. Click the **Use** drop-down list, and then click one of the following options:

   ● **Current Open Documents** creates a contact sheet using the documents you currently have open in Photoshop.

   ● **Folder** creates a contact sheet using images stored in a folder. If you click this option, the Browse button becomes available, which you use to navigate to the desired folder.

   ● **Selected Images From Bridge** creates a contact sheet using the images currently selected in the Adobe Bridge (see Chapter 1 for more information on working with the Bridge).

3. If you clicked Folder, click the **Browse** button and navigate to the folder that contains the images you want to print.

4. In the Document area, specify the size of the media to which you'll be printing the contact sheet, as well as the resolution at which the contact sheet thumbnails will be printed. If your printer uses default margins, the default 8 × 10-inch size works well with 8½ × 11-inch paper.

5. Type a value in the **Resolution** field. This is the resolution at which the thumbnails will be created and therefore printed. The default value of **300** pixels will give you excellent detail. Alternatively, you can type a lower resolution. Note that if you change the resolution, the resolution you specify only applies to the contact sheet and will not change the resolution of the original images.

6. Click the **Mode** down arrow, and click one of the following color mode options: **Grayscale**, **RGB Color**, **CMYK Color**, or **Lab Color**.

TIP

You can also access the Contact Sheet II dialog box from within the Adobe Bridge by clicking the thumbnails of the images you want to include with the contact sheet, and then clicking **Tools**, clicking **Photoshop**, and clicking **Contact Sheet II**.

If your images have long file names, select a small font size; otherwise, the caption will be truncated.

TIP

Store your contact sheets in a loose-leaf binder for ready reference when you need to find a specific image.

7. Accept the **Flatten All Layers** option (it is selected by default) to create a composite thumbnail of all layers.

8. In the Thumbnails area, click the **Place** down arrow, and then click **Across First** or **Down First**.

9. Accept the default **Use Auto-Spacing** option, and Photoshop evenly spaces the thumbnails across rows and columns. If you deselect this option, the Vertical and Horizontal text boxes become available, enabling you to enter the values by which you want the thumbnails spaced.

10. Type a value in the **Rows** and **Columns** text boxes to determine how many thumbnails will be placed in each row and how many columns will comprise the contact sheet. The number of rows and columns you specify ultimately determines the size of each contact sheet image.

11. Click the **Rotate For Best Fit** check box to have thumbnails rotated for best fit. This option will rotate any portrait thumbnails to landscape mode, which might make them difficult to view if you pack several rows and columns of thumbnails on a contact sheet.

12. Accept the default **Use Filename As Caption** option, and Photoshop will list the applicable file name beneath the thumbnail. If you deselect this option, the contact sheet will display only images.

13. Click the **Font** down arrow, and select the font that will be used to display the caption text.

14. Click the **Font Size** down arrow, and select a size from the drop-down list. Alternatively, you can enter a value in this field.

15. Click **OK** to process the contact sheet. Note that this may take some time, depending on the number of images you are committing to the contact sheet. The contact sheet is redisplayed in the Photoshop document pane. You will have multiple contact sheets if you selected more images than will fit on a single page.

16. Select each contact sheet in turn, click **File**, and click **Print**. Click **OK** to print.

NOTE

Alternatively, you can click a thumbnail in the Adobe Bridge, click **Tools**, click **Photoshop**, and then click **Picture Package**.

Create a Picture Package

If you use Photoshop to edit photos for clients or to create images for friends and relatives, you can create a picture package. A picture package prints more than one copy of an image on a sheet. You can mix different sizes, for example, one 5 × 7-inch and two 3 × 5-inch photos on one 8 × 10 sheet. Figure 8-2 illustrates a picture package.

1. Open the desired image.

2. Click **File**, click **Automate**, and click **Picture Package**. The Picture Package dialog box is displayed.

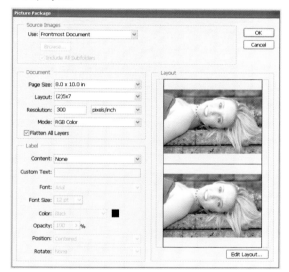

3. Accept the default **Foremost Image** option to create a picture package from the currently active document. Alternatively, you can click the **Use** down arrow, and click one of the following:

   - **File** to browse to a file from which to print a picture package

   - **Folder** to browse to a folder of images and print one picture package for each file in the folder

   - **Selected Images From Bridge** to print a picture package for each image currently selected in the Bridge

TIP

To preserve your photos, consider purchasing a fixative, which you spray over the printed image. The fixative protects the image from fading, smudging, and fingerprints. Purchase a clear fixative, such as Krylon Preserve It digital photo and paper protectant (www.krylon.com). It is available in both gloss and matte finish.

4. Click the **Page Size** down arrow, and click the desired size from the drop-down list.

5. Click the **Layout** down arrow, and click the desired layout from the drop-down list.

6. Type the desired print resolution in the Resolution field. Specify a resolution no greater than the resolution of the image for which you're creating the picture package.

7. In the Label area, click the **Content** down arrow, and click an option from the drop-down list. Note that the last four options are derived from the file's metadata. If you click **Custom Text**, the Custom Text field becomes available, enabling you to enter the text you want displayed as an image caption.

8. If you click one of the caption options, select the remaining options for the **Font**, **Font Size**, **Color**, **Opacity**, **Position**, and **Rotate** fields.

9. Click **OK** to create the picture package.

10. Click **File**, click **Print**, and then click **OK** to print the picture package.

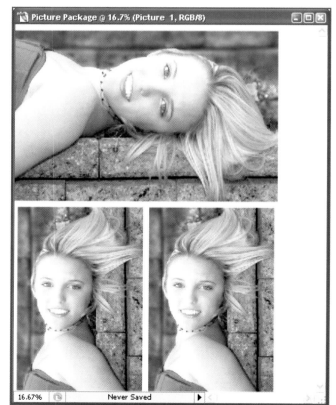

Figure 8-2: You can create a picture package with multiple images on a single sheet.

CREATING A DIGITAL QUICKMAT

Many of the images you'll create in Photoshop will be keepsakes you'll want to print on high-quality paper and then frame. When you frame a photograph, adding a matte greatly enhances the look of the photo. Professional frame shops charge a substantial fee for cutting mattes to fit your photographs; however, now there is a way to create digital mattes for your images. QuickMats 2 is an application that you can use to create a digital matte for any image. The application ships with matte presets that you open in Photoshop. After you have a matte open, you add the image to it. In the Layers palette, drag the image layer to the bottom of the stack. Then use actions that come with the QuickMats 2 application to select an individual matte. After you select the inner or outer matte, you can sample a color from within the image and apply it to the matte. This makes it possible for you to direct the viewer's attention to a specific part of the image. You can also apply a texture to the matte to make it resemble leather, canvas, lace, and so on. After you frame an image matted with this system, you'll have a hard time telling it from an image that was matted conventionally. Your viewers will have a hard time noticing the difference as well. If you print and frame a lot of images, Digital QuickMats 2 will save you the expense of having mattes cut at a professional frame shop.

Save Images

After editing an image in Photoshop, your next step is to save the file. You can save an image to most of the currently available image file formats. If you're going to edit the image at a future date, save the image in Photoshop's native PSD format to preserve the layers. You can also save the image in another format that supports layers for editing in another "layer-friendly" image-editing application, such as Corel Photo-Paint.

Use the Save As Command

After editing a file in Photoshop, you may want to save the file using a different image format. If you're a digital photographer and you edit Camera RAW images in Photoshop, this will almost always be the case. You can save an edited image using any of the popular image file formats (found in the Format drop-down list) for print or monitor display.

1. Click **File** and click **Save As**. The Save As dialog box appears.

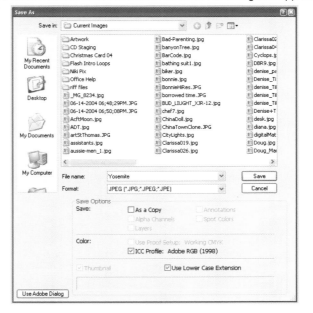

SAVING A DOCUMENT

When you edit an image in Photoshop, you'll want to save it. You can save the file using the image's native format. If the image's native format does not support layers, however, you'll need to flatten the layers before you can save the file in its native format.

1. Open the desired image file.

2. Edit the file using the techniques discussed in Chapter 6.

3. If necessary, flatten the image.

4. Click **File** and click **Save**.

NOTE

A detailed discussion of each file format is beyond the scope of this book. For in-depth information on each file format, press **F1** to summon Photoshop's online Help.

2. Enter the desired file name.

3. Click the **Format** down arrow, and click a format from the drop-down list.

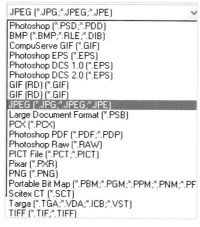

JPEG (*.JPG;*.JPEG;*.JPE)

Photoshop (*.PSD;*.PDD)
BMP (*.BMP;*.RLE;*.DIB)
CompuServe GIF (*.GIF)
Photoshop EPS (*.EPS)
Photoshop DCS 1.0 (*.EPS)
Photoshop DCS 2.0 (*.EPS)
GIF (RD) (*.GIF)
GIF (RD) (*.GIF)
JPEG (*.JPG;*.JPEG;*.JPE)
Large Document Format (*.PSB)
PCX (*.PCX)
Photoshop PDF (*.PDF;*.PDP)
Photoshop Raw (*.RAW)
PICT File (*.PCT;*.PICT)
Pixar (*.PXR)
PNG (*.PNG)
Portable Bit Map (*.PBM;*.PGM;*.PPM;*.PNM;*.PF
Scitex CT (*.SCT)
Targa (*.TGA;*.VDA;*.ICB;*.VST)
TIFF (*.TIF;*.TIFF)

4. Click **Save**. Depending on the image format, an additional dialog box appears enabling you to specify options for the file format in which you are saving the document. The following illustration shows the TIFF Options dialog box.

5. If necessary, click **OK** to exit the selected format's Options dialog box, and click **Save** to save the file.

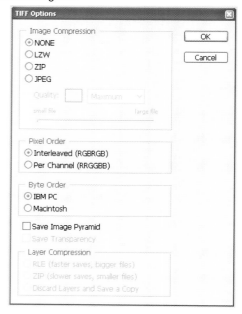

Save a Layered File

If you add layers when editing an image, you can preserve the layers when you save the file. You can save a layered file in any format that supports layers; however, if you're going to edit the document exclusively in Photoshop, save the layered file using Photoshop's native PSD file format.

1. Click **File** and click **Save As**. The Save As dialog box appears.

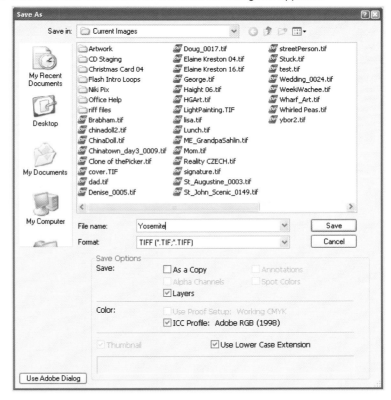

2. Type a file name for the document.

NOTE

When saving an image with layers using the Photoshop PSD format, a dialog box appears with the **Maximize Compatibility** check box selected. It is recommended that you leave this check box selected, as it saves the document in a format that enables you to edit it in other applications that support the PSD format. If you deselect this option and your image has adjustment layers or options not supported by other applications, these layers or features may not be available in these applications.

TIP

Keywords can be used to search for a document. Open the Adobe Bridge, click the **Metadata** tab, and then click the **triangle** icon in the upper-right corner of the Keywords tab. Click **Find** from the drop-down list to open the Find dialog box. In the Criteria area, click the first down arrow, and then click **Keywords**. Replace "Enter Text" with the keyword(s) you want to use as search criteria.

3. Click the **Format** down arrow, and click the desired file format from the drop-down list. To preserve layers, save the file in one of the following formats: Photoshop (*PSD, PDD), Photoshop PDF (PDF, PDP), or TIFF (*TIFF, *TIF). Note that the second format is Adobe's PDF (Portable Document Format), which enables you to send your images as a PDF document that can be viewed by anyone who has the Adobe Reader.

```
Photoshop (*.PSD;*.PDD)
BMP (*.BMP;*.RLE;*.DIB)
CompuServe GIF (*.GIF)
Photoshop EPS (*.EPS)
Photoshop DCS 1.0 (*.EPS)
Photoshop DCS 2.0 (*.EPS)
GIF (RD) (*.GIF)
GIF (RD) (*.GIF)
JPEG (*.JPG;*.JPEG;*.JPE)
Large Document Format (*.PSB)
PCX (*.PCX)
Photoshop PDF (*.PDF;*.PDP)
Photoshop Raw (*.RAW)
PICT File (*.PCT;*.PICT)
Pixar (*.PXR)
PNG (*.PNG)
Portable Bit Map (*.PBM;*.PGM;*.PPM;*.PNM;*.PFN
Scitex CT (*.SCT)
Targa (*.TGA;*.VDA;*.ICB;*.VST)
TIFF (*.TIF;*.TIFF)
```

4. In the Save Options area, click **Save As A Copy** to save a copy of the original document. When you click this option, the file name of the document is appended with "Copy." This option is not necessary if you've given the document a different name from the original file name in step 2.

5. In the Color area, click one of the following options: **Use Proof Setup (Working CMYK)** or **ICC Profile [Profile currently assigned to image]**. Note that one or both of these options may not be available depending on the file type you use to save the document.

6. Click **Save** to save the document with layers intact.

Add File Information and Metadata

When you save an image you've edited in Photoshop, you can add information to the file that can be read by other Photoshop users. In addition, some of the information you enter as metadata (information about the document that is embedded with the document) can be viewed by users who access the image's Properties dialog box after selecting the file outside of Photoshop.

1. Open the desired image.

NOTE

If you save the document as a Photoshop PSD file, the metadata appears in different tabs when users view the document's properties. The following illustration shows the Properties dialog box (as viewed with the Windows XP operating system) for a PSD file.

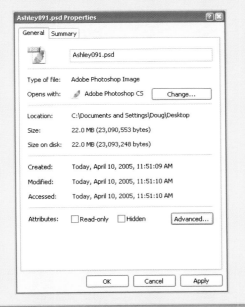

TIP

Click the other section titles to view other file information, such as the digital camera information, the EXIF data (data created by a digital camera, such as camera model, exposure setting, and so on), and more. You can also enter metadata in the Origin section, such as the date the image was created and the creator.

2. Click **File** and click **File Info**. The file information dialog box appears.

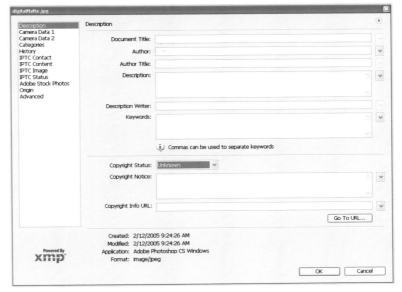

3. In the **Description** area, type a title for the document, the author's name, a description of the image, and keywords in the applicable fields.

4. Click **OK** to add the metadata to the document.

Create a Digital Copyright

When you create a digital copyright, it appears in the Summary dialog box when the image's properties are accessed. Other Photoshop users can also view your digital copyright by clicking **File** and clicking **File Info**.

1. Open the image you want to copyright.

2. Click **File** and click **File Info**. The file information dialog box appears.

3. In the Description area, enter the desired metadata, as outlined in the previous section (see "Add File Information and Metadata").

4. Click the **Copyright Status** down arrow, and then click **Copyrighted** from the drop-down list.

NOTE

Metadata for an image thumbnail you select in the Adobe Bridge is displayed in the Metadata tab. In fact, you can select several photos and then type copyright information or other information, such as your name and address, in the applicable section of the Metadata tab, and the information will be applied to the selected images. A pencil icon appears to the right of any metadata item that you can edit.

5. In the Copyright Notice text box, type the desired information, for example, Copyright 2005, Doug Sahlin, All rights reserved.

6. In the Copyright Info URL text box, type the URL to the copyright owner's Web site (if applicable). After entering this information, the Go To URL button becomes active. Other Photoshop users can click this button to view the URL while they are online.

7. Click **OK** to apply the digital copyright.

Save Document Metadata as a Template

If you frequently use the same metadata, you can save it as a template. After saving metadata as a template, it appears on a list in the file information dialog box.

1. Open an image file.

2. Click **File** and click **File Info**.

3. Type the information you want to save as a metadata template.

4. Click the **Options** icon in the upper-right corner of the dialog box, and click **Save Metadata Template**. The Save Metadata Template dialog box appears.

5. Type a name for the metadata template, and then click **Save**.

Import Document Metadata

After you save a metadata template, it appears on a list that you can access from within the file information dialog box. You can apply the template metadata to any document.

1. Open the desired file.
2. Click **File** and click **File Info**. The file information dialog box appears.
3. Click the **Options** icon in the upper-right corner of the dialog box to reveal the menu pictured in the illustration. Any metadata templates you've created appear at the top of the list.
4. Click the desired template to fill the applicable fields with metadata from the template. If desired, you can edit the metadata.
5. Click **OK** to apply the metadata to the document.

My copyright info
Save Metadata Template...
Delete Metadata Template...
Show Templates...

Create a PDF Presentation

You can quickly create a PDF presentation using the PDF Presentation command, which enables you to create a PDF slide show, including the option to add transitions between slides and to specify which images are used to create the PDF document. A PDF presentation is viewed in Full Screen mode without the Acrobat interface.

1. Open the desired files.
2. Click **File**, click **Automate**, and then click **PDF Presentation**. The PDF Presentation dialog box appears.

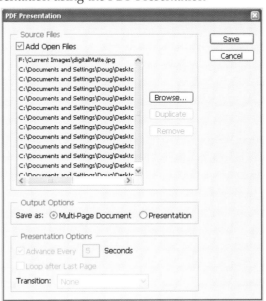

NOTE

You view the PDF slide show using the full version of Adobe Acrobat or using Adobe Reader, which can be downloaded for free from Adobe's web site.

3. Click **Add Open Files** to include all open files in the PDF.

4. In the Output Options area, click **Presentation**.

5. In the Presentation Options area, accept the default **Advance Every** option, which automatically advances to the next page after the number of seconds entered in the adjacent text field. The default is five seconds, but you can change the default by typing the desired value. Alternatively, you can click the **Advance Every** check box to disable this option, whereupon viewers will have to click the **DOWN ARROW** key to advance to the next slide.

6. Click the **Loop After Last Page** check box to loop the PDF presentation back to the first page after the last page is displayed.

7. Click the **Transition** down arrow, and select a transition option from the drop-down list.

8. Click **Save**. The Save dialog box appears.

9. Type a name for the slide show.

10. Click **Save** again. The Save Adobe PDF dialog box appears.

11. Accept the default options and then click **Save PDF**.

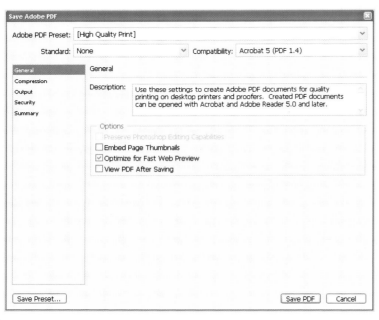

| Blinds Horizontal |
| Blinds Vertical |
| Box In |
| Box Out |
| Dissolve |
| Glitter Down |
| Glitter Right |
| Glitter Right-Down |
| None |
| Random Transition |
| Split Horizontal In |
| Split Horizontal Out |
| Split Vertical In |
| Split Vertical Out |
| Wipe Down |
| Wipe Left |
| Wipe Right |
| Wipe Up |

NOTE

The options in this dialog box are specific to Adobe Acrobat and therefore are beyond the scope of this book. For more information on the settings in this dialog box, see *How To Do Everything with Adobe Acrobat 7.0* or *Adobe Acrobat 7.0 QuickSteps*, both of which are published by McGraw-Hill Osborne.

How to...

- Optimize Using the Save For Web Dialog Box
- Making Part of an Image Transparent
- Work with Image Maps
- Using Layers to Create Image Maps
- Set Output Options
- Working with Rollovers and States
- Create an Animation
- Optimizing Animations
- Importing Files and Folders as Animations
- Slice an Image
- Saving Sliced Images

Chapter 9
Preparing Your Images for the Web

This chapter shows you how to use Photoshop's and ImageReady's tools for preparing images for display on the World Wide Web. You will learn how to optimize images and create animations, image maps, and rollover effects using Photoshop and ImageReady.

Optimize Images for the Web

Images for use on the Web need to be efficient—the file size needs to be as small as possible without a noticeable loss in image quality. Smaller file sizes result in images that are transmitted and displayed faster, thereby reducing the time it takes a web page to load. Three factors determine the file size of an image (for a set width and height): the file format (usually GIF, JPEG, or PNG), the number of colors (determined, in part, by the file format chosen), and the resolution of the image (in pixels per inch). Of the file types, GIF and JPEG formats are the most common. PNG is not as widely supported, although newer browsers support it. Characteristics of these common file types include:

9

TIP

The Save For Web dialog box automatically converts the image resolution to 72 pixels per inch (ppi), long considered the highest resolution needed for web work. If you wish to use a different image resolution, you must use Save As instead of Save For Web.

NOTE

When you save an image for the Web, you should first resize the image to Web-friendly dimensions whereby the width in the horizontal image or the height in a vertical image does not exceed 600 pixels.

TIP

The display option tabs provide multiple views of the image so that you can visually judge the effect of different optimization settings. You can display up to four versions of the image, each with different optimization settings.

- **GIF (Graphic Interchange Format)** images use an indexed palette of a maximum of 256 colors. Images with large areas of solid color and sharp detail work best as GIFs. GIF also supports transparency, allowing the area under the transparent portions of the GIF to be visible.

- **JPEG (Joint Photographic Experts Group)** format compresses an image to reduce the file size. When images are compressed in the JPEG format, data is lost—specifically, similar colors are removed from the image during compression. The amount of data lost depends on the amount of compression applied. JPEG supports 24-bit color, which yields approximately 16 million colors.

- **PNG (Portable Network Graphic)** comes in two varieties: PNG-8, which is similar to GIF; and PNG-24, which is similar to JPEG but uses lossless compression (no colors are removed).

You set the file type, number of colors, and resolution when you save images.

Optimize Using the Save For Web Dialog Box

Photoshop gives you two methods for saving images for the Web. The first is to use the Save As option in the File menu and select either the CompuServe GIF or JPEG formats. (This method is not available in ImageReady.) However, a more complete set of options is available using the Save For Web dialog box.

1. With an image open in Photoshop, click **File** and then click **Save For Web**. The Save For Web dialog box appears, as shown in Figure 9-1.

2. Depending on your image type, read one of the following sections to learn how to optimize your image. The optimization options vary by file type.

Figure 9-1: This Save For Web dialog box shows the 2-Up tab selected.

The Slice Select tool selects slices in the current image

The Zoom tool changes the magnification

Set the number of optimization versions displayed

The Hand tool moves the image in the selected window

The Eyedropper tool selects a color

Shows the color selected by the Eyedropper

Shows or hides slice borders

Preview the image with the selected optimization options

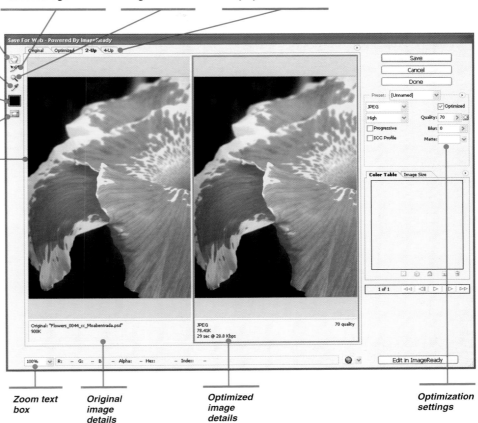

Zoom text box

Original image details

Optimized image details

Optimization settings

TIP

Not all of Photoshop's editing options are available in indexed color mode, so it can be advantageous to work in RGB mode and then convert the image to indexed color when it is saved. Photoshop will convert the image to indexed color when the image is saved as a GIF or PNG-8.

NOTE

An *algorithm* is a procedure or formula for solving a problem. Photoshop uses algorithms for color reduction and dithering, among other things.

OPTIMIZE A GIF OR PNG-8 IMAGE

GIF and PNG-8 images are similar and use an indexed color palette. The optimization options are shown in Figure 9-2.

MAKING PART OF AN IMAGE TRANSPARENT

With GIF, PNG-8, and PNG-24 images, you can select a color to be transparent in the final image. This is commonly done when you're displaying a web page image over a web page with a colored background. Choose the same color for the transparency in the image as the background color of the web page, and the image appears to be part of the background.

SELECT A COLOR TO BE TRANSPARENT

1. If your image is not in indexed color mode, click **Image**, click **Mode**, and then click **Indexed Color**. The Indexed Color dialog box appears.

2. Click the **Palette** down arrow, and click **Custom**.

   -Or-

   If your image is already in indexed color mode, click **Image**, click **Mode**, and then click **Color Table**. In either case, the Color Table dialog box appears.

3. Click the **Eyedropper** tool and then click the color in the image that you want to be transparent. The corresponding color swatch in the Color Table becomes transparent.

4. Click **OK** to close the Color Table dialog box. If necessary, click **OK** again to close the Indexed Color dialog box. The image will appear unchanged in Photoshop; however, the transparency will be apparent when you add the image to a web page.

Figure 9-2: These are the optimization options for GIF and PNG-8 images.

Use Color Reduction Algorithm to select the type of color palette

Use Optimized File Format to select the file format

Colors sets the number of colors in the image

Lossy sets the degree of color reduction

Saved Sets Of Optimized Settings contains preconfigured optimization settings

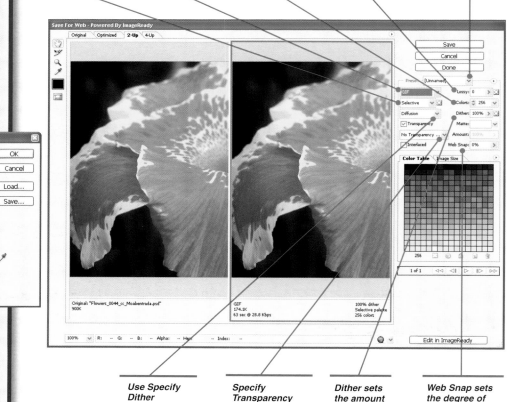

Use Specify Dither Algorithm to select the type of dither

Specify Transparency Dither Algorithm to select the type of transparency

Dither sets the amount of dither to apply

Web Snap sets the degree of matching to the Web-Safe palette

Dithering is a technique that Photoshop uses to combine pixels of different colors to create new colors that are unavailable in the selected color table. Dithering is used to prevent banding and to ensure smooth color blending in images.

TABLE 9-1: COLOR REDUCTION ALGORITHMS

NAME	WHAT IT DOES
Perceptual	Creates a palette that gives precedence to colors for which the human eye has greater sensitivity.
Selective	Favors broad areas of color and the preservation of web-safe colors.
Adaptive	Samples and uses the colors in the image rather than creating a full-spectrum palette.
Restrictive (Web)	Limits the palette to the 216 web-safe colors.
Custom	Use to create a custom palette by selecting the colors for the palette from the Color Table dialog box.
Black & White	Uses only black and white, which produces an effect similar to the halftones that are used in newspapers.
Grayscale	Uses only shades of gray, including black and white.
Mac OS	Uses the default Macintosh 8-bit system palette.
Windows	Uses the default Windows 8-bit system palette.

To optimize a GIF or PNG-8 image in Photoshop:

1. With your image open in Photoshop, click **File** and then click **Save For Web**.
2. Click the **2-Up** tab so that you can see the original and modified images side-by-side.
3. Click the **Optimized File Format** down arrow, and click **GIF** or **PNG-8**.
4. Select the desired options, as shown in Figure 9-2.
5. Click the **Color Reduction Algorithm** down arrow, and click the desired color-reduction algorithm (see Table 9-1).
6. Click the **Dither Algorithm** down arrow, and click the desired option (see Table 9-2).

TABLE 9-2: DITHERING ALGORITHMS

NAME	WHAT IT DOES
Diffusion	Applies a random pattern across adjacent pixels. You control the amount of dither using the Dither slider. More dither increases the number of colors and the file size.
Pattern	Applies a square pattern similar to a halftone.
Noise	Applies a random pattern similar to Diffusion but without diffusing the pattern across adjacent pixels.

7. If you want an area of your GIF or PNG-8 image to be transparent, click the **Transparency** check box.
8. If you are using transparency, click the **Transparency Dither Algorithm** down arrow, and click the desired transparency dither algorithm.
9. If you specify a dither algorithm, click the **Dither** right arrow, and drag the slider to specify the percentage of dithering. If you have a large variety of colors in the original image, specifying a larger amount of dithering may help reduce the file size.
10. If you want your GIF or PNG-8 image to be interlaced, click the **Interlaced** check box. This causes the image to load in a web page in several passes rather than in a single pass, which enables viewers with a slow connection to see part of the image immediately.
11. For GIF images, drag the **Lossy** slider to specify the lossy value. Specifying a high lossy value removes more colors from the compressed image, resulting in a smaller file size with poorer image quality.
12. Click the **Colors** down arrow, and select the number of colors you want in your GIF or PNG-8 image. You can also click the **Colors** spinners to specify the number of colors in the compressed image. Fewer colors mean a smaller file size.

TIP

When you're using the Save For Web dialog box to optimize images for the Web and you create settings you'd like to use on other images, you can save them. After creating the settings, click the **Optimize Menu** button located to the right of the preset that was the basis for your settings, and click **Save Settings**. In the Save Optimization Settings dialog box, type a name for your settings, and click **Save**. Your saved settings will appear as a preset on the Optimize File Format drop-down menu.

TIP

The Compression drop-down list in the Save for Web dialog box for a JPEG file offers preset compression settings. You can also set the level of compression using the Quality slider. This gives you greater control over the compression level and resulting file size.

13. Click the **Matte** down arrow, and select the desired matte color from the drop-down list (see Table 9-3). This sets the color against which transparent pixels will be dithered, creating a smooth blend of transparent pixels with the matte colors.

TABLE 9-3: MATTE DESCRIPTIONS

NAME	WHAT IT DOES
None	Makes pixels with more than 50 percent transparency fully transparent and pixels that are 50 percent or less fully opaque.
Eyedropper Color	Uses the color selected with the Eyedropper tool.
Black or White	Uses black or white, respectively, for the matte color.
Other	Allows you to select a color using the Color Picker dialog box.

14. If you've selected a matte option, drag the **Amount** slider to specify the value.

15. Set the amount of web snap by dragging the **Web Snap** slider. This shifts the colors in the image to the closest web-safe color—the higher the value, the more colors will be shifted.

16. When you're satisfied with your selections, click **Save**. The Save Optimized As dialog box appears.

17. In the Save In drop-down list, select the location for your image, and type the file name in the File Name text box. Verify the file type and then click **Save**.

OPTIMIZE A JPEG IMAGE

JPEG files are recommended for photographs and continuous-tone images because they support more colors than the GIF format.

1. With your image open in Photoshop, click **File** and then click **Save For Web**.

2. Click the **Optimized File Format** down arrow, and click **JPEG**.

3. Choose the options you want:

   • Click the **Compression Quality** down arrow, and select an option from the drop-down list. Higher compression settings produce fewer colors and smaller images.

   • If you want the image to download in successive passes rather than in one pass, click the **Progressive** check box.

NOTE

Color profiles are used to bridge the differences between the different types of display devices and printers. Each device, such as a computer monitor or a printer, has a range of colors that it is capable of displaying. This is the color space of the device. Color profiles enable each device to display the image as consistently as possible.

NOTE

Matte, the opposite of transparency, fills transparent pixels with a chosen color to display a solid background rather than a transparent one.

TIP

You can optimize a PNG-24 image by clicking **PNG-24** from the Optimization drop-down list. The PNG-24 format is similar to JPEG format, but PNG-24, unlike JPEG, uses a lossless compression algorithm. This means that PNG-24 images tend to be larger, but PNG-24 can preserve 256 levels of transparency.

- If you want to preserve the ICC profile (the color space) for the image, click the **ICC Profile** check box. (If it is unavailable to you, that means your image does not have an ICC profile.)

- If you want the image optimized, click the **Optimized** check box. This feature, which is not supported by older browsers, creates a slightly smaller file.

- If you want to use a compression setting not specified in the Compression Quality drop-down list, drag the **Quality** slider to set the compression amount.

- Drag the **Blur** slider to set the amount of blur. This applies a Gaussian-type blur (an adjustable hazy effect caused by adding detail to the pixels) to the image and decreases the file size. Recommended values are 0.1 to 0.5.

- Drag the **Matte** slider to select the matte color. The matte color is the fill color for pixels that were transparent in the original image.

4. When you're satisfied with your selections, click **Save**. The Save Optimized As dialog box appears.

5. Click the **Save In** down arrow, and navigate to the folder in which you want to save the image.

6. Type the file name in the File Name text box, and click **Save**.

SAVE OPTIMIZED IMAGES

The process for saving optimized images is similar to that for saving any other image.

1. Click the **Save** button in the Save For Web dialog box. The Save Optimized As dialog box appears.

2. Click the **Save In** down arrow, and navigate to the folder in which you want to save the file.

3. Type the file name in the File Name text box.

4. Click the **Save As Type** down arrow, and click the desired format type from the drop-down list.

5. Click the **Settings** down arrow, and click the desired option from the drop-down list.

6. Click **Other** to view and select additional options.

TIP

When saving an optimized image in ImageReady, you have additional options with regards to slices: whether to save all slices in the image, save only selected slices, or save only slices you have created.

TIP

With image maps, you can have multiple hyperlinks for a single image. You can also make image maps using slices of an image. Each slice is a single hyperlink.

TIP

Use these three tools (as shown next) to define *hotspots* (the area in the image that has a hyperlink) in an image. The **Rectangle Image Map** tool is used to define rectangles and squares. The **Circle Image Map** tool is used to define ovals and circles. The **Polygon Image Map** tool is used to define irregular areas.

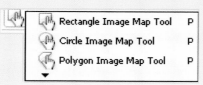

7. If there are slices in your image, click the **Slices** down arrow, and click one of the following options:

   - **All Slices** saves all the slices in the image.
   - **Selected Slices** saves only the selected slices.
   - **All User Slices** saves only the user slices in the image.

8. Click **Save**.

Work with Image Maps

You use image maps to define one or more areas of an image as a hyperlink. You can make image maps by selecting areas using the Image Map tools (ImageReady only) or by using layers where each layer is a single hyperlink.

To create an image map using the Image Map tools:

1. Open your image in ImageReady, or if it's open in Photoshop, click **File** and then click **Edit In ImageReady**.

2. Click the relevant Image Map tool in the Toolbox:

   - With the **Rectangle** or **Circle Image Map** tools, click to set one corner of the image map area, and drag diagonally to set the opposite corner.

   - With the **Polygon Image Map** tool, click to set the starting point of the image map area, move the pointer to the next point, and then click to create a line between the points. Click to define additional points in the image map section. When you've defined the last point for the image map section, double-click to connect the last point to the first point, as shown in Figure 9-3.

3. Click **Windows** and then click **Image Map**. The Image Map palette is displayed.

4. Type a name for the image map in the Name text box.

5. Click the **URL** down arrow, and type the URL for the image map. If you've previously entered a URL, it will appear in the drop-down list. The URL can be an absolute reference (including the protocol, such as http, and the domain name) or a relative reference (the page and directory name, if applicable).

Image maps can be either client-side or server-side. Client-side image maps are interpreted by the browser (the client), and server-side image maps are interpreted by the server. Client-side image maps are the default in ImageReady and are faster than server-side image maps, since it's not necessary to contact the server to display the image. Server-side image maps do not work with multiple-slice images.

With the Rectangle and Circle Image Map tools, press **SHIFT** to constrain the area to a square or circle, respectively. Press **ALT** to draw the area from its center. With the Polygon Image Map tool, press **SHIFT** to constrain segments to 45-degree increments.

Using _blank always opens a new browser to display the page. This is useful when you want to keep the browser displaying your web site open while displaying a page from another web site.

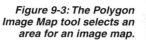

Figure 9-3: The Polygon Image Map tool selects an area for an image map.

6. Click the **Target** down arrow, and select a target frame from the drop-down list. If the page is part of a frameset, this can be the name of one of the frames in the frameset. Select from among these options:

   - **_blank** opens a new browser to display the page.
   - **_self** displays the page in the same frame as the calling file.
   - **_parent** displays the page in the current top-level (parent) frame.
   - **_top** replaces all the current frames with the new page.

7. Type the alternate text for the image in the Alt text box. The alternate text will be displayed in place of the image if the user has chosen to display text only in his or her browser, or it will be displayed as a Tool Tip if the user has chosen to display images.

8. Click **File** and then click **Save Optimized As**. The Save Optimized As dialog box appears. Click the **Save In** down arrow, and navigate to the folder in which you want to store your files.

9. Click the **Save As Type** down arrow, and click **HTML And Images (*.html)**. This will save your image and the HTML code for the image map. You can save just the image or just the HTML code by selecting an option from the Save As Type drop-down list.

QUICKSTEPS

USING LAYERS TO CREATE IMAGE MAPS

When you use layers to create an image map, each hotspot is the shape of the content of the layer. If the content changes in size, so does the hotspot. This allows you to create precise irregular-shaped hotspots that don't require modification if the image is edited. The Layers palette is used extensively when creating layers for image maps, so if it isn't displayed on the screen, click **Window** and then click **Layers**.

1. Select the layer to use for the hotspot in the Layers palette.

2. Click **Layer** and then click **New Layer Based Image Map Area**.

3. Enter the **URL** and other information in the Image Map palette.

10. If you already have a web page for your image map, select it from the list. If you are creating the web page, type the name in the File Name text box. Click **Save**.

11. To add areas to your image map, use the Image Map tools, and resave your work. Click **File** and then click **Update HTML** to update your HTML code as you work.

Set Output Options

Use the Output Settings dialog box to set the output options for Photoshop and ImageReady. In ImageReady, you can also apply your saved output settings to other files. In Photoshop, open the Output Settings dialog box from the Save Optimized, Save Optimized As, or the Save For Web dialog boxes. Only the Save For Web dialog box allows you to save custom settings. When you save custom settings, they appear on the Preset drop-down list.

1. With an image open in Photoshop, click **File** and then click **Save For Web**.

2. Click the **Optimize** menu button to the right of Preset, and then click **Edit Output Settings**. The Output Settings dialog box appears.

You can select the different groups of output options from the drop-down list located below the presets in the Output Settings dialog box. For example, you can click HTML to set HTML output options. The HTML options are listed in Table 9-4.

TABLE 9-4: DESCRIPTIONS OF HTML SETTINGS

HTML OPTIONS	DESCRIPTION
Output XHTML	Ensures the generated code conforms to the XHTML standard. If selected, some other options (such as Tag Case) are unavailable due to XHMTL requirements. XHTML has more stringent syntax than HTML.
Tags Case	Sets the case of the HTML tags. The options are Lowercase, Uppercase, and Mixed Case (leading caps).
Attribute Case	Sets the case of the HTML tag attributes. The options are Lowercase, Mixed Case, Mixed With Initial Lower, and Uppercase.
Indent	Sets the type and amount of indent for indented lines. The options are Tabs, None, 1 Space, 2 Spaces, 4 Spaces, and 8 Spaces.
Line Endings	Sets the line endings for different operating systems. The options are Automatic, Mac (Macintosh), Win (Windows), and Unix.
Encoding	Sets the character encoding for the generated code. The options are Automatic (iso-8859-1), Western (iso-8859-1), Mac OS Roman (x-mac-roman), and Unicode (utf-8). The iso-8859-1 character set is the standard set of characters used in Western European languages. Unicode (utf-8) is a better choice if you need to support other languages.
Include Comments	Includes HTML comments within the HTML <!-- --> delimiters. Comments help you understand what is happening on the page.
Always Add ALT Attributes	Includes the ALT attribute for those HTML tags where it is applicable, such as the image (IMG) tag. Web accessibility standards require the ALT attribute for all non-text elements. The ALT value will be empty, so you will need to enter the tag information separately.
Always Quote Attributes	Places quotes around the values of HTML tag attributes. HTML does not require quotes, but XHMTL and XML (Extensible Markup Language) do.
Close All Tags	Inserts the closing HTML tags for all tags that require them. HTML is generally forgiving of unclosed tags, but XHTML and XML are not.
Include Zero Margins On Body Tag	Adds the Margin attribute set to 0 to the BODY tag. This starts the page content in the upper-left corner of the browser with no margin. This is not supported by all browsers.

3. Click the **Next** button. The Slices section appears. You can also click the down arrow below the Settings field, and click **Slices** from the drop-down list. Click one of the following options for slices in your document:

- **Generate Table** creates an HTML table for displaying the slices.

- **Empty Cells** sets the rules for how empty table cells are generated: GIF, IMG W&H (GIF spacer image using the Image tag (IMG) with width and height specified); GIF, TD W&H (GIF spacer image using the Table Data tag (TD) with width and height specified); and NoWrap, TD W&H (text is not wrapped, using the Table Data tag with width and height specified).

- **TD W&H** sets when width and height values will be generated. The options are Auto, Always, and Never.

- **Spacer Cells** controls whether or not a row of spacer cells will be generated. Some browsers allow space between cells, which destroys the effect of slices. A row of spacer cells at the top or bottom of the table can help

WORKING WITH ROLLOVERS AND STATES

Rollovers are an effect that occurs when an event is triggered by some user action; for example, an image may change when the pointer is rolled over it. Every image has a normal state—the image that is displayed when the web page is first loaded. Additional states (images) can be displayed based on a mouse action, such as rolling or clicking. Rollovers are a combination of images and HTML and JavaScript code—all of which ImageReady creates when you use the application to optimize an image for the Web. Rollovers are commonly used as menu buttons on web pages.

To create a rollover, create an image with two layers in Photoshop or ImageReady. Edit the image in ImageReady. Then create a new layer-based slice, and in the Web Content palette, click the layer that will be displayed when viewers of your web page move their cursors over the slice. Click the **Create Rollover State** button, and choose the state that will cause the layer to be displayed. The default state is **Over**, which occurs when users move their cursor over the slice. You can also choose other states by right-clicking the rollover state in the Web Content palette and then choosing the desired state from the context menu.

ensure that the table will have the overall width specified. The options are: Auto, Auto (Bottom), Always, Always (Bottom), and Never.

- **Generate CSS** generates a Cascading Style Sheet (CSS) to display the slices rather than a table. Not all browsers fully support style sheets, which limits this method. You should test this with your target browser. When you click the Generate CSS option, the Referenced option becomes available.

- **Referenced** sets how the CSS elements will be referenced in the code: By ID (a unique ID value set in the code), Inline (style elements set in the DIV tag), or By Name (classes referenced by a unique ID).

- **Default Slice Naming** provides options, through a series of drop-down lists, for automatically generating file names for each slice.

4. Click the **Next** button. The Background section appears. You can also click the down arrow below the Settings field, and then click **Background** from the drop-down list. This option places a background image on the web page. The background can be an image or a solid color. If you want to use an image, you can type the path to the image in the Path text box, or you can click the **Choose** button and browse to an image file. If you prefer a solid color, click the **Color** down arrow, and click an option from the drop-down list.

Your choices are None, Matte (the current matte color), Black Or White, or Eyedropper Color (to select one of the current palette colors); or you can click **Other** to choose a color with the Color Picker.

5. Click the **Next** button. The Savings File section appears. You can also click the down arrow below the Settings field, and click **Saving Files** from the drop-down list. In the File Naming section, a series of drop-down menus are used to specify how the various files generated are named when you save the document. Accept the defaults, or choose a different option from the drop-down lists.

6. After clicking the desired file naming options, specify settings for the following options:

- **Filename Compatibility** enables you to specify the operating systems with which the files will be compatible. Your native operating system is chosen by default. You can choose to generate files compatible with Windows, Mac OS 9, and Unix.

- **Put Images In Folder** enables you to store the images in a separate folder from the HTML documents. Accept the default **Images** folder option, or you can type a different name.

- **Copy Background Image When Saving** creates a copy of the specified background image when the document is saved.

- **Include Copyright** includes a copyright notice with the generated files.

7. Click **Save**. The Save Output Settings dialog box appears.

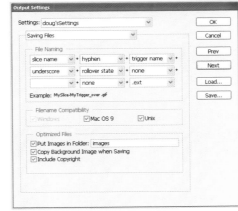

8. Type a name for the output settings file, and then click **Save**.

Animate Your Images

You can create animations as layered images (PSD files) in Photoshop or ImageReady. You can save the finished animation as a GIF, which doesn't require a browser add-in to display properly; as a QuickTime movie; or as a Macromedia Flash animation (a SWF file). The latter two options require browser add-ins.

TIP

You can download the free Flash player from Macromedia at http://macromedia.com. The Flash player is required to view Flash animations in web browsers and is included with most browser downloads. The free QuickTime player is available from Apple at http://www.apple.com/quicktime. It is required to view QuickTime movies in web browsers.

Create an Animation

The Animation palette, shown in Figure 9-4, is used in conjunction with the Layers and Web Content palettes to create animations. To create an animation:

1. Create a new image in Photoshop or ImageReady.
2. Create a layer for the static elements—the elements that do not move in the animation.
3. Create layers for each of the moving elements.
4. Save the image as a PSD file. This step is optional but recommended, as you'll have an original version of the file with no animation applied.
5. Click **Window** and then click **Animation**. The Animation palette is displayed.

6. Click the first frame and then click the **Duplicate Selected Frame** button in the Animation palette.
7. Click the frame you just created, and, in the Layers palette, click the layer you want to animate.
8. Click the **Move** tool and, in the document window, move the object to the desired position.
9. Repeat steps 7 and 8 for other objects you want to animate on the frame.
10. Repeat step 6 to add other frames to the animation, and then repeat steps 7 and 8 to animate the objects in each frame.
11. Set the duration of time each frame will be displayed by clicking the **Frame Delay Time** button at the bottom of the animation thumbnail and then clicking a preset from the menu. Selecting **Other** opens the Set Frame Delay dialog box, where you can set display times not available in the menu.
12. To set how many times the animation will run, click **Looping Options**. The Looping Options menu opens, and you can select **Once, Forever,** or **Other**. If you select Other, the Set Loop Count dialog box appears, and you can set the desired number of repeats.
13. Click **File** and then click **Save As**. Save the document with a different name than you used in step 4, and you'll have a version of the document with animation applied.

CAUTION

On the Animation palette you cannot change the size of an object in successive frames by clicking **Layer** and then clicking **Transform**. When you use the Transform command on an object in one frame, the transformation is applied to the other frames in the animation. If your objects need to be resized to fit the image, do so before creating additional frames.

TIP

You can set the delay times for single frames or for a selected group of frames. To set the delay time for a selected group, click the first frame and then press SHIFT while you click the last frame. Click the **Frame Delay Time** button in any selected frame to set the time for all the selected frames.

Figure 9-4: You use the Animation palette to set options for your animation.

Select First Frame selects the first frame of the animation

Play/Stop Animation starts or stops the animation playback

Tween opens the Tween dialog box

Delete Selected Frames removes selected frames from the animation

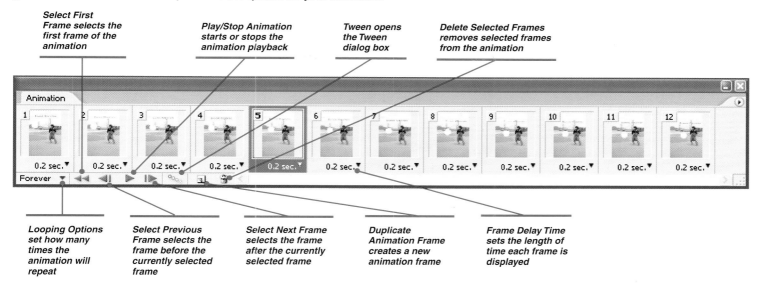

Looping Options set how many times the animation will repeat

Select Previous Frame selects the frame before the currently selected frame

Select Next Frame selects the frame after the currently selected frame

Duplicate Animation Frame creates a new animation frame

Frame Delay Time sets the length of time each frame is displayed

USE TWEENING

The creation of animations can be simplified by the use of *tweening*. Tweening creates intermediate frames in an animation. You create the start and end frames, and tweening creates the specified number of frames in *between* those frames; hence, the term tweening. Tweening can be applied to single or contiguous frames:

● If applied to a single frame, you select whether to tween between it and the previous or following frame.

● If you select two contiguous frames, the tweened frames are placed between the selected frames.

● If you select more then two contiguous frames, the intermediate frames are modified.

● If you select the first and last frames, they are treated as contiguous. This is useful for smoothing animations that loop more than once.

1. In the Animation palette, select the frames to tween.

2. Click the **Tween** button. The Tween dialog box appears.

OPTIMIZING ANIMATIONS

You should optimize animations as GIF images only, since this is the only image format that supports them. If you optimize an animation as a JPEG or PNG, only the current frame of the animation will be displayed. In addition to the optimization options available for all GIF images, with animations, you can limit optimization to only the areas that change between frames, which greatly reduces the size of the final file. ImageReady also applies a special dithering algorithm to prevent flickering.

1. Click the Animation palette **Menu** button on the upper right of the palette, and then click **Optimize Animation**. The Optimize Animation dialog box appears.

2. Choose from the following options:

- **Bounding Box** crops each frame to the area that has changed from the preceding frame. This option is recommended because it makes for a smaller file, but it isn't supported by all GIF editors. If your animations will be edited in other programs, you should determine if this feature is supported; otherwise, deselect it.

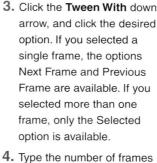

Dock to Palette Well	
New Frame	Alt+Shift+Ctrl+F
Delete Frame	
Delete Animation	
Copy Frame	
Paste Frame…	
Select All Frames	
Tween…	
Reverse Frames	
Optimize Animation…	
Make Frames From Layers	
Flatten Frames Into Layers	
Match Layer Across Frames…	
Create New Layer for Each New Frame	
✔ New Layers Visible in All Frames	
Palette Options…	

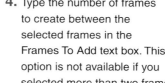

Optimize Animation

Optimize By
☑ Bounding Box
☑ Redundant Pixel Removal
OK
Cancel

- **Redundant Pixel Removal** makes all pixels that are unchanged from the previous frame transparent. This option is also recommended to reduce the final file size. This feature requires that the Transparency option in the Optimize palette be selected.

3. Click the **Tween With** down arrow, and click the desired option. If you selected a single frame, the options Next Frame and Previous Frame are available. If you selected more than one frame, only the Selected option is available.

4. Type the number of frames to create between the selected frames in the Frames To Add text box. This option is not available if you selected more than two frames. In that case, only the selected frames are tweened.

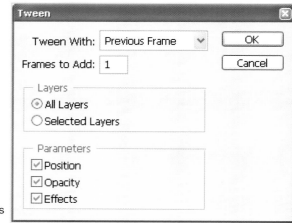

Tween

Tween With: Previous Frame
Frames to Add: 1
OK
Cancel

Layers
⦿ All Layers
◯ Selected Layers

Parameters
☑ Position
☑ Opacity
☑ Effects

5. Click the desired Layers option: **All Layers** modifies all the layers in the selected frames; **Selected Layer** modifies only the layers selected in the Layers palette. Static layers do not need to be modified by tweening, but you may have objects on multiple layers that do.

6. Accept the parameters, which are all selected by default. You can also clear a parameter check box to deselect the parameter and not apply it to the tweening. You have the following tweening parameters with which to work:

- **Position** varies the position of the objects evenly between the starting and ending frames.

- **Opacity** varies the opacity of the objects evenly between the starting and ending frames. This is useful for making smooth fades.

- **Effects** varies the layer-effect parameters evenly between the starting and ending frames. For example, a drop shadow effect could be used to give the impression of a light source moving across the animation, thereby changing the angle of the shadow.

7. Click **OK** to apply your settings.

NOTE

If you chose one of the looping options, the animation will play repeatedly until you click the Stop button.

NOTE

To preview the animation in a browser from within Photoshop, click **File** and then click **Save For Web**. The Save For Web dialog box appears. Click the **Preview In Browser** button to open the animation in your preferred web browser.

VIEW ANIMATIONS

You can view animations in Photoshop, ImageReady, or a web browser. In ImageReady or Photoshop:

1. Open the animation and the **Animation** palette.

2. Click the **Play** button. The animation runs in the document window.

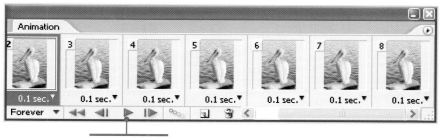

Play/Stop button

3. While the animation is playing, the Play button changes to the Stop button. Click the **Stop** button to stop the animation.

4. To view the animation in a web browser, click the **Preview In Browser** button in the Toolbox (Image-Ready only). Figure 9-5 shows an animation as previewed in Internet Explorer. The animation and generated HTML is shown in the browser, as in Figure 9-5.

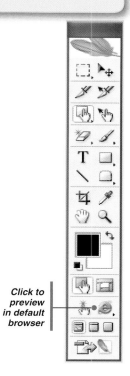

Click to preview in default browser

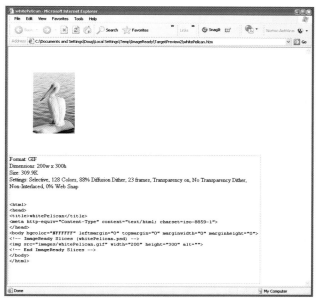

Figure 9-5: When the animation runs in a browser, the HTML code is also displayed.

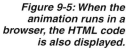

9

UICKSTEPS

IMPORTING FILES AND FOLDERS AS ANIMATIONS

ImageReady imports and edits animation formats created in other programs such as GIFs, MOV (QuickTime), AVI (Windows Media), and FLIC (various programs) files plus folders containing bitmap images to use in animations.

To import Photoshop files as frames in ImageReady:

1. Click **File** and then click **Open**. The Open dialog box appears.

2. Select the Photoshop file you want to open, and click **OK**.

3. Click **Window** and then click **Animation**.

4. Click the Animation palette **Menu** button, and click **Make Frames From Layers** from the drop-down list.

To import a folder of files as frames in ImageReady:

1. Put only the files you want to be animation frames in the folder.

2. Click **File**, click **Import**, and then click **Folder As Frames**. The Browse For Folder dialog box appears.

3. Select the folder to import, and click **OK**. The files will be placed in the Animation palette as frames and in the Layers palette as layers.

Continued...

NOTE

RFC stands for Request For Comments. When an Internet standard is proposed, the initial draft is released as a Request For Comments. Interested parties, such as manufacturers and industry groups, comment on the standard. Eventually the standard is finalized with the RFC number.

SAVE ANIMATIONS

From within ImageReady or Photoshop, you can save an animation as an animated GIF, a QuickTime movie, or a Macromedia Flash (SWF) file. You can also save each frame of the animation as a separate file. The procedure for saving an animation as a GIF is basically the same as for saving any other GIF image. You first optimize the image and then save it.

To save an animation as a QuickTime movie:

1. If you've created the animation in Photoshop, click **File** and click **Edit In ImageReady**.

2. Click **File**, click **Export**, and then click **Original Document**. The Export Original dialog box appears.

3. Click the **Save As Type** down arrow, and click **QuickTime Movie**.

4. Click the **Save In** down arrow, navigate to the folder in which you want to save the file, and type the name for the file in the File Name text box.

5. Click **Save**. The Compression Settings dialog box appears.

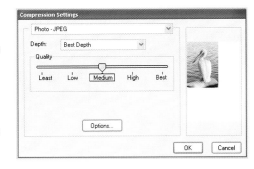

6. Click the **Compression Codec** down arrow, and click the desired format. A number of standard video and graphic codecs are available, including codecs you may have purchased or downloaded. A codec compresses the file when you save it and decompresses the file when you open it in the associated player. The default, **Photo-JPEG**, will work in most situations. The remaining options vary based on the format selected.

7. If the **Depth** down arrow is displayed, click it to select the bit depth for the file.

8. If the **Quality** slider is displayed, drag it to set the amount of compression for the file. **Best** creates the largest file size and the highest quality animation, while **Least** creates the smallest file size with the poorest quality animation.

9. If the **Options** button appears, click it to open a dialog box with options for the selected format. For Photo-JPEG, the only option is **Optimize For Streaming**. If you select this, you can also make the file RFC 2035-compatible (a format for JPEG-compressed

IMPORTING FILES AND FOLDERS AS ANIMATIONS (Continued)

To import MOV, AVI, and FLIC files for editing in ImageReady:

1. Click **File**, click **Open**, and then choose the file to open.
2. Click **OK**. The Open Movie dialog box appears.

3. Select the range of frames to import:
   - Click **From Beginning To End** to select all the frames.
   - Click **Selected Range Only** to import some of the frames. Select the frames to import by holding down **SHIFT** and moving the slider, or by clicking the previous and next arrows in the animation window.
4. Click the **Limit To Every** check box, click **Frame**, and choose a value in the drop-down list to skip frames in the selected range.
5. Click **OK** to import the selected frames.

NOTE

The files will be imported alphabetically. You may need to modify the file names to ensure the files are placed as frames in the correct order. You can also reorganize the frames in the Animation palette after they are imported.

video). Streaming video starts playing in a browser before the file has been completely downloaded and continues playing while the full file downloads in the background. The video will start playing in the minimum amount of time, enhancing the user experience.

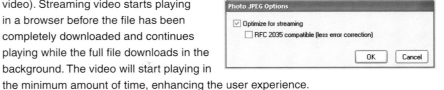

10. Click **OK** to save the file.

CREATE A SWF ANIMATION

Macromedia Flash is one of the most popular formats for animations on the Web. ImageReady makes it easy to create Flash animations (SWF files) that can be imported into Macromedia Flash or added to web pages.

Click **File**, click **Export**, and then click **Macromedia Flash SWF**.

–Or–

1. Click **File**, click **Export**, and then click **Original Document**. The Export Original dialog box appears. Click the **Save As Type** down arrow, and then click **Macromedia Flash SWF** from the drop-down list. Click **Save**. The Macromedia Flash (SWF) Export dialog box appears.
2. Click the **Preserve Appearance** check box to retain the appearance of text and shape layers that cannot be exported natively to the SWF file. ImageReady will rasterize (convert a vector-based object to a graphic) these objects to retain the appearance of the PSD file. Text and shape layers will be lost if this option isn't selected.
3. Click the **SWF bgcolor** down arrow, and select a background color from the palette. You can use the current foreground and background colors, any color from the current palette, or a color selected with the Color Picker.

4. Click the **Generate HTML** check box to generate the HTML needed to display the SWF file in a web browser.

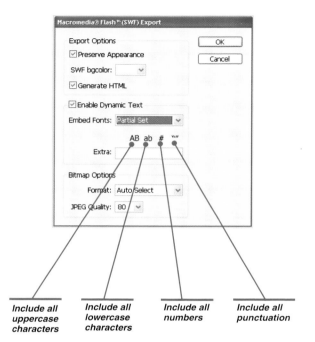

Include all uppercase characters

Include all lowercase characters

Include all numbers

Include all punctuation

5. Click the **Enable Dynamic Text** check box to map PSD text to SWF dynamic text. SWF dynamic text is lost when the file is opened in Flash, so this option is only useful if the animation will only be on the Web.

6. If Enable Dynamic Text is selected, click the **Embed Fonts** down arrow to set the text options. No characters will be embedded if you select **None**. **Full Set** embeds the entire character set. If you select **Partial Set**, you must choose which characters you want to embed:

   - All uppercase characters
   - All lowercase characters
   - All numbers
   - All punctuation

7. If you embed a partial set, you can type other characters you want to embed in the **Extra** text box.

8. Click the **Format** down arrow, and select the format for bitmap images from the drop-down list. **Auto Select** will choose the best format based on the number of colors. **Lossless-8** will generate 8-bit images with no color loss. **Lossless-32** will generate 32-bit images with no color loss. **JPEG** generates JPEG images.

9. If you selected Auto Select or JPEG, click the **JPEG Quality** down arrow, and drag the slider to set the amount of compression. Lower values compress the file more, creating smaller file sizes at the expense of image quality; while higher values compress the file less, creating larger file sizes with better-quality graphics.

10. Click **OK**. The Export As Macromedia SWF dialog box appears.

11. Click the **Save In** down arrow, and navigate to the folder in which you want to save the files.

12. Accept the default file name, or type a file name in the File Name text box.

13. Click **Save**.

TIP

In ImageReady, you can export any or all of the frames in an animation as individual files. Click **File**, click **Export**, and then click **Animation Frames As Files**. Follow the prompts in the Export Animation Frames As Files dialog box to complete the task.

Work with ImageReady

ImageReady is the workhorse for producing web graphics. Some of its capabilities have been covered in the previous sections; the following sections will cover its advanced features, including slices and rollovers.

Slice an Image

With Photoshop and ImageReady, you can *slice* an image. This means that you can "cut" an image into sections. You can apply different effects to each slice or designate each slice as a hyperlink. To the user, the slices appear as a single image. You have four types of slices to choose from:

- **Auto** slices are created automatically. These are the areas in an image that are not defined by one of the other slice types.
- Use the Slice tool to create **user** slices.
- Select layers in the Layers palette to create **layer-based** slices.
- Use the Web Content palette to create **table** slices.

VIEW SLICES

Slices can be viewed in Photoshop, ImageReady, and the Save For Web dialog box. You can distinguish between different types of slices by looking at the lines that define them and the color of their symbols:

- User and layer-based slices have solid lines and blue symbols by default.
- Auto slices have dotted lines and gray symbols by default.

Slices are numbered starting with the slice nearest the upper-left corner of the image and moving to the lower-right corner—a numeric symbol is in the upper-left corner of each slice. As you add or remove slices, the numbering for individual slices will change to reflect the changes. Each slice also has a *badge*, or icon, that displays the properties of the slice.

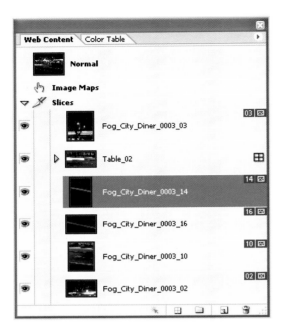

To display or hide the badges
in ImageReady:

1. Click the Web Content palette **Menu** button, and click **Palette Options**. The Web Content Palette Options dialog box appears.

2. Click the **Show Slice Badges** check box to hide slice badges (if currently displayed) or to show slice badges (if currently hidden).

CREATE USER SLICES

To create a user slice:

1. Click the **Slice** tool in the Toolbox.

2. Click the **Style** down arrow, and click the desired option. This option determines how the slices you create are drawn. Choose from the following options:

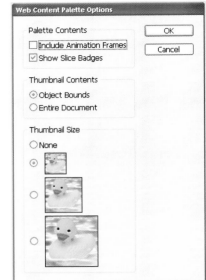

- **Normal** uses dragging to set the slice area.

- **Fixed Aspect Ratio** uses a fixed width-to-height ratio, which you set by typing values in the Width and Height text boxes. Set the size of the slice by dragging, and the slice is proportionate to the values you type in the Width and Height text boxes.

- **Fixed Size** creates a slice of a specific size in pixels that you type in the Width and Height text boxes.

3. With Normal and Fixed Aspect Ratio slices, drag to select the area of the slice.

4. With a fixed-size slice, click to create the slice, and then drag the selection outline to the desired area.

You can also create user slices using guides.

1. Place the guides on your image.

2. In Photoshop, click the **Slices From Guides** button in the Options bar.

3. In ImageReady, click **Slices** and then click **Create Slices From Guides**.

NOTE

Slices are always rectangular. You cannot have an oval or irregularly shaped slice.

TIP

Press **SHIFT** while you drag to constrain the slice to a square, and press **ALT** while you drag to draw from the center.

In ImageReady, you can create a slice from a selection.

1. Use the **Rectangular Marquee** tool to select an area of the image. The selection area can be any shape.

2. Click **Select** and then click **Create Slice From Selection**. The slice will be a rectangle large enough to contain the entire selected area.

CREATE LAYER-BASED SLICES

A layer-based slice consists of the entire selected layer. These are useful for rollovers. If you apply an effect, such as a drop shadow, to the layer to create a rollover state, the slice automatically adjusts to include the pixels created by the effect. To create a layer-based slice in Photoshop or ImageReady, click the layer in the Layers palette. Then click **Layer** and click **New Layer Based Slice**.

USE THE WEB CONTENT PALETTE

The ImageReady Web Content palette has several uses: it displays information about slices, image maps, and animation frames; and you can use it to create, edit, and set options for rollovers. Figure 9-6 shows the Web Content palette with slice and image map information displayed. To display the Web Content palette, click **Window** and then click **Web Content**.

The Web Content palette displays all slices and image maps, and contains a menu with a number of options for working with rollovers, slices, and image maps. As with other Photoshop palettes, you can show or hide content by clicking an object's eyeball icon. Learn more about the Web Content palette in the following sections.

| Dock to Palette Well |
| New Rollover State |
| Duplicate Image Map |
| Delete Image Map Area |
| Delete Rollover |
| Delete All Rollovers |
| Create Layer-Based Rollover |
| Copy Rollover State |
| Paste Rollover State |
| Find All Remote Slices... |
| Find Remote Slices For State... |
| Rollover State Options... |
| ✔ New Layers Visible in All States/Frames |
| Palette Options... |

OPTIMIZE SLICES IN IMAGEREADY

Slices are optimized using the same tools as with other graphic files. You can use the Save For Web dialog box in Photoshop or the Optimize palette in ImageReady.

Figure 9-6: The Web Content palette displays slice and image map information.

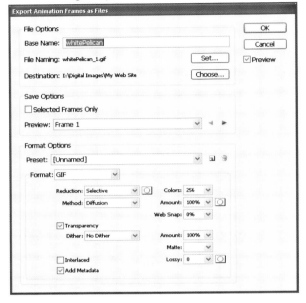

To optimize a slice in ImageReady:

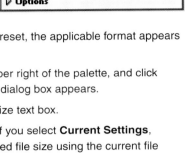

1. Click one or more slices with the Slice Select tool. You can also click a slice in the Web Content palette.

2. Click **Window** and then click **Optimize**. The Optimize palette is displayed.

3. Click the **Preset** down arrow, and click the desired preset. The presets are the same as in the Save As Web dialog box. When you select a preset, the applicable format appears in the Format text field.

4. Click the Optimize palette **Menu** button on the upper right of the palette, and click **Optimize To File Size**. The Optimize To File Size dialog box appears.

5. Type the file size in kilobytes in the Desired File Size text box.

6. In the Start With area, select the relevant option. If you select **Current Settings**, ImageReady will optimize the image to the specified file size using the current file format. If you select **Auto Select GIF/JPEG**, ImageReady will automatically select GIF or JPEG as the file format with the necessary settings to optimize the file.

7. In the Use area, select the relevant option to apply the optimization: **Current Slice**, **Each Slice**, or **Total Of All Slices**.

8. Click **OK** to apply your settings.

You can also copy optimization settings from one slice to another.

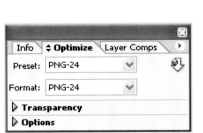

1. Select the slice with the optimization settings to be copied.

2. To apply these setting to a second slice, drag the **droplet** icon, found on the Optimize palette, to the second slice.

How to...

- Work with the Actions Palette

- Record an Action to Automate a Multistep Task

- 🖉 Using Modal Controls and Tools

- Play and Undo Actions

- 🕲 Setting Playback Options

- Edit Actions

- 🖉 Rerecording and Duplicating Actions and Commands

- Use the Batch Command

- 🕲 Changing Action Options

- Create a Droplet from an Action

- 🕲 Creating Droplets in ImageReady

- Crop and Straighten Photos

- 🕲 Fitting an Image

- Create a Picture Package

- 🕲 Adding Copyright Information to an Image

- Create a Web Photo Gallery

- Create a Panorama with Photomerge

Chapter 10
Saving Time with Actions and Automation

This chapter covers the Photoshop and ImageReady tools used for automating repetitive tasks. You can use the Actions palette to create sequences of commands that can be saved and applied to images. Working with Photoshop's Automate menu, which simplifies other complicated tasks, is also covered in this chapter.

Automate Sequences of Frequently Used Commands

When working with graphics, you may frequently need to apply the same sequence of commands to a series of images. Resizing an image to a standard size and applying layer styles or a filter are examples of such tasks. Your images may be processed in a batch (as a group) or individually. The Actions palette, available in both Photoshop and ImageReady, is the most flexible tool to use because you can create and save your own sequences of events.

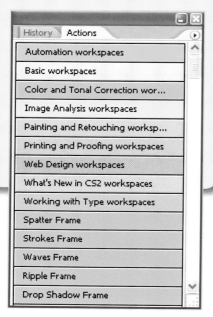

Work with the Actions Palette

Your primary tool for automating tasks is the Actions palette. The Photoshop Actions palette is shown in Figure 10-1. The Photoshop Actions palette has more user-recordable functionality than the ImageReady Actions palette shown in Figure 10-2. With Photoshop, you can also group actions into sets for better organization; ImageReady does not provide this ability.

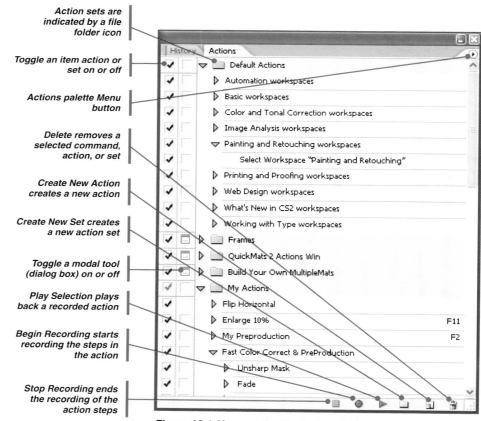

Action sets are indicated by a file folder icon

Toggle an item action or set on or off

Actions palette Menu button

Delete removes a selected command, action, or set

Create New Action creates a new action

Create New Set creates a new action set

Toggle a modal tool (dialog box) on or off

Play Selection plays back a recorded action

Begin Recording starts recording the steps in the action

Stop Recording ends the recording of the action steps

Figure 10-1: You use the Photoshop Actions palette to select and apply actions to your images.

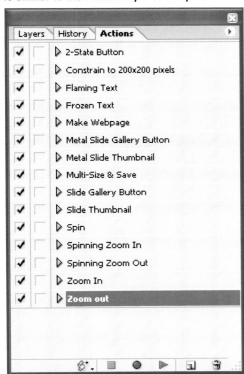

Figure 10-2: The ImageReady Actions palette is similar to the Photoshop Actions palette.

Record an Action to Automate a Multistep Task

You create an action by recording the steps to perform it using the menus and other tools. To record an action:

1. Open an image file.

2. In the Actions palette, click the **New Action** button.

   –Or–

   Click **New Action** in the Actions palette menu.

   In either case, the New Action dialog box appears. The Photoshop New Action dialog box, shown here, has options for the set name and button color. The ImageReady New Action dialog box doesn't have these options because they're not supported.

3. In the New Action dialog box, type a descriptive name for the action in the Name text box.

4. In Photoshop, click the **Set** down arrow, and choose the desired set from the drop-down list.

   –Or–

   Type the name of a new set in the Set text field.

5. Click the **Function Key** down arrow, and select a function key combination to run the action or set. (This step is optional.)

6. When you select a function key, you can also choose to use the **SHIFT** and/or **CTRL** keys with it by clicking the **Shift** and/or **Control** check boxes. This gives you more keyboard combinations to start the action.

7. In Photoshop, click the **Color** down arrow, and choose a display color for the action when using the Actions palette in Button mode.

8. Click **Record**.

NOTE

In Photoshop you can create *sets* of actions. A set is a group of actions. You may have an action that resizes an image and another action that applies a layer style. You can group these two actions as a single set. When you apply this set to an image, you select the set rather than the individual actions. In ImageReady, you have to apply the actions separately.

QUICK**FACTS**

USING MODAL CONTROLS AND TOOLS

A *modal control* is a dialog box used in an action. A *modal tool* is a command that requires the user to perform an action, such as pressing **ENTER** or double-clicking, before continuing. An example of a modal tool is the Crop tool. After you select an area to crop, you have to press **ENTER** or double-click the selected area to complete the crop.

You can have commands that use modal controls and modal tools to pause the action and wait for the user to enter values in a dialog box or to perform an action. You can also have commands that use the dialog box settings defined in the action and perform the action for the user (the action doesn't pause).

You set modal controls and tools by clicking the **Toggle Dialog On/Off** box icon next to the action name in the Actions palette. The icon appears when a dialog box will be displayed or when user actions will be required. The Toggle Dialog On/Off box is only available if any of the commands in the action have dialog boxes or user actions associated with them. If all the commands have dialog boxes or user actions, the dialog box icon is gray when selected. If some of the commands don't have

dialog boxes or user actions, the icon is red.

Toggle Item On/Off box

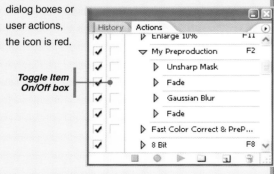

Your Actions palette is now in Record mode. All the operations you perform from this point until you click the Stop button will be part of your action. When you stop recording, your action will be listed in the Actions palette.

Play and Undo Actions

You apply an action to an image by *playing* the action. You can play a single command, an entire action, or a set of actions. You can exclude commands by clearing the Toggle Item On/Off check box for the commands. If a modal control is displayed, you can set values in it as part of the action.

To play an action:

1. Open the image file.
2. To play a complete action, select the action name in the Actions palette.
3. To play part of an action, click the **triangle** icon to the left of the action to display all commands associated with the action, and then click the desired command to start it from the Actions palette.
4. Click the **Play** button or click **Play** in the Actions palette menu.

To play single commands in an action:

1. Click the command you want to play.
2. Press **CTRL** while you click the **Play** button in the Actions palette.

   –Or–

   Press **CTRL** while you double-click the command in the Actions palette.

To undo an action using the History palette:

Drag the individual commands to the **Delete Current State** icon.

You can also:

- In Photoshop, click the button that looks like a camera in the History palette to take a snapshot before you start the action, and then restore the action from the snapshot.
- In ImageReady, click **Edit** and then click **Undo [action name]**.

TIP

In Photoshop you can turn off all modal controls and tools for a set by clearing the Toggle Dialog On/Off box next to the set name.

SETTING PLAYBACK OPTIONS

You can play actions at three speeds: normal, step-by-step, and with a set delay between each step. Slowing down an action will help you find any problems with the commands. To set the playback options:

Playback Options

Performance
- ● Accelerated
- ○ Step by Step
- ○ Pause For: [ ] seconds

☑ Pause For Audio Annotation

[OK]
[Cancel]

1. Click the Actions palette **Options** button, and then click **Playback Options**. The Playback Options dialog box appears.
2. Click one of the following Performance options:
- **Accelerated**, which is the normal (default) speed
- **Step By Step**, which stops after each step
- **Pause For**, which pauses after each step for the number of seconds you type in the Seconds text box

If you have audio annotations for your action, you can select **Pause For Audio Annotation** to ensure that each annotation will complete before the next command runs.

Edit Actions

You can edit actions in a number of ways. You can **rearrange** actions and commands, **record** additional commands, **insert** non-recordable commands, **rerecord and duplicate** actions and commands, **delete** actions and commands, and **change** action options (see the QuickSteps "Changing Action Options").

REARRANGE ACTIONS AND COMMANDS

You can rearrange the order in which commands play within an action and the order in which actions are displayed within the Actions palette by dragging them from their current location to a new location in the Actions palette.

RECORD ADDITIONAL COMMANDS

To add additional commands to an action:

1. Click an action in the Actions palette. The new commands are appended at the end.

   –Or–

   In the Actions palette, click the **triangle** icon to the left of the desired action to expand and display all commands associated with the action, and then click a command. The new commands are inserted after the selected command.
2. Click the **Record** button or click **Start Recording** in the Actions palette.
3. Run the additional commands you want recorded.
4. Click the **Stop** button when the commands have been recorded.

INSERT NON-RECORDABLE COMMANDS

You cannot record commands using the painting and toning tools, tool options, or commands from the View and Window menu groups. You can insert these commands into your actions, during recording or after. No values are included when you do this, so if the command has a dialog box, it will be displayed. You cannot disable the display of any dialog boxes for inserted commands.

To insert a menu item into an action:

1. Select the point in the action where you want to insert the menu item by clicking an action name. The menu item will be inserted at the end of the action.

RERECORDING AND DUPLICATING ACTIONS AND COMMANDS

You can change the values used in modal controls or modal tools in an action by rerecording the action. You can make a copy—and keep the original—by duplicating the action. To rerecord an action, click the action and then click **Record Again** in the Actions palette menu.

CHANGE A MODAL CONTROL (DIALOG BOX)

1. Change the values in the dialog box when it appears.
2. Click **OK** to set the new values. If you click **Cancel**, the old values are retained.

To change a modal tool, use the tool differently and then press **ENTER** to change the effect. You can press **ESC** to cancel the change.

RERECORD A SINGLE COMMAND

1. Click the **triangle** icon to the left of the desired action's name.
2. Double-click the command in the Actions palette to open the applicable dialog box.
3. Change the values for the command.
4. Click **OK**.

DUPLICATE AN ACTION OR COMMAND

- Press **ALT** while you drag the action or command to a new location in the Actions palette.

  –Or–

- Select the action or command, and then click **Duplicate** in the Actions palette menu.

  –Or–

- Drag the action or command to the New Action button.

–Or–

Click the **triangle** icon to the left of the action to display all actions associated with the command, and then click a command. The menu item will be inserted after the end of the command.

2. Click the Actions palette **Options** button, and then click **Insert Menu Item**. The Insert Menu Item dialog box appears.

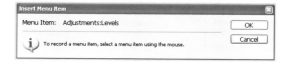

3. Click a menu item.
4. Click **OK**. The menu item is added to the action.

DELETE ACTIONS AND COMMANDS

To delete an action or command, click the action or command in the Actions palette, and then do one of the following:

- Click the **Delete** button, and then click **OK** in the confirmation dialog box that appears.
- Press **ALT** while you click the **Delete** button to skip the confirmation dialog box.
- Drag the action or command to the **Delete** button.
- Click **Delete** in the Actions palette menu.

Work with the Automate Menu

The Automate menu in Photoshop contains a number of options for performing complex tasks, with dialog boxes being displayed for entering values during the carrying out of the operation.

Use the Batch Command

You apply an action to a folder, including subfolders, with the Batch command. With batch processing, you can leave all the files open, save the changes to the original files, and then close the files or save the modified files to a new location.

TIP

To rename an action, you can also double-click the action name in the Action palette, and type the new name.

QUICKSTEPS

CHANGING ACTION OPTIONS

You can change the name of an action, the keyboard shortcut, and the button color (in Photoshop only) using the Action Options dialog box.

1. Select the action in the Actions palette.

2. Click the Actions palette **Menu** button beneath the Close icon, and click **Action Options**. The Action Options dialog box appears.

- To rename an action, type over the existing name in the Name field.

- To choose a keyboard shortcut, click the **Function** down arrow, and click a function key name.

- To change the color, click the **Color** down arrow, and click the desired color.

3. Click **OK** to close the Action Options dialog box.

To use the Batch command:

1. Click **File**, click **Automate**, and then click **Batch**. The Batch dialog box appears, shown in Figure 10-3.

2. Click the **Set** down arrow, and then choose the action set from the drop-down list.

3. Click the **Action** down arrow, and choose the action from the drop-down list. (If you have added any recorded actions, they will be listed in the Action list along with the preset actions that ship with Photoshop.)

4. Click the **Source** down arrow, and then choose the source from the drop-down list:

- **Folder** to select a folder containing files and/or subfolders. Click **Choose** to open the Browse For Folder dialog box to select the folder.

- **Import**, which displays the From drop-down list. The options shown here in addition to PDF Image will depend on what digital camera or scanner drivers you have installed on your system.

- **Opened Files** to perform the action on all open files.

- **Bridge** to perform the action on the files selected in the Bridge.

5. With the Folder and Bridge options, you have an additional set of options, listed in Table 10-1, that you can select.

TABLE 10-1: FOLDER AND BRIDGE OPTIONS

OPTION	ACTION
Override Action "Open" Commands	Applies Open commands in the action to the batch files, not the file names set in the action. The action must include an Open command, as the Batch command will not automatically open the source files. If the action is designed to apply to open files or if the action requires specific files to be opened, this option should not be selected.
Include All Subfolders	Processes all files in any subfolders.
Suppress File "Open" Option Dialogs	Hides any File Open Options dialog boxes, which is useful when processing camera RAW files. The default or previously selected settings in the dialog boxes will be used.
Suppress Color Profile Warnings	Hides any color policy messages.
Destination: None	Leaves the files open unless the action includes a Save command.

Figure 10-3: You use the Batch dialog box to set the options for batch processing.

6. Click the **Destination** down arrow, and click one of the following destination choices:

   ● **None** leaves the files open unless the action includes a Save command.

   ● **Save And Close** saves the processed files in the same location, overwriting the original file.

   ● **Folder** saves the processed files to a new location. Click **Choose** to specify the new location.

With the Save And Close and Folder options, you can also select the Override Action "Save As" Commands check box. This saves files to the destination folder using the Save As commands in the action. The action you're using must include a Save As or Save command, or no files will be saved.

7. If you selected Folder as the destination, choose the file-naming convention using the **File Naming** drop-down lists. Click one of the down arrows, and then click one of the serial number options. Type the starting number for the files in the Starting Serial # text box.

8. If you selected Folder as the destination, click the relevant operating system check boxes in the bottom of the File Naming area. Your computer's operating system is selected by default. You can also choose to make the file names compatible with Macintosh and Unix operating systems.

9. Click the **Errors** down arrow, and click the desired method for handling errors:

   ● **Stop For Errors**, which stops the action if an error occurs

   ● **Log Errors To File**, which continues the action when an error occurs and writes the error information to a log file

10. If you've chosen to use an error log file, click **Save As** to set the location for the error log. You can read the error log with a text editor, such as Notepad.

11. Click **OK**.

Figure 10-4: You use the Create Droplet dialog box to set the options for creating droplets.

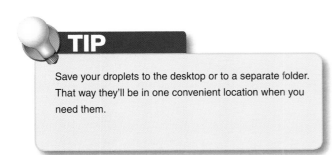

Save your droplets to the desktop or to a separate folder. That way they'll be in one convenient location when you need them.

Create a Droplet from an Action

Droplets are icons to which you drag a file to carry out an action. You first create the action using the steps described in the previous section (see "Work with the Actions Palette"), and then create a droplet from the action. You can save the droplet to the desktop or to another location on your computer. When you drag a file to the droplet, it will open the application needed to carry out the action.

To create a droplet from an action:

1. Click **File**, click **Automate**, and then click **Create Droplet**. The Create Droplet dialog box appears, shown in Figure 10-4. Many of the options are the same as in the Batch dialog box and behave in the same way.

2. Click **Choose**. The Save dialog box appears.

3. Click the **Save In** down arrow, and navigate to the location in which to save the droplet.

4. Type the name for the droplet in the File Name text box.

5. Accept the default **Format** option.

6. Click **Save**.

7. Click the **Set** down arrow, and click the action set for the droplet. This will only contain "Default Actions" if you have not created your own action sets to automate your image-editing tasks.

8. Click the **Action** down arrow, and choose the action for the droplet. The action options are explained in Table 10-1.

9. Open the **Destination** drop-down list, and choose one of the destination choices:

   - **None** leaves the files open unless the action includes a Save command.

   - **Save And Close** saves the processed files in the same location, overwriting the original files.

   - **Folder** saves the processed files to a new location. Click **Choose** to specify the new location.

10. If you selected Folder as the destination, choose the file-naming convention using the **File Naming** drop-down lists. Click one of the down arrows, and then click one of the serial number options. Type the starting number for the files in the Starting Serial # text box.

CREATING DROPLETS IN IMAGEREADY

You can also create droplets in ImageReady, although fewer options are available. To create a droplet:

Drag the action from the Actions palette to the desktop.

–Or–

1. Open the **Actions** palette and select the action you want.

2. Click the Actions palette **Options** button, and click **Create Droplet**. The Save This Action As A Droplet dialog box appears.

3. Click the **Save In** down arrow, and navigate to the location in which you want to save the droplet.

4. Type a name for it in the File Name text box.

5. Click **OK**.

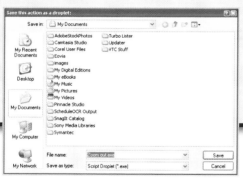

TIP

For best results with the Crop And Straighten Photos tool, leave at least one-eighth of an inch between the photos and have a uniform color behind the photos (usually the scanner cover). Crop And Straighten Photos works best with images with clearly delineated edges.

---

11. If you selected Folder as the destination, click the relevant operating system check boxes in the bottom of the File Naming area. Your computer's operating system is selected by default. You can also choose to make the file names compatible with Macintosh and Unix operating systems.

12. Click the **Errors** down arrow, and then click a method for handling errors:

  ● **Stop For Errors** stops the action if an error occurs.

  ● **Log Errors To File** continues the action when an error occurs and writes the error information to a log file.

13. If you've chosen to use an error log file, click **Save As** to set the location for the error log. You can read the error log with a text editor, such as Notepad.

14. Click **OK**.

Crop and Straighten Photos

When you scan a group of photographs, it can be easier to scan several at once, rather than one at a time. This creates a single image file that you need to cut into separate images for each photo. Each photo will probably need to be straightened also, as it's difficult to have all the photos lined up evenly on the scanner bed. This is what the Crop And Straighten Photos tool does—crops the individual images, creating a separate file for each one, and straightens each one at the same time.

To use the Crop And Straighten Photo tool:

1. Open your scanned image.

2. Select the images to process: the entire image is the default; or you can draw a selection border around just the photos you want to crop and straighten.

3. Click **File**, click **Automate**, and then click **Crop And Straighten Photos**. Photoshop breaks the scanned image into individual photos.

4. Save each image.

QUICKSTEPS

FITTING AN IMAGE

You can resize an image to a set image size using the Fit Image command. This resamples the image and resizes it to the selected size while retaining the aspect ratio. If you have an image that is 400 pixels high by 200 pixels wide and you resize it using the Fit Image command to 200 pixels by 200 pixels, the final image will be 200 pixels high by 100 pixels wide. The aspect ratio (2:1) remains the same, and the longer dimension (in this case, the height) is reduced to the specified dimension (200 pixels) and the shorter dimension is reduced proportionally. You can also use Fit Image to enlarge an image to fit into a larger document.

1. Open your image in Photoshop.

2. Click **File**, click **Automate**, and then click **Fit Image**. The Fit Image dialog box appears with the current measurements displayed.

3. Type the new values in the **Width** and **Height** text boxes.

4. Click **OK**.

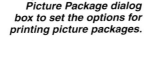

NOTE

If you use the Fit Image command to enlarge an image, do not increase the image greater than 10 percent; otherwise, image degradation will occur.

Create a Picture Package

When you print an image, you want to use the paper as efficiently as possible. You don't want to print one 4 × 5-inch picture on an 8.5 × 11-inch sheet of paper. You use the Picture Package feature in Photoshop to place multiple copies of an image, or multiple images, in multiple sizes on a single sheet of paper. This is similar to the picture packages you get from a portrait studio.

You use the Picture Package dialog box, shown in Figure 10-5, to create a picture package. You can use Picture Package with a currently open image or select the desired image file to create your picture package. To open the Picture Package dialog box:

Click **File**, click **Automate**, and then click **Picture Package**.

–Or–

In the Bridge, select the images you want to include in a picture package, click **Tools**, click **Photoshop**, and then click **Picture Package**.

Figure 10-5: You use the Picture Package dialog box to set the options for printing picture packages.

If you have not already selected images to include in your picture package, you can now select a single image or multiple images, and you can select your images from several sources.

To select your images:

1. Click the **Use** down arrow, and choose one of the following options as the source image or images for your picture package:

   - **File** uses an image file that's not currently open

   - **Folder** opens a folder of images

   - **Frontmost Document** uses the active image open in Photoshop

   - **Selected Images From The Bridge** uses the images you've selected in the Bridge (the Bridge must be open for this option to be available)

2. If you choose File or Folder, the Browse button becomes active. Click **Browse** to open:

   - The **Select An Image File** dialog box (if you chose File)

   - The **Browse For Folder** dialog box (if you chose Folder)

Before adding or changing images, you first should set the properties of the picture package.

To set the properties:

1. Click the **Page Size** down arrow, and click the size of paper you will use for the picture package. The choices are 8.0 × 10.0 inches, 10.0 × 16.0 inches, and 11.0 × 17.0 inches. These are a mix of standard photographic paper and office paper sizes. Click the option that's closest to, but not larger than, the size of paper loaded in your printer's feed tray.

NOTE

If you choose Folder as your image source, you can also place a check mark in the Include All Subfolders check box to include all the subfolders in the selected folder.

2. Click the **Layout** down arrow, and click the layout for your image or images on the page. The choices displayed will depend on the size of paper you chose from the Page Size drop-down list. The drop-down list for the 8.0 × 10.0 page size is shown here.

(2)5x7
(1)5x7 (2)2.5x3.5 (4)2x2.5
(1)5x7 (2)3.5x5
(1)5x7 (8)2x2.5
(1)5x7 (4)2.5x3.25 (2)1.5x2
(1)5x7 (4)2.5x3.5
(4)4x5
(2)4x5 (2)2.5x3.5 (4)2x2.5
(2)4x5 (8)2x2.5
(2)4x5 (4)2.5x3.5
(4)3.5x5
(20)2x2
(16)2x2.5
(8)2.5x3.5
(4)2.5x3.5 (8)2x2.5
(9)2.5x3.25

3. Accept the default resolution, or type a different resolution for the printed image in the Resolution text box. The default option of **300** pixels/inch is a good choice.

4. Accept the default unit of measure (pixels/inch), or click the **Unit** down arrow, and click a different unit of measure.

5. Click the **Mode** down arrow, and click a color mode from the drop-down list:

   - **Grayscale** will produce an image with only gray tones, including black and white.
   - **RGB Color** is the color mode used by computer monitors.
   - **CMYK Color** is the color mode used by commercial printers but not for photographic prints (CMYK stands for Cyan, Magenta, Yellow, and Black).
   - **Lab Color** is a color mode used by Photoshop to convert between other color modes. (Lab color images can be printed by PostScript Level 2 and 3 printers. If you don't have one of these printers, you should use a different color mode.)

Unless you want a grayscale image, you should use RGB Color if you're printing the image on an inkjet printer, or use CMYK Color if you're outsourcing the printing to a commercial service center that uses CMYK printers.

6. Click the **Flatten Image** check box if you want all the layers in your image merged. This doesn't affect the original image, only the picture package. This option is most meaningful if you have added a label to the image, which is described in the following steps. If you flatten the image, you will not be able to edit any labels in your saved picture package. If you don't flatten the image, you will be able to edit the labels, but your picture package file will be larger.

You edit the file information that can be printed with your picture package in the dialog box shown in Figure 10-6. Click **File** and then click **File Info** to display the dialog box.

Figure 10-6: You use the file information dialog box to save information about an image as part of the image.

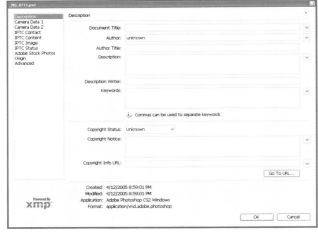

To protect your images, you can add a digital watermark to them. Photoshop includes a filter from Digimarc Corporation (www.digimarc.com). After registering with Digimarc, you get a unique Digimarc ID, which you can embed in your finished images.

7. If you want a label to be printed with your image, click the **Content** down arrow, and then click the desired label from the drop-down list. The label will be printed with each individual image. Your choices are:

   • **None** doesn't print a label.

   • **Custom Text** enables the Custom Text text box. Type the desired text in the Custom Text text box, which will be printed with the image.

   • **Filename** prints the file name of the image.

   • **Copyright** prints the copyright information that is part of the image file.

   • **Description** prints the description information that is part of the image file.

   • **Credit** prints the credit information that is part of the image file.

   • **Title** prints the title information that is part of the image file.

8. If you selected **Custom Text** from the Content drop-down list, type the text in the Custom Text text box.

9. Click the **Font** down arrow, and click the desired font. Your choices are **Courier**, **Arial**, and **Times New Roman**.

10. Click the **Font Size** down arrow, and choose the size of the font.

11. Click the **Color** down arrow, and choose the color for the text. Your choices are **Black**, **White**, and **Custom**—chosen with the Color Picker dialog box.

12. Drag the **Opacity** slider to set the opacity of the text. You can have any setting from 0 (transparent) to 100 (opaque) percent.

13. Click the **Position** down arrow, and click the desired option to determine the location of the text in the image. Your choices are **Centered**, **Top Left**, **Bottom Left**, **Top Right**, and **Bottom Right**.

14. Click the **Rotate** down arrow, and click the desired option to determine the angle of the text. Your choices are **None**, **45 Degrees Right**, **90 Degrees Right**, **45 Degrees Left**, and **90 Degrees Left**.

15. Click **OK**. Photoshop assembles the picture package.

16. Click **File** and then click **Print**. Photoshop prints the picture package.

17. Click **File** and then click **Save As**. The Save As dialog box appears, enabling you to save the picture package in the desired format for future use. (This step is optional.)

ADDING COPYRIGHT INFORMATION TO AN IMAGE

When an image is used on the Web, it's easy for anyone to download the image and use it in their work. There's no way to prevent this, but you can embed your copyright information in the image file so that you can at least prove ownership of the image.

1. Open your image in Photoshop.

2. Click **File** and then click **File Info**. The file information dialog box appears.

3. Click the **Copyright Status** down arrow, and click one of the following options:

- **Unknown** is used when the copyright status is not known.

- **Copyrighted** is used when you own the copyright or know who the copyright holder is (this might be an organization for which you work).

- **Public Domain** is used when the image is in the public domain, that is, when no copyright holder exists.

4. If you chose Copyrighted, type the copyright text in the Copyright Notice text box. You can also select existing text (created for images previously copyrighted in Photoshop) by clicking the down arrow to the right of the Copyright Notice text box. The text should be something like your name followed by "All Rights Reserved." You could also include contact information, such as your e-mail or mailing address, and the year.

5. Type the URL of the web site containing the detailed information about your terms of copyright in the Copyright Info URL text box (if applicable). This site would display your terms of use, such as restrictions on using the image or requiring credit for the image.

6. Click **OK**.

CREATE A MULTI-IMAGE PICTURE PACKAGE

So far, you have built your picture package using a single image. You can also have multiple images in your picture package. To add or change the images in your picture package:

1. Prior to selecting an image, follow the steps in the "Create a Picture Package" section of this chapter to create the desired picture package layout.

2. Click one of the placeholders in the layout pane of the Picture Package dialog box. The Select An Image File dialog box appears.

3. Click an image file to place in your picture package, and then click **Open**. The image is placed in the space that you clicked in the Picture Package dialog box, as shown here. If you selected Folder as the source for your images, that folder is the default location for the Select An Image File dialog box, but you can change the location using the **Look In** drop-down list.

You can repeat the previous steps until all the placeholders have an image. If you've selected a single image, all placeholders will have that image. You can add images in any combination until your picture package is the way you want.

4. Click **OK**. Photoshop creates a new image, which is your picture package. You can save this image or manipulate it just like any other Photoshop image.

5. If you want to save your picture package, click **File** and then click **Save**.

6. In the Save As dialog box, navigate to the folder in which you want to save the file, type the file name in the File Name text box, click the **Format** down arrow, and choose the file format. These are the same steps for saving any Photoshop image.

7. Click **Save** to save the picture package.

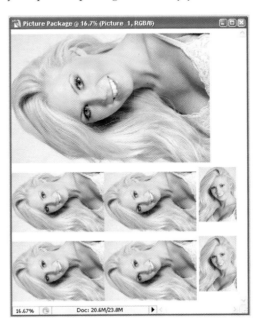

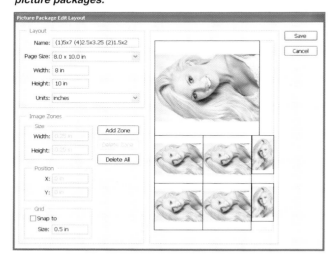

Figure 10-7: You use the Picture Package Edit Layout dialog box to create and save custom layouts for your picture packages.

CREATE A CUSTOM PICTURE PACKAGE LAYOUT

You can also customize the picture package layout. To customize the layout:

1. Click the **Edit Layout** button in the Picture Package dialog box. The Picture Package Edit Layout dialog box appears, shown in Figure 10-7.

2. Type a descriptive name for your custom layout in the Name text box.

3. Click the **Page Size** down arrow, and choose a paper size. More choices are available in this dialog box than are found in the Page Size drop-down list accessed from the Picture Package dialog box. As an added bonus, you can create a custom page size as well.

4. If you've clicked Custom from the Page Size drop-down list, click the **Units** down arrow, and click the unit of measurement to use. Then type the dimensions of your custom page in the **Width** and **Height** text boxes.

Next, you set the size and position of the zones (the image areas in the layout). The defaults are the zones in the layout that was selected in the Layout drop-down list accessed from the Picture Package dialog box. You can add and delete zones and change the size of a zone.

To change a zone's size or placement:

1. Click **Add Zone** to add a new image area.

2. Click the zone outlines to display a bounding box with handles. Drag the handles to the size you want. The width and height will appear in the Width and Height text boxes as you drag. You can also type the position using the X and Y text boxes. These values are measured from the upper-left corner. To place the image in the upper-left corner of the page, the position would be X = 0 and Y = 0. To place the image in the lower-right corner of the page, X would be the width of the page minus the width of the image zone; Y would be the height of the page minus the height of the image zone.

4. If you want the image zones to be aligned with a nonprinting grid on the page, click the **Snap To** check box, and type the grid spacing in the Size text box.

5. To create a new zone, click the **Add Zone** button, and then enter the dimensions and placement as described previously. You can also delete all the existing zones by clicking the **Delete All** button; or click the zone and click **Delete Zone** to delete a single zone. Then you can create new zones.

6. Click **Save**. The Enter The New Layout File Name dialog box appears.

7. Type the name for your layout in the File Name text box. Leave the default folder selection in the Save In text box (this will save your layout with the existing picture package layouts).

8. Click **Save**. Your new layout will now appear in the Layout drop-down list in the Picture Package dialog box, where you can select it.

Create a Web Photo Gallery

There are many reasons to put your photos on the Web. It's a great way to share photos with family and friends, or perhaps you have a portfolio of artwork you want online. When you use the Web Photo Gallery command, Photoshop creates the HTML needed for a home page containing thumbnail images, each of which is a hyperlink to a page with the full-sized image. You have a set of style templates to choose from for the layout of the pages, and you can customize an existing layout or create a new layout.

Figure 10-8: You use the Web Photo Gallery dialog box to create web pages that display your images on the Web.

To create a web photo gallery:

1. Click **File**, click **Automate**, and then click **Web Photo Gallery**. The Web Photo Gallery dialog box appears, shown in Figure 10-8.

2. Click the **Style** down arrow, and click the desired style for your web photo gallery. When you select a style, a small preview is displayed in the dialog box.

The styles fall into three general categories:

- **The thumbnail images are displayed vertically along the left side of the page**, with the full-size image displayed in the center. These styles are Centered Frame 1– Basic, Centered Frame 1 – Feedback, Centered Frame 1 – Info Only, and Centered Frame 2 – Feedback.

- **The thumbnail images are displayed horizontally along the bottom** of **the page**, with the full-size image displayed in the center. These styles are Horizontal– Feedback, Horizontal Gray, Horizontal Neutral, and Horizontal Slideshow.

- **The home page shows all the thumbnails**. To see a full-size image, click one of the thumbnails. These styles are Simple, Table 1, and Table 2.

TIP

When you set the general options for your web photo gallery, you specify how file extensions are generated and whether the width and height are specified in the HTML tag Photoshop generates for each image in your web photo gallery.

TIP

Specifying the width and height of the images in your web photo gallery is recommended. When these attributes aren't included, objects move around on a web page when it's loaded—the browser doesn't know the size of the images until they are loaded, so it doesn't know where to place objects around them. When the width and height are specified, the browser reserves that space for the images and places the other content accordingly.

TIP

When you set banner options for images in your web photo gallery, you specify what information is displayed in the web browser's title bar when your photo gallery is displayed. You can display the web site name, the photographer's name, contact information, or the date the web photo gallery was created.

In addition to the basic layout, some of the styles include information about the image and the ability for the person viewing the page to leave feedback about the page, which is then e-mailed to you. Figure 10-9 shows the Centered Frame 1 – Feedback style. At the bottom of the web page are links for Image Info and Image Feedback.

Figure 10-9: The Web Photo Gallery greatly simplifies creating web pages for your images.

When your web page visitors click the **Image Info** tab, the optional image information is displayed. Click the **Close** tab to hide this information. When they click the **Image Feedback** tab, a form is displayed in which the viewer can leave feedback about the image. The viewer can save the feedback, and it will be displayed in the feedback form; or the viewer can e-mail it to the person who created the web page. Click **Close** to close the feedback form.

10

TIP

The thumbnails options for the web photo gallery are used to set the size of the thumbnails in your photo gallery. You can specify the thumbnail size, whether it has a border, and whether a title is displayed below the thumbnail.

TIP

The custom colors options for the web photo gallery set the colors of the background, banner, text, active link, link, and visited link on the web pages. A link is *active* when the pointer is over it and *visited* after you have viewed the page to which it links.

TIP

If you set security options, you can display text over an image, which identifies the image if someone has the audacity to steal the image from your photo gallery and try to display it elsewhere. You specify the text and font attributes, as well as the opacity of the text.

Once you've selected a style for your web photo gallery, select the remaining options.

3. If you are using a style that includes feedback, type your e-mail address in the E-Mail text box. This is the address to which e-mail from your web photo gallery will be sent.

4. Click the **Use** down arrow, and click the location of your source image files. You can choose **Folder** or **Selected Images From File Browser**.

5. If you chose Folder from the Use drop-down list, click the **Browse** button. The Browse For Folder dialog box appears. Navigate to the folder that contains your images, and click **OK**. You can also click the **Include All Subfolders** check box to include all the subfolders in the folder you've selected.

6. Click the **Destination** button. The Browse For Folder dialog box appears.

7. Navigate to the folder where you want to save your completed web photo gallery. You can also click the **Make New Folder** button to create a new folder for the web photo gallery.

8. Click **OK**.

9. Click the **Options** down arrow, and choose the options for your web photo gallery. The most important option is the **Large Images** option. You use this option to determine the size of the image that is displayed when a thumbnail in your photo gallery is clicked.

10. Click **OK**. Photoshop generates the thumbnails and other files required and saves the pages in your destination folder. The home page will be in the folder you specified, and folders will be created for your full-size images, thumbnails, and web pages. Your default web browser will open and display your completed web photo gallery.

Create a Panorama with Photomerge

You have probably had an occasion in which a view was spectacular, but your camera just couldn't get it all. With Photomerge, you can combine two or more images into a single panoramic image. To create a panorama:

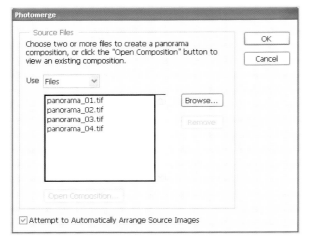

1. Click **File**, click **Automate**, and then click **Photomerge**. The Photomerge dialog box is displayed.

2. Click the **Use** down arrow, and click one of the following options: **Files**, **Folder**, or **Open Files**. Open Files uses the files that are currently open in Photoshop.

3. If you click Files or Folder, the Browse button becomes available. Click **Browse**, and the Open dialog box appears (if you clicked File); the Browse For Folder dialog box appears if you clicked Folder.

4. Click the images or folder of images to include in your panorama. Your selected images are listed in the Photomerge dialog box.

5. Click **OK**. The merged image is opened in the Photomerge dialog box, shown in Figure 10-10. If Photoshop didn't properly merge the images, you can manually move the images until they are blended properly, as outlined in the "Manually Merge Images" section of this chapter.

6. When you have the merged image the way you want it, click **OK**. The Photomerge dialog box closes, and your merged image appears as a new image. You work with this image in the same way you would any other Photoshop image.

7. Click **File** and then click **Save**. The Save As dialog box appears.

8. Click the **Save In** down arrow, and navigate to the folder in which you want to save the image.

9. Type the name of the merged image in the File Name text box.

10. Click the **Format** down arrow, and choose the file format for the merged image.

11. Click **Save**.

Figure 10-10: You use the Photomerge dialog box to create and work with merged images.

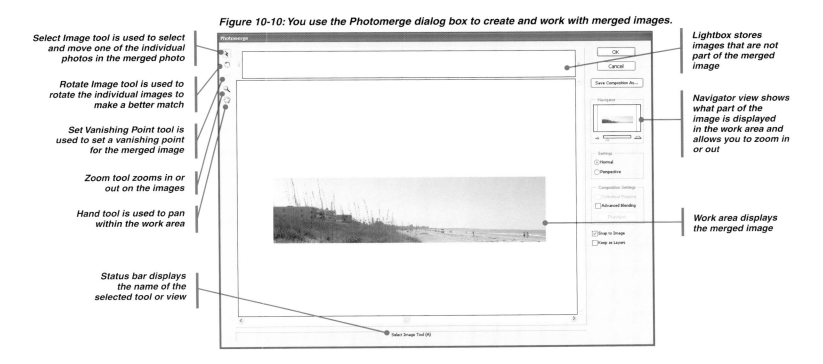

Select Image tool is used to select and move one of the individual photos in the merged photo

Rotate Image tool is used to rotate the individual images to make a better match

Set Vanishing Point tool is used to set a vanishing point for the merged image

Zoom tool zooms in or out on the images

Hand tool is used to pan within the work area

Status bar displays the name of the selected tool or view

Lightbox stores images that are not part of the merged image

Navigator view shows what part of the image is displayed in the work area and allows you to zoom in or out

Work area displays the merged image

MANUALLY MERGE IMAGES

You work with your merged files in the Photomerge dialog box work area. You can change the order of the images by dragging them in the work area, or you can drag them to the lightbox to use later. You can work with this dialog box in the following ways:

- Click the **Zoom** tool or use the Navigator view tools to zoom in or out of the image.

- In the Settings area, click the **Perspective** option to apply a perspective correction to the image. This is an effect you should use by trial and error—see if you like your image better with the Normal option or with the Perspective option selected.

- If you've chosen the Perspective option, click the **Vanishing Point** tool to set a vanishing point for the merged image. Each photo has its own vanishing point (the point to which parallel lines, like railroad tracks, appear to meet). The default is to use the vanishing point from the center image. Click a different image in your composition

TIP

Keeping your images as separate layers by clicking the **Keep As Layers** check box gives you the ability to make corrections to each image after it has been merged into a panorama. This way, you have much more flexibility in fine-tuning the images. For example, slight variations in exposure (where one image is slightly lighter or darker than the other) are easily corrected when each image is a layer. If an image is a single layer, you will need to select the area in the image that needs changing before applying the correction.

to change the vanishing point. The vanishing point image is highlighted in blue when you click it with the Vanishing Point tool, and the perspective of your panorama changes accordingly.

- In the Composition Settings area, click the **Cylindrical Mapping** check box to reduce the "bow-tie" effect that the Perspective option can create. Cylindrical Mapping is only available if you select the Perspective option.

- In the Composition Settings area, click the **Advanced Blending** check box to reduce color inconsistencies in the image created by exposure differences. It is applied to individual images after they are placed. You should try to adjust individual images to make them as close as possible before merging them, but this option is good for fine-tuning the image once the individual images have been placed.

- Click **Preview** to see the effects of the composition settings options. This puts the Photomerge dialog box in Preview mode, where you can see the effects of your settings, but you cannot adjust any of the settings. Click **Exit Preview** to close the preview.

- Click the **Snap To Image** check box to automatically align the images when Photoshop detects an overlapping area. For best results, your images should all have areas that overlap.

- Click the **Keep As Layers** check box to keep your individual images as separate layers in the merged image. This way, you can modify the individual images after you have created and saved the merged image.

A

actions
    applying with Batch command, 224–226
    automating, 221–222
    changing options for, 225
    creating droplets from, 227–228
    creating sets of, 221
    editing, 223–224
    playing and undoing, 222
    renaming, 225
    rerecording, 224
    setting playback options for, 223
Actions palette, working with, 220–221
Adaptive color reduction algorithm, effect of, 199
Add Anchor Point tool, using, 105
additive RGB, definition of, 24
adjustment layers, working with, 150–151
Adobe Photo Downloader, retrieving photos with, 43–44
Adobe Services, ordering online prints from, 182
Airbrush option, effect of, 20
algorithms
    for color reduction, 199
    definition of, 197
    for dithering, 199
All Programs menu, selecting, 3
ALT+BACKSPACE (erase) shortcut, using, 66
Always Add ALT Attributes HTML setting, description of, 205
Always Quote Attributes HTML setting, description of, 205
anchor points
    editing, 105
    selecting, 106
    using, 74
angle gradients, applying, 119
animation frames. See also frames
    exporting in ImageReady, 214
    setting delay times for, 208
animations
    creating, 208
    importing files and folders as, 212–213
    optimizing, 210
    previewing, 211
    saving, 212–213
    tweening, 209–210
    using looping options with, 211
    viewing, 211
anti-aliasing
    applying to text, 164
    explanation of, 59–60
    using with Magic Eraser tool, 118
    using with Magic Wand tool, 53–54
Apple, Web address for, 207
areas
    excluding with selections, 59

selecting with Magic Wand tool, 53–54
    selecting with Magnetic Lasso tool, 56–57
    selecting with Polygonal Lasso tool, 55–56
Art History Brush tool, using, 124–125
artwork, creating with paths, 108
aspect ratio of selections, constraining, 53
Attribute Case HTML setting, description of, 205
Auto Color options, changing, 141–142
Auto Levels options, changing, 141–142
Automate menu
    Batch command on, 224–226
    Create Droplet option on, 227
    Crop And Straighten Photo tool on, 228
    Picture Package option on, 229–235
AVI files, importing, 213

B

background and foreground colors
    matching with Eyedropper tools, 135
    restoring defaults for, 17, 113
    setting, 20–21
    swapping, 17
    switching between, 113
background elements, extracting, 66–69
Background Eraser tool, using, 70–71, 116–117
background layers. See also layers
    unlocking, 78
    using Gradient tool with, 118–121
backgrounds
    creating for CD labels, 99
    creating layers from, 79
badges, displaying and hiding in ImageReady, 216
Baseline Shift option, applying to text, 164
Batch command, using, 224–226
Bevel effects, using with text, 172–173
beveling frames, 92–93
Bezier handle, example of, 105
Bi-Cubic interpolation, using, 133–134
Bilinear interpolation, using, 133
bitmaps, overview of, 25–26, 104
Black & White color reduction algorithm, effect of, 199
black and white foreground, restoring, 21
black-and-white photos, scanning, 42
blend modes, 97–98
Blending Options feature
    using with CD labels, 102
    using with frames, 90–91
    using with layer styles, 94
Blur tools, using, 153
blurring images, 151–153
borders, converting selections to, 61
bounding boxes
    manipulating, 167–168
    resizing, 162
breaks in text, preventing, 165
Bridge

changing detail displayed with thumbnails in, 39
    changing file display in, 38
    changing thumbnail size in, 37
    changing views in, 38
    displaying find results in, 39
    finding stock photos with, 45
    opening and closing palettes in, 37
    opening images with, 7
    resizing panes in, 37
    returning to Photoshop CS2 from, 32
    viewing, selecting, and opening files with, 31–32
Bridge view, refreshing, 31
Bridge workspaces, saving and loading, 37
brightness, choosing for RAW files, 49
browsers, opening, 203
brush groups, changing, 113
brush libraries, saving and loading, 115
brush presets, managing, 115
brush sizes, changing, 19
brush tips
    changing, 19
    resizing, 114
Brush tools
    changing options for, 19–20
    editing layer masks with, 86
    effects of, 18
    identifying, 17
    painting with, 112–114
    using with CD labels, 102
    using with layer masks, 85
brushes
    adding dynamic elements to, 114
    creating, 114
    customizing, 113
    deleting, 115
    loading from context menus, 20
    renaming, 114
    resetting defaults for, 115
    using Airbrush option with, 20
buttons. See Toolbox

C

Camera RAW dialog box
    displaying, 48
    options in, 50
Cancel and Reset buttons, switching between, 49, 66
canvas size, changing, 134–135
canvases, creating from presets, 8
CD labels, creating, 99–102
Channel Mixer
    experimenting with values in, 155
    using instead of grayscale images, 30
channels, toggling through, 139
Channels feature, using with histograms, 137
Character palette, formatting type with, 162–164
characters, displaying while typing, 169

Circle Image map tool, defining hotspots with, 202
circles, constraining areas to, 203
circular guide, creating for CD labels, 100
circular selections, making with Marquee tool, 52
Cleanup tool, using with extractions, 69
client-side image maps, using, 203
clipping images to black or white, 48
clipping paths, using, 108–109
Clone Stamp tool, copying pixels with, 153–154
Close All Tags HTML setting, description of, 205
closed paths, creating text in, 169
CMYK (Cyan, Magenta, Yellow, Black) color space
    converting images to, 30
    significance of, 24
    using, 29
Color Balance command, using, 145
color casts, removing, 145
color correcting images
    with curves, 139–143
    with levels, 138–139
    with Red Eye tool, 144
    with Variations command, 145–146
color filters, finding, 148
color management, using when printing, 180–182
Color Mode feature, using with gradients, 120
color modes
    choosing, 28–30
    converting, 30
color photos, scanning, 42
Color Picker
    replacing colors in, 113
    using, 99, 104
color profiles, using, 201
Color Range command, using, 57–58
color ranges, adding to and selecting, 148
color reduction algorithms, examples of, 199
Color Sampler tool, setting, 143
color space, changing for photos, 49
colors
    altering, 139–143
    blending with Gradient tool, 118–121
    changing, 154–155
    changing hue and saturation for, 147–148
    inverting in images, 21
    matching, 149
    removing from images, 23
    sampling with Eyedropper tools, 117
    selecting for strokes, 109
    selecting for transparency, 198
    working with, 24
commands
    rearranging and recording, 223–224
    rerecording, 224
Commit feature, using with type, 161
compression, overview of, 27
Compression Quality feature, using with JPEGs

for Web, 200
contact sheets, creating, 182–184
context menus
contiguous selections, making with Magic Wand
 tool, 54
contrast, choosing for RAW files, 49
controls, working with, 11–12
copying
 files, 40
 images, 36
 layers, 77, 80
 merged layers, 78–79
copyrights, creating, 191–192, 231, 233
Crop And Straighten Photos tool, using, 228
Crop tool
 constraining to specific dimensions, 132
 effects of, 18
 identifying, 17
 using with photos, 132
 using with selections, 62
cropping
 RAW files, 49
CSS (Cascading Style Sheets), generating, 206
cursor preferences, changing, 5
curved paths, drawing, 105
curves, drawing with Pen tool, 74
Curves command, using, 139–143

D

Defringe command, using with pixels, 63
deleting
 brushes, 115
 files, 40
 layer masks, 87
 layers, 82
 with selections, 62
Desaturate feature, using, 23
desktop shortcuts, creating, 5
Diffusion dithering algorithm, effect of, 199
digital copyrights, creating, 191–192
digital photos, importing, 43
digital QuickMats, creating, 187
digital watermarks, protecting images with, 232
dimension versus resolution, 28
Direct Selection tool, using, 105
Display And Cursors preferences, setting, 4
dithering
 algorithms for, 199
 explanation of, 29, *199*
docking palettes, 13
document title bar in workspace, location of, 3
documents
 copying layers from, 80
 copying selections to, 66
 displaying information about, 7
 navigating in, 10
 opening in ImageReady, 6

saving, 188
 searching with keywords, 190
Dodge/Burn/Sponge tools
 effects of, 18
 identifying, 17
dpi (dots per inch), significance of, 28
drop shadows
 adding to layers, 89
 creating, 170–171
 visibility of, 88
drop-down lists and controls, using, 11
droplets
 creating from actions, 227–228
 creating in ImageReady, 228
Dust & Scratches filter, using, 157–158
dynamic brushes, creating, 114

E

Edge Touchup tool, using with extractions, 69
Edit mode, verifying, 162
elliptical selections, making with Marquee tool, 52
Emboss effects
 using with CD labels, 101–102
 using with text, 172–173
Encoding HTML setting, description of, 205
Enter Quick Mask mode, accessing, 17
Eraser tools
 Background Eraser, 70–71, 116–117
 effects of, 18
 Magic Eraser, 70, 117–118
Exit Quick Mask mode, accessing, 17
exposure, choosing for RAW files, 48
Extract dialog box, erasing highlights and fills
 in, 66
Extract filter
 resetting, 67
 using, 68
 using with background elements, 66–67
extractions, cleaning up, 69
Eyedropper tools, 17–18
 adjusting levels and curves with, 142–143
 matching foreground and background color
  with, 135
 sampling colors with, 117
 selecting temporarily, 135
 using, 113, 136

F

feathering, explanation of, 59–60
file display, changing in Bridge, 38
File Handling preferences, setting, 4
file information, adding, 190–191
file names, using small fonts with, 184
files
 advisory about renaming of, 36
 creating, 6
 Dust & Scratches, 157–158

importing as animations, 212–213
 labeling, 34–36
 managing with Bridge, 7
 opening, 7
 rating, 35–36
 renaming, moving, copying, and deleting, 40
 renaming in folders, 36
 saving, 46–47
 searching for, 40
 selecting, 7, 34
 sorting and rearranging, 33
 Unsharp Mask, 151–152
 viewing, selecting, and opening with Bridge,
  31–32
fill versus opacity, *95–96*
Filter Gallery, using, 125–126
filter parameters, editing, 126
filters
 accessing, 4
 Gaussian Blur, 152
 Liquify filter, 127–128
 photo filters, 148
 redoing, 100
 using Extract filter with background elements,
  66–67
Find dialog box, searching for files with, 40
find results, displaying in Bridge, 39
finding and replacing text, 166–167
Fine/Coarse setting, using, 146
Fit Image command, using, 229
Flash player
 creating animations with, 213–214
 downloading, 207
Flatten Image feature, using with picture packages,
 231
flattening images, 83
FLIC files, importing, 213
flyout menus
 accessing, 17
 using, 12
Folder and Bridge options, actions for, 225
folders
 importing as animations, 212–213
 renaming images in, 36
fonts, changing, 163
foreground and background colors
 restoring defaults for, 113
 setting, 20–21
 swapping, 17
 switching between, 113
frame area, defining, 90
frames. *See also* animation frames
 beveling, 92
 creating with layer effects, 90–94
 moving and resizing, 93–94
 positioning and cropping, 93–94
Free Transform command

applying, 130
 straightening photos with, 130–131
 using with frames, 93
Freeform Pen tool
 selecting, 107
 using, 107
freehand selections, sketching, 54–55
Freeze Mask tool, using with Liquify filter, 128
fringe pixels, removing, 63. *See also* pixels
Full Screen mode
 using, 16–17
fuzziness, applying to color ranges, 58

G

Gaussian Blur filter, using, 152
General preferences, setting, 4
GIF images, optimizing for Web, 197–200
Global Light feature
 using with drop shadows, 171
 using with layer effects, 93
glow, applying to text, 173
Go To Bridge in workspace, location of, 3
Gradient Editor, opening, 120
gradient masks, creating, 86–87
Gradient tool, using, 118–121
Gradient/Paint Bucket tools
 effects of, 18
 identifying, 17
Grayscale color reduction algorithm, effect of, 199
grayscale images
 versus Channel Mixer, 30
 converting color images to, 30
 creating, 28
grid, straightening images with, 131
Grow command, expanding selections with, 70
guides, creating user slices with, 216–217
Guides, Grid And Slices preferences, setting, 5

H

Hand tool
 effect of, 18
 navigating and zooming documents with, 10
handles, displaying for printing, 179
Healing Brushes
 effects of, 18
 fixing small areas with, 155–156
 identifying, 17
Help system, accessing, 11
highlights, adjusting, 150
histograms
 adjusting levels for, 138–139
 viewing tonal ranges with, *136–138*
History Brush
 identifying, 17
 using for touch-ups, 158
 working with, 23
History palette

undoing actions with, 222
using, 21–22
Horizontal Type tool
labeling photos with, 161
using with CD labels, 102
hotspots, defining, *202*
HSL (hue, saturation, and luminance), working
with, 24
HTML settings, descriptions of, 205
hue
changing, 147–150
working with, 24
hyphenating and justifying text, 164–165

I

ICC (International Color Consortium) profiles,
printing images with, 182
image canvases, creating from presets, 8
image colors, changing, 154–155
image maps, working with, 202–204
image rotation, setting for RAW files, 49
image sizes
changing, 28
using presets with, 9
image states, viewing with History palette, 21
ImageReady
creating droplets in, 228
exporting animation frame in, 214
importing Photoshop files as frames in, 212–213
opening current documents in, 6
slicing images in, 215–218
images. *See also* photos; picture packages; stock
photos
adding copyright information to, 233
altering tonality and color of, 139–143
applying actions to, 220
applying filters to parts of, 126
clipping to white or black, 48
converting color modes for, 30
copying and moving, 36
cropping to nonrectangular selections, 62
displaying versions of, 196
distorting areas of, 128
extracting, 68
fitting, 229
flattening, 83
flattening for picture packages, 231
increasing size of, 133
inverting colors in, 21
keeping as separate layers, 240
making transparent, 198
matching, 149
merging, 239–240
navigating in Full Screen mode, 12
opening, 37
opening and creating, 6–8
placing marquee selections around, 52

printing, 178
printing parts of, 181
removing colors from, 23
renaming in folders, 36
resizing and trimming, 132–134
resizing for printing, 176
retouching and repairing, 153–154
rotating and flipping, 130–131
sampling foreground and background colors
from, 20
saving for Web, 196
scanning, 41–43
searching for, 40, 45
selecting for picture packages, 230
selecting with Bridge, 32
sharpening and blurring, 151–153
slicing in ImageReady, 215–218
switching between versions of, 21
using History Brush with, 23
viewing, 35
viewing tonal ranges of, 136–138
importing document metadata, 193
Include Comments HTML setting, description
of, 205
Include Zero Margins On Body Tag HTML setting,
description of, 205
Indent HTML setting, description of, 205
indexed color mode
converting images to, 30
using, 29–30
Inner Glow effect, applying to text, 173
interpolation, types of, 133

J

JPEG images
compression problems with, 27
managing, 26
optimizing, 200–201
Jump To Image Ready tool, identifying, 17
justifying and hyphenating text, 164–165

K

Keep As Layers feature, using, 240
kerning, applying to text, 164
keyboard
starting Photoshop from, 3
zooming with, 9
keyboard shortcuts, creating, 5
keywords, searching documents with, 190

L

labeled images, viewing, 35
labels
creating for CDs, 99–102
creating for photos, 161
removing, 33
renaming, 34–35
Landscape orientation, selecting, 177

Lasso tools
identifying, 17
using, 54–57
layer effects
combining, 93
creating frames with, 90–94
editing, 91
working with, 87–88
layer fill, reducing, 92
layer groups
creating, 82–83
masking, 88
layer masks
adding selections to, 86
definition of, *84*
deleting, 87
disabling temporarily, 87
editing, 86
painting and creating, 85
layer order, rearranging, 80–81
Layer Style dialog box
displaying, 93
using, 171
Layer Style dialog box, displaying, 100, 170
layer styles
adding type effects with, 170–173
copying, 65
finding and using, 171
saving and loading, 94–95
layer-based slices, creating, 217
layered files, saving, 189–190
layers. *See also* background layers; linked layers;
merged layers; visible layers
adding drop shadows to, 89
adding strokes to, 91
applying, 87
copying from other applications to, 80
copying selections to, 65
copying type effects between, 172
creating and copying, 77
creating from backgrounds, 79
creating from selections, 78
creating image maps with, 204
definition of, *75*
deleting, 82
dragging, 80
editing with, 78–82
flattening, 83
hiding and revealing, 76
hiding with layer masks, 86
linking and unlinking, 78
merging, 83–84
moving into layer groups, 83
naming, 100
removing from layer groups, 83
renaminig, 77
saving files with, 47

selecting for matching, 149
separating images in, 240
Layers palette, components of, 76
leading, changing, 163
left bracket key ([), decreasing brush tip sizes
with, 114
letters, displaying while typing, 169
Levels dialog box, displaying, 138
libraries, creating for brushes, 115
line art, scanning, 42–43
Line Endings HTML setting, description of, 205
linear gradients, applying, 119
lines, following pens with, 105
Link Layers button, clicking, 78
linked layers, merging, 84. *See also* layers
Liquify filter, using, 127–128
Looping Options feature, using with animations,
208
looping options, using with animations, 211
lossy algorithm, JPG compression as, 27
luminance, working with, 24

M

Mac OS color reduction algorithm, effect of, 199
Magic Eraser tool
making selections with, 70
using, 117–118
Magic Wand tool
effects of, 18
identifying, 17
using, 53–54
Magnetic Lasso tool
identifying, 54
selecting areas with, 56–57
Magnetic Pen tool, using, 106–107
magnification, changing, 9
Marquee tools
effects of, 18
identifying, 17
making selections with, 52
masks. *See* gradient masks; layer masks
Match Color command, using, 149
mattes
descriptions of, 200
versus transparency, 201
Maximize Compatibility option, using with saved
layered files, 190
Measure tools, using, 17–18, 131
Memory And Image Cache preferences, setting, 5
menu bar, 3, 6
menu commands, assigning keyboard shortcuts
to, 15
merged layers, copying, 78–79. *See also* layers
merging images, 239–240
merging layers, 83–84
metadata

adding, 190–192
importing, 193
saving as templates, 192
storing in XMP format, 33
Moab Paper Company, Web address for, 179
modal controls, 222-224
monitors, calibrating for printing, 180
Motion Blur filter, using, 153
MOV files, importing, 213
Move tool
effects of, 18
identifying, 17
using with selections, 67
moving
files, 40
images, 36
Multi-Page Document feature, using, 193
Multiply mode, using, 97–98
music note shape, using with CD labels, 101

N

Navigator palette, using, 10
Nearest Neighbor interpolation, using, 133
nodes, identifying, 104
Noise dithering algorithm, effect of, 199
noncontiguous selections, making with Magic
Wand tool, 54
Notes tool, 17, 18
numeric lists, sliding, 12

O

online Help, using, 11
opacity, 95-97
Open dialog box, displaying, 6
optimized images, saving, 201–202
options bar in workspace, location of, 3
Options dialog box, using with Brush tool, 19
Output Settings dialog box, using, 204–207
Output XHTML setting, description of, 205

P

Page Setup command, using, 176–177
Paint Bucket tool, using, 121
paintbrush, optimizing, 20
painting with Brush tool, 112–114
Palette Well
location of, 3
using, 13
palettes
and indexed color images, 29
location of, 3
manipulating with Palette Well, 13
opening and closing in Bridge, 37
panes in Bridge, resizing, 37
panoramas, creating with Photomerge, 238–240
paper
and print sizes, 231

selecting for printing, 179
Paragraph palette, formatting paragraphs with,
164–165
paragraph type, entering, 162
Patch tool
fixing large areas with, 156–157
identifying, 17
Path Selection tools
effects of, 18
identifying, 17
using, 169
paths
adding strokes to, 109
converting, 111
creating artwork with, 108
creating text on, 168
drawing with Pen tool, 105
editing text on, 169
filling, 109
moving text along, 170
stroke and fill paths, 109–110
types of, 108
using with Pen tool, 74, 104
Pattern dithering algorithm, effect of, 199
Pattern Stamp tool, using, 157
patterns
copying pixels from, 157
creating, 122–123
previewing and saving, 123
PDF documents, creating, 193
PDF presentations, creating, 193–194
Pen tools
creating selections with, 74
drawing curves with, 74
effects of, 18
identifying, 17
types of, 111
using, 104–106
Pencil tools
effects of, 18
identifying, 17
Perceptual color reduction algorithm, effect of, 199
photo filters, using, 148
Photomerge, creating panoramas with, 238–240
photos. See also images; picture packages; stock
photos
changing color space for, 49
changing resolution for, 49
cropping, 132
displaying pixels in, 26
labeling with Horizontal Type tool, 161
preserving, 186
resizing, 50
retrieving with Adobe Photo Downloader, 43–44
scanning, 41
straightening, 130–131
trimming, 135

Photoshop CS2, starting and closing, 2–3
Picture Package feature, using, 229–235
picture packages. See also images; photos; stock
photos
creating, 185–186
pixels. See also fringe pixels
and bitmaps, 25–26
copying from patterns, 157
copying with Clone Stamp tool, 153–154
deleting, 62
displaying, 26
erasing, 116–118
relationship to compression, 27
selecting within range of colors, 57
zooming, 8
playback options, setting for actions, 223
Plug-ins And Scratch Disks preferences, setting, 5
PNG-8 images, optimizing for Web, 197–200
PNG-24 images, optimizing, 201
point type, entering, 160–161
points, 104-106
Polygon Image map tool, defining hotspots with,
202–203
Polygonal Lasso tool
identifying, 54
selecting areas with, 55–56
Portrait orientation, selecting, 177
ppi (pixels per inch), significance of, 26, 28
preferences, setting, 3–5
presentations, creating, 193–194
Preserve Luminosity feature, using, 149
Preset Manager, using, 124–125
preset styles, loading, 95
presets
creating, 9
creating image canvases from, 8
managing for brushes, 115
saving for brushes, 113
print and paper sizes, examples of, 231
Print With Preview command, using, 178–179
printing
calibrating monitors for, 180
with desktop printers, 176–179
displaying for printing, 179
with fine art papers, 179
images, 178
parts of images, 181
picture packages, 229
resizing images for, 176
single copies of pages, 180
using color management for, 180–182
vector-based graphics, 180
prints, ordering online from Adobe Services, 182
programs, accessing, 4
proof setups, using, 182
Protect Foreground Color option, using with
Background Eraser tool, 117

Q

Quick Masks
painting selections with, 72–73
switching to, 85
QuickTime movies, saving animations as, 212
QuickTime player, downloading, 207

R

radial gradients, applying, 119
raster images overview of, 25–26, 104
rated images, viewing, 35
rating files, 35–36
RAW images, working with, 47–50
Reconstruct button, undoing transformations
with, 128
Record Again option, using with actions and
commands, 224
Rectangle Image map tool, defining hotspots
with, 202
Rectangular and Elliptical Marquee tools,
switching between, 52
rectangular selections, making with Marquee
tool, 52
Red Eye tool
color correcting images with, 144
identifying, 17
redoing changes, 22
reflected gradients, applying, 119
repairing images, 153–157
replacing and finding text, 166–167
Reset and Cancel buttons, switching between,
49, 66
resetting settings, 147
resizing
bounding boxes, 162, 167
images, 28, 132–135
images for printing, 176
photos, 50
resolution
changing, 28
changing for photos, 49
choosing for printing, 177
versus dimension, 28
for scanning photos, 41
for Web images, 231
Restrictive (Web) color reduction algorithm, effect
of, 199
retouching images, 153–154
RFC (Request For Comments), significance of, 212
RGB (Red, Green, Blue) color space, 197
converting images to, 30
significance of, 24
using, 28–29
using with picture packages, 231
right bracket key ([), increasing brush tip sizes
with, 114

rollovers, working with, 206
rotating
    bounding boxes, 167
    images, 130–131
Rubber Band feature, using, 105

S

saturation
    changing, 147–150
    choosing for RAW files, 49
    working with, 24
Save As dialog box, displaying, 46, 187–188
Save For Web dialog box, using, 196–202
saving
    documents, 188
    files, 46–47
    layered files, 189–190
    optimized images, 201–202
    RAW files, 50
    sliced images, 217
Scale Vertically and Horizontally options,
    applying to text, 164
scanning, 41–43
scratches. *See* Dust & Scratches filter
Screen mode, using, 98–99
screen modes, selecting, 16–17
selection borders, moving, 59
selections
    adding to, 55, 60
    adding to layer masks, 86
    constraining, 53
    converting, 110
    converting to borders, 61
    copying to new documents, 66
    copying to new layers, 65
    creating layers from, 78
    creating with Pen tool, 74
    cropping to, 62
    definition of, *51*
    deleting with, 62
    deselecting, 58, 90
    duplicating contents of, 67
    excluding areas with, 59
    expanding, 70
    expanding and contracting, 61
    filing with foreground color, 90
    inverting, 59
    loading, 64
    making, 60
    making with Lasso tools, 54–57
    making with Magic Eraser tool, 70
    making with Magic Wand tool, 53–54
    making with Marquee tool, 52
    moving, 53
    moving contents of, 67
    painting with Quick Masks, 72–73
    previewing for color ranges, 58

resizing, 61
restoring, 146
saving, 63
selecting and deselecting, 61
subtracting from, 61
touching up with Quick Masks, 72–73
transforming, 60
using Gradient tool with, 118–121
Selective color reduction algorithm, effect of, 199
sepia-tone photos, creating, 158
server-side image maps, using, 203
settings, resetting, 147
shadows, 49,150
shape layers, creating, 104
Shape Layers feature, using, 104
Shape tools
    effects of, 18
    identifying, 17
    using, 110–112
    using with CD labels, 101
Sharpen tools, using, 153
sharpening images, 151–153
shortcut menus
    loading brushes from, 20
    using, 12
shortcuts, creating, 5
Similar command, expanding selections with, 70
Slice tools
    effects of, 18
    identifying, 17
sliced images, saving, 217
slices
    creating user slices, 216
    optimizing in ImageReady, 217–218
    viewing with ImageReady, 215–216
Slices option, description of, 205
slicing images, explanation of, *215*
sliders, using, 11
Smart Highlighting feature, using, 69
Smoothness feature, using with patterns, 123
Smudge tools, using, 153
snapshots, making and renaming with History
    palette, 22
sorting files, 33
Space drop-down menu, using with RAW files, 49
Spelling Checker, using, 166
Spot Healing Brush tool, using, 154–155
squares, constraining areas to, 203
Stamp tools, 17,18
Standard Screen mode, using, 16, 17
Start menu, starting Photoshop from, 2
states, working with, 206
statistical information, with histograms, 137
Status bar
    information displaying in, 7
    zooming with, 10

Step Backward and Forward commands, using, 22
stock photos, finding, 44–46. *See also* images;
    photos; picture packages
Straighten tool, using with RAW files, 49
Stroke effect, using, 88
strokes
    adding to layers, 91
    adding to paths, 109
    replacing, 92
    selecting foreground colors for, 109
Styles palette, using, 171
subtractive CMYK, definition of, 24
swatches, using, 12
SWF animations, creating, 207, 213–214

T

Tags Case HTML setting, description of, 205
task automation. *See* actions; Actions palette
temperature, choosing for RAW files, 48
templates, saving document metadata as, 192
text. *See also* type effects
    adding to CD labels, 102
    adjusting height of, 164
    applying glow to, 173
    committing, 161
    creating, 160–162
    creating on paths, 168
    creating within closed paths, 169
    editing, 162–164
    editing on paths, 169
    finding and replacing, 166–167
    hyphenating and justifying, 164–165
    moving along paths, 170
    preventing breaks in, 165
    transforming, 167–168
    using Bevel and Emboss effects with, 172
    warping, 167
text masks, creating, 174
Text tools
    effect of, 160
    effects of, 18
    identifying, 17
    selecting, 160
Threshold command, rendering black-and-white
    images with, 43
thumbnails
    adjusting in Bridge, 39
    opening, 31
    rearranging, 33
    resizing in Bridge, 37
    varying sizes of, 44
tint, choosing for RAW files, 48
tweening, using with animations, 209–210
type. *See* text
type effects. *See also* text
    adding with Layer Styles, 170–173
    copying between layers, 172

Type preferences, setting, 5

U

undoing changes, 21, 22
Units And Rulers preferences, setting, 5
Unsharp Mask filter, sharpening images with,
    151–152
user slices, creating, 216

V

Variations command, color correcting images
    with, 145–146
vector shapes, overview of, 26–27
vector-based graphics
    description of, 104
    printing, 180
visible layers, merging, 84. *See also* layers
Visit Adobe.com tool, identifying, 17

W

warping text, 167
watermarks, protecting images with, 232
Web
    optimizing GIF and PNG-8 images for, 197–200
    optimizing JPEG images for, 200–201
    resolutions of images for, 231
    saving images for, 196–202
    saving images optimized for, 201–202
Web accessibility standards, complying with, 204
Web Content palette, using, 217–218
web photo galleries, creating, 235–237
Welcome screen, displaying, 2
white balance, choosing for RAW files, 48
White Balance tool, identifying, 47
Windows color reduction algorithm, effect of, 199
working paths, using, 108
workspace
    components of, 3
    customizing and retrieving, 14
    setting preferences in, 3–5
    troubleshooting layout of, 14

X

XMP metadata, lack of support for, 33

Z

zones, managing in picture packages, 234–235
Zoom too
    effects of, 18
    identifying, 17
zooming
    effect of, 8
    with keyboard, 9
    keyboard shortcut for, 26
    line art to 100 percent, 42
    with Navigator palette, 10
    with Zoom tool, 9

International Contact Information

AUSTRALIA
McGraw-Hill Book Company Australia Pty. Ltd.
- TEL +61-2-9900-1800
- FAX +61-2-9878-8881
- http://www.mcgraw-hill.com.au
- books-it_sydney@mcgraw-hill.com

CANADA
McGraw-Hill Ryerson Ltd.
- TEL +905-430-5000
- FAX +905-430-5020
- http://www.mcgraw-hill.ca

GREECE, MIDDLE EAST, & AFRICA
(Excluding South Africa)
McGraw-Hill Hellas
- TEL +30-210-6560-990
- TEL +30-210-6560-993
- TEL +30-210-6560-994
- FAX +30-210-6545-525

MEXICO (Also serving Latin America)
McGraw-Hill Interamericana Editores S.A. de C.V.
- TEL +525-1500-5108
- FAX +525-117-1589
- http://www.mcgraw-hill.com.mx
- carlos_ruiz@mcgraw-hill.com

SINGAPORE (Serving Asia)
McGraw-Hill Book Company
- TEL +65-6863-1580
- FAX +65-6862-3354
- http://www.mcgraw-hill.com.sg
- mghasia@mcgraw-hill.com

SOUTH AFRICA
McGraw-Hill South Africa
- TEL +27-11-622-7512
- FAX +27-11-622-9045
- robyn_swanepoel@mcgraw-hill.com

SPAIN
McGraw-Hill/Interamericana de España, S.A.U.
- TEL +34-91-180-3000
- FAX +34-91-372-8513
- http://www.mcgraw-hill.es
- professional@mcgraw-hill.es

UNITED KINGDOM, NORTHERN, EASTERN, & CENTRAL EUROPE
McGraw-Hill Education Europe
- TEL +44-1-628-502500
- FAX +44-1-628-770224
- http://www.mcgraw-hill.co.uk
- emea_queries@mcgraw-hill.com

ALL OTHER INQUIRIES Contact:
McGraw-Hill/Osborne
- TEL +1-510-420-7700
- FAX +1-510-420-7703
- http://www.osborne.com
- omg_international@mcgraw-hill.com